EUL VERLAG

Reihe: Controlling · Band 18

Herausgegeben von Prof. Dr. Volker Lingnau, Kaiserslautern, Prof. Dr. Albrecht Becker, Innsbruck, und Prof. Dr. Rolf Brühl, Berlin

Dr. Jörn Sebastian Basel

Heuristic Reasoning in Management Accounting

A Mixed Methods Analysis

With a Foreword by Prof. Dr. Rolf Brühl,
ESCP Europe Wirtschaftshochschule Berlin

Bibliografische Information der Deutschen Nationalbibliothek

Die Deutsche Nationalbibliothek verzeichnet diese Publikation
in der Deutschen Nationalbibliografie; detaillierte bibliografische
Daten sind im Internet über <http://dnb.d-nb.de> abrufbar.

Dissertation, ESCP Europe Wirtschaftshochschule Berlin, 2011

ISBN 978-3-8441-0160-7
1. Auflage Juli 2012

© JOSEF EUL VERLAG GmbH, Lohmar – Köln, 2012
Alle Rechte vorbehalten

JOSEF EUL VERLAG GmbH
Brandsberg 6
53797 Lohmar
Tel.: 0 22 05 / 90 10 6-6
Fax: 0 22 05 / 90 10 6-88
E-Mail: info@eul-verlag.de
http://www.eul-verlag.de

Bei der Herstellung unserer Bücher möchten wir die Umwelt schonen. Dieses
Buch ist daher auf säurefreiem, 100% chlorfrei gebleichtem, alterungsbestän-
digem Papier nach DIN 6738 gedruckt.

Foreword

Traditionally, research in economics and management science is dominated by a model of the human being as rational decision maker. These idealized humans are capable of managing complex cognitive tasks like a computer and do not err. However, empirical research in judgment and decision making has shown that real humans systematically violate assumptions of this unbounded rationality. Although the heuristics-and-bias-approach is directed against the idealized model of human rationality, it shares its normative yardstick. With a new approach this view is challenged: The fast-and-frugal-approach goes a step further and maintains that – under certain conditions – heuristics are more effective and efficient. Rationality is therefore a matter of adaption to the environment (ecological rationality) and no reference to rationality assumptions like axioms of expected-utility-theory is made.

Heuristics are short-cuts and deliberately ignore information, for instance through examining fewer cues or integrating less information. However, this collides with a view on management accountants and controllers as rational agents which seems to suggest that all available information should be considered. As their role as information supplier is often accompanied with the task to assist managers in their judgment and decision making, they have huge influence on these processes. Therefore, it is of high relevance to know if, how, and which heuristics management accountants and controllers use. Furthermore, we need to know which individual and situational factors influence their usage of heuristics. With a series of studies, Jörn Basel sheds light to these research questions and addresses some central claims of the fast-and-frugal-approach in his dissertation.

He starts with a thorough theoretical analysis and unfolds different strands of cognitive research. Central to his discussion are dual-process-approaches which are debated in cognitive psychology. Scholars of these approaches claim that we should distinguish between two distinct processes (or systems) of the human mind. Following this interpretation, heuristics are processes which are described as intuitive, automatic, fast, and unconscious. They are routinized cognitive processes which are based on experience in certain social environments and thus often exhibit ecological rationality.

In the empirical part of his dissertation, Basel experimentally shows that management accounting students and practitioners use heuristics in an investment setting. Although they are told to use all information, they use a phase strategy and select information in a lexicographic manner. A verbal protocol analysis of this experiment clearly reveals the different strategies in their judgment and decision making. Strikingly, a test for the decision making style of the participants does not show any effects. However, in a setting where accountability of the results is introduced participants with high dependency do buy more information compared to the first study. This is contrasted to the finding that overall participants still use not all available information. If these results are corroborated in future studies, we could conclude that heuristics are a general strategy for social actors in complex settings. However, as the external validity of experiments is often debated, these issues have to be tackled with other research designs as well.

Therefore, in his fifth study, Basel interviews managers and management controllers of firms in order to validate his findings and make his arguments more plausible. Basically, the interviewees confirm that they use heuristics with a phase strategy. However, due to the qualitative setting and the small sample size of this concluding study, we should be cautious in generalizing these findings.

Nevertheless, Basel is able to show the fruitfulness of his approach which can be framed with the help of a distinction by Herbert Simon. Future research should take a closer look on the processes of judgment and decision making (procedural rationality), because in real management accounting settings it is often difficult to judge about the optimal outcome (substantial rationality).

Overall, Jörn Basel's ambitious and innovative dissertation picks up an up-to-date topic in behavioural accounting research which not only is of relevance for researchers but as well for practitioners. I am convinced that both researchers and practitioners will benefit from reading this fine piece of research and I wish this book all the success it deserves.

Prof. Dr. Rolf Brühl

Chair of Management Control

ESCP Europe Business School Berlin

Preface

Writing a doctoral thesis can be likened to running a marathon. Both require proper regular training, a good portion of endurance (and maybe a little talent) and ideally a supportive training group including the guidance of an experienced coach. During my academic studies I consider myself fortunate to have found all these prerequisites in an optimum environment.

Speaking first of an experienced coach, in my academic supervisor, Prof. Dr. Rolf Brühl at ESCP Europe Business School in Berlin, I had the good fortune of having an intellectual mentor who both supported and challenged me in my academic work. Attending conferences together and many stimulating chats over a cup of coffee made my doctoral experience at his chair a truly enjoyable one. My dissertation deals mainly with intuitive decision making and I think that both our positive gut feelings proved to be right when we started this project on heuristic reasoning (maybe an additional proof for the surprising benefits of System 1-thinking?). Speaking of good mentors and advice givers during my academic studies, I am also grateful that Prof. Dr. Bernhard Hirsch (Universität der Bundeswehr, Munich) accepted the role of my second supervisor. He and his team in Munich share the same interests in behavioral research in accounting and he accompanied my work during many fruitful joint colloquia. In line with this, I also want to thank Prof. Dr. Markus Bick for his uncomplicated and friendly behaviour in his role as the chair of the commission at the ESCP Europe during the review process.

Prof. Dr. Brühl also supported my stay as a visiting scholar at the Fisher School of Accounting at the University of Florida in 2010. This delightful experience was possible thanks to an invitation from Prof. Dr. Robert Knechel, Director at the International Center for Research in Accounting and Auditing, to whom I would also like to express my gratitude. Additional financial support for that stay came from Club International ESCP Europe, which I greatly appreciate.

Secondly, speaking of good and effective training, my personal training (and sometimes competition) highlights included the attendance of several international conferences in amazing places such as Pittsburgh, Tel Aviv, Vienna and Rome. In particular the research colloquia and summer schools helped me greatly to sharpen my research questions and to reflect critically on my methodology. Specifically I would like to thank faculty and participants of the following events for their feedback and constructive comments: ESCP Europe research colloquia, Berlin 2008-2011; Summer School on Bounded Rationality at the Max Planck Institute for Human Development, Berlin, 2009; EAA Doctoral Colloquium, Siena, 2011 and the ERMAC Doctoral Colloquium, Vienna, 2011. Of course I must also thank all the participants and companies that participated in my experiments and in the interviews. I really appreciate that many of them were willing to spend some of their precious time for a bar of chocolate.

Thirdly, speaking of a good training group, I thank all the doctoral students at ESCP Europe who helped me with my research or who participated in our daily Klausener-Platz lunch breaks. In particular I would like to mention members of the chair of management control team including Dr. Nils Horch, Dr. Mathias Osann, Max Kury, Michael Hanzlick and our tremendous student research assistants Steffi Friedemann, Mathias Schumann and Inan Ince. Special thanks also go to Dr. Florian Dost and Jens Sievert for their support in Study I of my thesis and for always having a good supply of sweets in their office. I assume they know that, like a marathon runner, you need a boost of carbohydrate at some point in order to keep going... Overall I strongly believe that such a pleasant working atmosphere and such friendly and supportive colleagues are one, or even the key, contributors to success when striving for a long term goal such as a doctoral thesis (or a marathon).

And finally speaking of endurance, I must clearly state that writing this dissertation at the ESCP Europe in Berlin and finishing my studies in Konstanz, Toronto and Heidelberg, would not have been possible without the ongoing and incredible support of my beloved parents Dr. Sigrid Basel-Gedeon and Rainer Basel. They were a permanent source of motivation and the best counsellors one could imagine. I would also like to thank my sister Meike and her family and my brother Stefan for their support – I am thankful to have such a wonderful family. This preface would not be complete without thanking another special person. Dear Viktoria, thank you so much for all your encouragement and your patience during my doctoral studies.

Jörn Sebastian Basel

Berlin, June 2012

Content

Foreword V

Preface VII

Content IX

List of Figures XIII

List of Tables XV

List of Abbreviations XVII

1 Introduction 1

1.1 On making (rational) decisions in management accounting 1

1.2 Derivation of the research questions 3

1.3 Research methods 7

1.4 Research procedure 9

1.4.1 Experimental methods 9

1.4.2 Verbal protocols 9

1.4.3 Interviews 10

2 Judgment and decision making and heuristics in (management)
   accounting 15

2.1 Rationality in management research 15

2.2 Explaining social action 19

2.3 From unbounded- to bounded- to ecological rationality 21

2.3.1 Money as utility and the origin of modern decision sciences 21

2.3.2 Unbounded rationality and optimization under constraints 25

2.3.3 Bounded rationality 26

2.3.4   Heuristics and biases 28

2.3.5   Satisficing decisions and what is actually bounded in rationality 33

2.3.6   Fast and frugal heuristics 36

2.3.7   Bounded minds and ecological rationality 40

2.3.8   Critique of fast and frugal decision strategies 43

2.4   Development of behavioral research in accounting 46

**2.5   Judgment and decision making and cognitive aspects in behavioral
        accounting research 51**

2.5.1   Information processing in the context of behavioral accounting 54

2.5.2   Research on heuristics in accounting research 58

2.6   Excursus: Assuring rationality – a German perspective 63

2.6.1   The actor model by Weber and colleagues 65

**2.7   Toward a theoretical framework of heuristic reasoning in management
        accounting 67**

2.7.1   Advances and trends in analyzing heuristics 67

2.7.2   Dual process models as a unifying approach 70

2.7.3   Clarifying some claims about intuition 75

2.7.4   The function of learning and expertise 79

2.7.5   The role of accountability and self-protection 82

2.7.6   Self-other decision making 86

2.7.7   Précis of theoretical framework regarding the application in management
        accounting 87

3   Synopsis and research design 91

3.1   Synopsis toward the empirical research design 91

3.2   Specifications of research design and research gap 96

3.2.1   Specification of the quantitative approach 96

3.2.2   Specification of the qualitative approach 97

3.2.3   Qualitative research in management accounting 101

3.2.4   Limitations of the applied mixed methods design........................103

3.3   Mixed methods in the context of testing theories............104

4   Step I: Experimental studies..109

4.1   Study: 1 can "less-be-more" in management accounting.................109

4.1.1   Introduction – heuristic reasoning in an investment decision 109

4.1.2   Method..114

4.1.3   Results..116

4.1.4   Discussion 123

4.2   Study 2: verbal protocol analysis of accounting problem solving.....126

4.2.1   Introduction – tracking decision processes with verbal protocols..............126

4.2.2   Method..131

4.2.3   Results..132

4.2.3.1 On the validity of the protocols 132

4.2.3.2 Code-based analysis of the protocols 133

4.2.4   Discussion 138

4.3   Study 3: on the accountability of accountants 140

4.3.1   Introduction – accountability in JDM research............................140

4.3.2   Method..143

4.3.3   Results..143

4.3.4   Discussion 150

**4.4   Study 4: Choice reversal in management accounting – a quasi-
         experimental demonstration...154**

4.4.1   Introduction – the sure-thing principle 154

4.4.2   Method..158

4.4.3   Results..159

4.4.3.1 Scenario 1 – Investment decision..159

4.4.3.2 Scenario 2 – Off-shoring decision 162

4.4.3.3 Scenario 3 – Fraud detection 164

4.4.3.4 Scenario 4 – Sunk costs 165

4.4.4   Discussion 167

5   Step II: Qualitative study 173

5.1   Understanding the decision process – a qualitative approach 173

5.2   Case selection and description 175

5.3   Data collection 178

5.3.1   Interview design and process 178

5.3.2   Transcription of the interviews 179

5.3.3   Analysis of the interviews 180

5.3.4   Some remarks on quality criteria in qualitative research 183

5.4   Qualitative results 186

5.4.1   General decision making procedures and rationality conceptualizations .. 187

5.4.2   Accounting functions 190

5.4.3   Heuristic types and implementation 191

5.4.4   Learning functions 193

5.4.5   Individual differences 194

5.4.6   Conclusion 196

6   Final summary and conclusion 199

6.1   Contributions and added value of the overall work 199

6.2   Limitations of the research design 204

6.3   Future research directions 205

6.4   Overall conclusion 209

Appendix 211

References 217

List of Figures

Figure 1: Process and influence characteristics of heuristic reasoning 7

Figure 2: Doctoral thesis structure 12

Figure 3: Outline and content of the thesis 14

Figure 4: Increased interest in the role of intuition-based on Factiva database 17

Figure 5: Explaining action with the deductive-nomological-model 20

Figure 6: Visions of rationality 24

Figure 7: Value (a) and weighting function (b) 30

Figure 8: Classic take-the-best algorithm 38

Figure 9: Accuracy of the take-the-best heuristic 39

Figure 10: Fitting versus predicting 40

Figure 11: Dominant psychological disciplines in behavioral accounting research ... 54

Figure 12: Classification of human information processing 56

Figure 13: Explaining social action within the actor model 67

Figure 14: Simon's scissors explicated 70

Figure 15: Heuristic reasoning and its reliance on intuition 79

Figure 16: Strategy selection theory 80

Figure 17: U-shaped progression of intuitive thinking in relation to expertise 82

Figure 18: Towards a theoretical framework of heuristics in management
           accounting 90

Figure 19: Theoretical embeddedness of the research design 106

Figure 20: The hierarchical structure of evolutionary explanations 107

Figure 21: Cue use depending on information load 122

Figure 22: Experimental results as a phased strategy from a dual process
           perspective 139

Figure 23: Cue acquisition as a complexity reduction mechanism 147

Figure 24: Coding scheme based on a deductive top-down process 181

Figure 25: Two stage thematic analysis procedure 183

Figure 26: Research design 187

Figure 27: Identified themes..198

List of Tables

Table 1: Some biases resulting from heuristics 32

Table 2: Summary of critique of the fast and frugal heuristics/ecological rationality
approach.. 46

Table 3: Development of behavioral research in accounting in the last 50 years 50

Table 4: JDM accounting articles by JDM approach: 1995-2002 53

Table 5: Heuristics as a research topic in major accounting publications*............... 60

Table 6: Publication of JDM experiments in accounting 61

Table 7: Various approaches and definitions of heuristic reasoning 68

Table 8: Characterization of Systems 1 and 2 72

Table 9: Absolute number of information used depending on amount of cues
presented... 117

Table 10: Percentage of cues used depending on amount of cues presented 118

Table 11: Crosstab – Relative cues used depending on absolute cues presented. 119

Table 12: Sum of rank differences depending on absolute cues presented 121

Table 13: Sum of rank differences depending on relative cues used (grouped) 121

Table 14: Results of the statistical analysis in Study 1 122

Table 15: JDM versus problem solving research 128

Table 16: Comparing Study 1 and verbal protocols with high information load....... 132

Table 17: Comparing Study 1 and verbal protocols with medium information load. 132

Table 18: Comparing Study 1 and verbal protocols with low information load 133

Table 19: Coding system for protocol analysis including example considerations.. 134

Table 20: Coding system suggested by Payne (1976a)... 135

Table 21: H1 – comparison of Study 1 and 3 in 20 cue condition 145

Table 22: H1 – comparison of Study 1 and 3 in 10 cue condition 145

Table 23: H1 – comparison of Study 1 and 3 in 5 cue condition 145

Table 24: H3 – Median split over factor score for "dependent" style...................... 148

Table 25: H3 – Tests of between-subjects-effects in- and excluding the factor
"dependent" style.. 149

Table 26: Results of the statistical analysis in Study 3 150

Table 27: Percentage of participants that recommended acquisition in condition 1
versus condition 2 in scenario 1 161

Table 28: Percentage of participants that recommended a project launch in condition
1 versus condition 2 in scenario 2 163

Table 29: Percentage of participants that recommend to report or not to report in
condition 1 versus condition 2 in scenario 3 165

Table 30: Percentage of participants that recommended to sell or not to sell in
condition 1 versus condition 2 in scenario 4 167

Table 31: Case descriptions 176

Table 32: Qualitative research process based on Eisenhardt (1989) 177

Table 33: Quality criteria for qualitative research based on Wrona (2005) 186

Table 34: GDMS responses of the eight cases 196

List of Abbreviations

Abbreviation	Meaning
ABC	Adaptive behavior and cognition
ANOVA	Analysis of variance
AOS	Accounting, Organizations and Society (Journal)
APA	American Psychological Association
BAR	Behavioral accounting research
BDT	Behavioral decision theory
BSC	Balanced scorecard
BRIA	Behavioral Research in Accounting (Journal)
CUT	Cardinal utility theory
df	Degrees of freedom
DN-model	Deductive-nomological-model
EUT	Expected utility theory
GDMS	General decision making style (measure)
JAR	Journal of Accounting Research (Journal)
JDM	Judgment and decision making
KPI	Key performance indicator
MA	Management accounting
MC	Management control
M&A	Merger and acquisition
M	Mean
MCS	Management control systems
MPI	Max Planck Institute
n	Size of group, cell
NDM	Naturalistic decision making
p	Significance level
PT	Prospect theory
R&D	Research and development
R^2	Percentage of variance explained
SD	Standard deviation
SEU theory	Theory of participative utility
SJDM	Society for Judgment and Decision Making
SSL	Strategy selection theory
SuC	Startup company
TTB	Take-the-best (heuristic)

*"It is one thing to show a man that he is in
error, and another to put him in possession
of the truth."*

John Locke (1689)

1 Introduction

1.1 On making (rational) decisions in management accounting

Making good choices and judgments in an increasingly complex and uncertain business world can be challenging. This is in particular true for management controllers,
whose role is seen by Weber and Schäffer (1999) as one of "assuring the rationality
of the management" in their task of "supplying information to the management on an
ongoing basis" (J. Weber, 2011a, p. 25).[1] Following this assumption, it appears that
management controllers somehow have a privileged access in terms of so-called
rational decision making and can face this kind of challenge in a particular way.

However, in line with the long history of research on biases in decision making
(e.g. Kahneman & Tversky, 2000), it seems unrealistic to presume that management
controllers differ from other professionals in the way they make decisions, especially
when using heuristics (cf. mental shortcuts, rules of thumb (Shah & Oppenheimer,
2008)) as a decision facilitating strategy. For instance, Kotchetova and Salterio
(2004, p. 548) recently pointed out that despite the fact that "processing of routine
transaction data is generally easy and error free, there are many accounting activities that may require estimates [...]. These estimates and projections are maybe sub-

---

[1] There is an ongoing debate (particularly in the German accounting community) regarding the
accurate description of the role and the tasks of management accountants and management controllers respectively. This thesis deals with the decision making processes of management controllers, whose task is defined by Weber (2011, p. 30) as "to inform the management about economic matters and activities" In this view, controllers not only provide information as "reliable re-
porters", they also ensure that the management adequately uses this information. According to
Weber (2011), the latter also represents the distinction between accountant and controller. However, it has to be noted that there is a tremendous amount of definitions and approaches, that
range from controllers as bean counters to controllers almost adequate to general managers (for
differences comparing Germany with Anglo-Saxon accounting tradition see Ahrens, 1999; for
general descriptions of the tasks and roles of management accountants/controllers see Anthony
& Govindarajan, 2001; Brühl, 2009; Byrne & Pierce, 2007; Horváth, 2009; Schmidt, 2011). For
the purposes of this thesis management accounting is used when referring to an institutional perspective (e.g. the management accounting community) and (management) controller is used
when referring to an individual perspective (e.g. the task of the management controller).

ject to both bias and noise (random error). "For example, many calculations of performance indicators in an investment decision lack a perfectly objective basis (for various reasons) and are subject to a substantive degree of individual estimates and thus to potential biases.

The objective of this thesis is thus to provide a more realistic description of the decision making behavior of management controllers and their use of heuristics, applying a mixed methods research design (Tashakkori & Teddlie, 2003). In a series of five studies, it is suggested that management controllers may not always act according to the laws of (economic) rationality, but under certain circumstances their decision making can be seen as an adaptive strategy to cope with a complex and uncertain environment (following the concepts of Gigerenzer, Todd, & the ABC Research Group, 1999; Payne, Bettman, & Johnson, 1993). Furthermore, the notion that managers tend to use intuitive decision making strategies, and management controllers are said to prefer more reflective strategies (J. Weber & Schäffer, 2008b), is linked with various streams of current psychological research, such as dual process theories (e.g. Evans & Frankish, 2010; Kahneman & Frederick, 2002; Sloman, 1996) or the influence of decision making styles (e.g. Betsch, 2008; Bruine de Bruin, Fischhoff, & Parker, 2007; Stanovich & West, 2000) that are currently seen as key issues with regard to judgment and decision making (JDM) research (Baron, 2008).

This behavioral-oriented approach towards heuristic reasoning represents a true gap in research as most existing research on decision making behavior in management accounting/control is guided either by rather static, economic models that make extensive use of free parameters (e.g. Balakrishnan & Sivaramakrishnan, 2002) or by normative approaches that regardless of frequency, only have limited empirical support (e.g., Schäffer & Weber, 2001). For instance, Luft (2011) points out that real decision makers differ from economic models in various ways (e.g. with respect to estimation of variables and parameter values) and suggests a shift towards more psychology-based models. Focusing on descriptions of real decision processes is also more successful for improving the decision making behavior of management controllers (Milkman, Chugh, & Bazerman, 2009), which represents one key factor regarding the relevance of this research topic.

1.2 Derivation of the research questions

In management control textbooks, controllers are often portrayed as prototypes of rational agents who prevent the management from making decisions based purely on their gut feelings, personal preferences and affective reactions. Link (2002), for example, points out that the management controller can be best described as the "chief information officer (CIO)" of the company. Weber and Schäffer (2011a; 1999, 2008a) see the task of the management controller as that of a consultant to the management, but also as a critical counterpart because that individual has to prevent the management from making irrational decisions (deficits of cognitive capabilities) and potential opportunism (deficits of willingness to act in favor of the company). In line with this argument, Brändle (2007) points out that these kinds of rationality deficits on the part of management represent a true bottleneck for every company. He highlights that the reason for this is because the rationality of the managers is bounded.[2]

Considering the extensive research on biases in judgment and decision making (for example Kahneman & Tversky, 2000), especially among so-called experts (Kahneman & Klein, 2009), it seems bold to claim a superior rationality for management accountants (at least according to the heuristics and biases program) within a company. In addition, it is not clear from the above sources how this "assuring of rationality" should actually work. If we take it to the extreme we might ask, why do we need management at all, if accountants make more rational (and thus better) decisions compared to the (top) management? Why does not the whole board of every *Fortune 500* company consist of management accountants making perfectly rational decisions? In other words: **How do management controllers cope with the challenge of increasingly complex tasks** and **when do they rely on heuristics in order to reduce complexity?**

In order to give a more realistic definition of the role of management controllers, it appears necessary to reflect briefly, what is meant by a rational decision (see section 2.3, p. 21ff, for an in depth discussion). In line with classical assumptions on rational-

---

[2]   It is important to note that this view on bounded rationality is not identical with its original meaning coined by Herbert Simon (1955), who saw bounded rationality as a general model for the cognitive capacities of humans (Jones, 1999).

ity, one of the most central aspects is consistency both of choice and preferences (Shafir & LeBoeuf, 2002). For example, if I prefer A over B and B over C I should also prefer A over C. In a more applied context, this would mean that a manager who prefers to buy shares from BMW over Audi and Audi over Mercedes, should also prefer to buy shares from BMW over Mercedes. Following the above given descriptions of management accountants, a manager might commit this logical lapse in making an investment decision. Choice between:

I.   BMW (A) and Audi (B) → manager invests in BMW (A)

II. Audi (B) and Mercedes (C) → manager invests in Audi (B)

III. BMW (A) and Mercedes (C) → manager invests in Mercedes (C)

Consistent with the above-mentioned definitions, in such a scenario the accountant should detect this case of irrationality and convince the decision maker that in scenario III, he should also prefer BMW over Mercedes. Many factors could have produced such an inconsistency. Framing effects or availability (Tversky & Kahneman, 1986) are just some frequently noted explanations (Bazerman & Moore, 2009) for violations of this normative standard. However, there is no empirical evidence that would exclude management accountants (or other experts), from committing these sorts of mistakes. On the contrary, some authors even argue that experts in particular are often victims of all sorts of irrational beliefs and biases (e.g. Ericsson, Andersson, & Cokely, 2006). In line with this extensive body of evidence of biases in (expert) decision making, there is still a lack of models that accurately describe the search strategies management accountants use in their tasks (Hogarth, 1991; Shields, 1980). The research question is thus: **What kinds of search strategies do management controllers use**?

One important distinction is of particular relevance in this case. The norm of consistency describes only the decision making process, and is not necessary linked with the outcome. This implies that one can make perfect rational decisions, but not ones which are necessarily the most successful (so the "irrational" manager might be successful in terms of his decisions).

Besides this, it is questionable if, in a complex environment, so-called "large worlds" consistency (Savage, 1954) is an appropriate standard. According to Gigerenzer and Gaissmaier (2011, p. 453) a "large world" refers to a "situation in which some relevant "information is unknown or must be estimated from samples, and the future is uncertain, violating the conditions for rational decision theory". "Large worlds" thus have to be distinguished from "small worlds", where all consequences and probabilities are known, such as in different versions of ultimatum games or the prisoner's dilemma (Binmore, 2007). Due to the fact that many, possibly subtle variables are constantly changing, it can be tricky to identify preference patterns in dynamic environments, where the comparison of A and B at time 1 (t1) can not simply be compared with the comparison of A and B at a second time 2 (t2). Therefore, what might appear as inconsistent at first glance can actually be consistent – it just depends on what kind of variables are taken into account.

In addition to this problem, it is also likely that management accountants may focus too much on the outcome of a decision and may miss the underlying logic. This tendency to focus too much on the outcome instead of the conditions when the decision was made, can be seen as well as a potential bias (Baron & Hershey, 1988). So a manager might act completely rationally from a logical point of view, but as his decisions lead to a bad outcome, he is paradoxically criticized for making irrational decisions (and the other way round). An example for this is the former CEO of Daimler, Jürgen E. Schrempp, who, during his time on the board of Daimler (1995 to 2005), took almost every chance to buy other companies (most well-known being the M&A with Chrysler), but was blamed later for being irrational in terms of his acquisition policy.

Some scholars suggest that efficient decisions in large worlds are not necessarily based on the classic norms of rationality. For instance Payne and colleagues (Payne, et al., 1993) or Gigerenzer and Selten (2002) point out that heuristics represent adaptive strategies (with working principle of exploiting the informational structure of the "large worlds" environment) that can be more successful in such a complex environments. In line with this stream of research, I derive the following research question: **Is there evidence of the adaptive character/ecological rationality of the decisions made by management controllers?**

Weber and Schäffer (1999) suggest the rationality working principle of management controllers as "instrumental rationality" (see also Tribe, 1973 for an early description of instrumental rationality). The degree of this kind of rationality is calculated by how efficient resources are allocated. This assumption means that accountants somehow have the ability to optimize the point at which costs (e.g. information costs) exceed the possible benefits. However, such as-if models are criticized by Selten (2002) for leading to an infinite regress, because this optimal stopping point again has also to be calculated, and these models are thus seen as a non-realistic model of actual human decision processes.

Even if this goal of optimization might not be reached, there is an ongoing debate if certain individual differences or decision making styles lead to more rational decisions (for an overview see Stanovich, 1999). Seeing the role of management controllers in "assuring the rationality" this issue is as well of high relevance in this community but it is rarely subject in behavioral accounting research (for an early study regarding this issue see Driver & Mock, 1975; Gul, 1984). Consequently the research question is: **What kind of role is played by individual differences, and to what degree is the task itself and its characteristics, such as accountability, responsible for the decision strategy?**

Overall, the objective of this work is thus twofold: firstly, to describe the use of heuristic reasoning in management accounting from a cognitive perspective, using a solid theoretical framework in experimental settings. Secondly, to explicate heuristics and the view of practitioners on the rationality (of financial decisions), also in a field study.

Following this approach, the empirically demonstrated gap in current behavioral accounting research regarding the use of novel perspectives of rational decision making (see Section 3.2.2, p. 97) can be closed. Arguing, that concepts such as ecological rationality and adaptive decision making (see Gigerenzer & Gaissmaier, 2011) have not been implemented into behavioral accounting research in an empirical way. Despite a long tradition of JDM research in this area (e.g. Dickhaut, 1976; or for an early summary Libby & Lewis, 1977), functionality and precise characteristics have rarely been studied (for an exception see Bedard & Wright, 1994). Most research in this area has so far typically focused on the replication and description of heuristics as departures from rational decision making, and as a lapse of human judgment (Hogarth, 1991; Trotman, Tan, & Ang, 2011).

Figure 1: Process and influence characteristics of heuristic reasoning

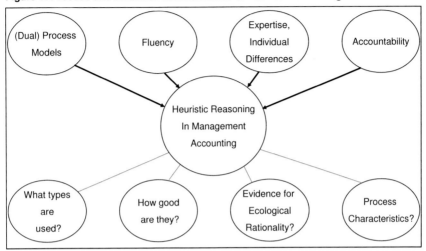

1.3   Research methods

Because the issue of heuristic reasoning (besides the well-known biases) and eco-logical rationality in management accounting is complex, and due to its current dy-namics, it is not a field with a large research history in terms of behavioral accounting research (only a few aspects have been touched for example by Bonner, 2008; Luft & Shields, 2009; Shields, 2002). It appears that a promising solution would be to de-velop a mixed methods design (Tashakkori & Teddlie, 2003), combining both quanti-tative (experimental, quasi-experimental) and qualitative (interviews, verbal proto-cols) methods, in order to achieve a more complete picture of adaptive decision making and ecological rationality in this field.

Quantitative methods, such as laboratory and web-based experiments allow the researcher to make exact hypotheses and to test some basic assumptions regarding the decision making process with regard to specific accounting issues (Birnbaum, 2000; Holland, 1986; Kempf, 2006). In JDM research, these are also the most com-monly used methods in the leading journals. This can be explained by the strong emphasis of most JDM research on cognitive and social psychology, fields which have traditionally been dominated by quantitative, experimental methods (Brehm, Kassin, & Fein, 2002; Sternberg, 2003).

Qualitative methods such as interviews, can be applied to include explorative questions as part of this research (Miles & Huberman, 1994; Yin, 2009). Additionally, they allow the cross-validation of results obtained using quantitative methods. This is of special interest because most of the participants in the experimental studies involved in this research are accounting students. Hence, one could argue that an accountant or manager working in a company would make completely different decisions compared to a Masters-level student or the like.

In addition to the interviews, verbal protocols also work as a further possibility for investigating the decision making process (Ericsson & Simon, 1993) and represent a kind of natural mixed method approach. Even though they have some well-documented limitations (Nisbett & Wilson, 1977) they can, in combination with other methods, provide fruitful insights into the decision making processes of management controllers (Ericsson, 2006).

The combination of the two paradigms, as laid out in the used mixed methods design, can be seen in line of what Reichenbach (1938) called "context of justification" and "context of discovery". "Justification" in this work, refers to empirical testing and the adoption of the concept of adaptive decision making, and ecological rationality into the management (accounting) context. "Discovery" refers to the inductive development of further hypotheses in order to develop a richer picture of the nature of adaptive decision making in large worlds.

- **Theoretical objective**: definition of terms and concepts (here: heuristic reasoning, ecological rationality, adaptive decision making) using current concepts and models of cognitive research (e.g. dual process models, fluency) and the integration of these concepts into existing management (accounting) research.

- **Explanation objective**: Test of key influence factors (like expertise, accountability, information load) on heuristic reasoning. Integration of the "two scissors" metaphor[3] by Herbert Simon (1990) into sensible explanations.

---

[3] According to Simon (1990, p. 7): "Human rational behavior (and the physical behavior of all physical symbol systems) is shaped by a scissors whose blades are the structure of task environments and the computational capabilities of the actor"

This approach can be seen as a further step with regard to exploring under which circumstances expertise (here that of management accountants) leads to efficient decisions and recommendations, and under what circumstances it also leads to biases (Kahneman & Klein, 2009). This could explain when, for example, heuristics are useful (Gigerenzer & Brighton, 2009) and when they might mislead the decision maker (Kahneman & Tversky, 2000). As mentioned before, management controllers make the perfect participants for this kind of research, because their self-concept is based on the assumption that they have a neutral and highly logical modus operandi. Furthermore, controllers spend a lot of their time analyzing reports, data and other kinds of information. They are responsible for the information which is finally presented to decision makers, or, as Ansari and Euske (1987, p. 549) write: "Management controllers make decisions so that the management can make decisions." It appears worth studying as to whether or not the prescriptive implications of the role of management accountants can be shown, both under controlled conditions, and with the help of structured interviews.

1.4 Research procedure

1.4.1 Experimental methods

In the quantitative section of this thesis (Chapter 4, p. 109ff), a series of three experimental studies and one web-based quasi-experimental study shed some light on how management controllers cope with the typical challenges they face – that is dealing with complexity in an uncertain environment, and how heuristics work in these environments as part of a potentially adaptive strategy.

An appropriate scenario to analyze their behavior represent investment decisions, in which several performance indicators have to be considered, before making any kind of recommendation to the management. An analysis of performance indicators is, for example, also a typical task associated with evaluating and generating the well-established Balanced-Scorecard (Kaplan & Norton, 1992). Possible variables that have an impact on this kind of decision making process and that are being tested are: information (over)load and costs, time pressure, accountability, and individual differences.

1.4.2 Verbal protocols

The results from paper-pencil based experiments are compared with verbal protocols

(see section 4.2, p. 125ff) (Ericsson, 2006; Ericsson & Simon, 1993), where participants solve the same task as in the experiment – however they are asked to voice
their thoughts while solving the problem. It can be expected that not all kinds of internal processes are accessible with regard to participants of the study (Hayes,
1986). Nevertheless, the stunning validity of verbal protocols has been recently
documented in a large scale meta-analysis by Fox and colleagues (2011). This kind
of method serves as an add-on approach used to cross-validate the paper-pencil
based experiments and, most importantly, to generate a richer description of the decision making process (Payne & Venkatraman, 2011).

In general it appears promising to include in these kinds of studies only students
or professionals who have some management accounting experience (e.g. third year
students, Masters level students)[4] as participants. Controlling for expertise and experience in these kind of studies is nevertheless a typical challenge (Ashton &
Kramer, 1980; Remus, 1986). The importance of verbal protocols (and other more
qualitatively-oriented approaches) as data, in addition to the commonly used quantitative methods, is stressed for instance by Simon (2000, p. 36). He advocates that
"economists must be trained in methods of observing and interviewing, of taking and
analyzing verbal think-aloud protocols, of extracting information about decision processes from written records, and of drawing conclusions reliably from multiple studies
of these kinds."

1.4.3   Interviews

To get a view from outside the controlled conditions of the experiments, it is also of
interest to include an explorative approach using more open techniques such as
structured interviews (e.g. Rubin & Rubin, 2005) and their thematic analysis (Braun
& Clarke, 2006) in this thesis (see Chapter 5, p. 172ff). Managers (who combine the
roles of CEOs and CFOs) from four startups and four experienced management controllers from medium and large companies, are questioned in standardized interviews about how they assure "rational decision making" in their companies. Startups

---

[4]   In general, it might also be better to speak of management accounting experience instead of
management accounting expertise, as some scholars have pointed out the difficulties regarding
the measurement of what actually constitutes an expert in business administration (see Ericsson,
Prietula, & Cokely, 2007).

are selected for two pragmatic reasons. Firstly, these companies face a high level of uncertainty and risk which is typical for "large worlds" (Davila & Foster, 2007). Secondly, it is assumed that hierarchies in startups are rather flat. Thus, it can be concluded that the decisions reported in the interview will have a high impact level and are not only relevant on a certain hierarchical level. Additionally, the decision strategies can be contrasted to those in found in the large companies.

In particular the independent variables from the experimental research are integrated into the design of the questions. For example, it will be asked how the participants' decision strategies change when they have to report their results to their stakeholders, versus when they have the freedom to act upon their own decision. Another issue of interest is how the management tries to deal with conflicting opinions that are based on the use of heuristics, and how they try to prevent themselves from introducing potential decision biases.

Besides the variables adopted as part of the quantitative approach, I will investigate the extent to which accountants, as experts, are reluctant to act upon rules (which is described as a potential bias by Kahneman and Lovallo (1993)). It is of interest to investigate if long experience leads to a reluctance to adopt new strategies or guidelines. It may be that experience-based heuristic reasoning is only successful to a degree, when people stop being adaptive.

Again, we must keep in mind that people are often misguided by the outcome bias of decisions. Therefore, if a manager only uses success as a feedback it might appear that he is failing to learn from a (changing) environment. The main focus of the qualitative approach is to consider under what circumstances heuristics and shortcuts are used in evaluating information in field settings. For example Bettman and Park (1980), using a experimental verbal protocol analysis, suggested that people use phased strategies when making decisions. A phased strategy implies that, based on a heuristic, inferior alternatives are eliminated, and only the remaining cues are evaluated extensively.

As illustrated in Figures 2 and 3, this thesis starts with a detailed discussion of what actually constitutes rationality in management research, and which crucial part is played by heuristics in terms of this issue (Chapter 2, p. 15ff). The next section of Chapter 2 links this discussion with the field of behavioral accounting research (BAR) and discusses key concepts within judgment and decision making (JDM) research in accounting (in particular section 2.7, p. 67ff) alongside the historical development of this subfield. The empirical research design is summarized in Chapter 3 (p. 91ff), together with a discussion of the used mixed methods approach. The first part of the empirical section of this work is a series of four experimental studies, analyzing heuristic reasoning in management accounting from various perspectives (Chapter 4, p. 109ff).

Figure 2: Doctoral thesis structure

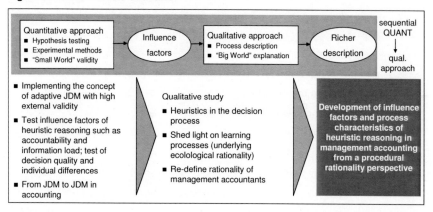

Study 1 (p. 112ff), an experimental study with n = 212 management accounting students, suggests that there is a strong preference for leaving out most of the cues and engaging instead in heuristic reasoning, even if the instructions for the task clearly ask the participant to consider all presented information. Comparing these strategies with the equally-balanced solution as a normative yardstick (Payne, 1976b) shows that, from the individual perspective, the often-quoted "less-is-more" (Gigerenzer, et al., 1999) effect is certainly not true.

Study 2 (p. 130ff) replicated Study 1 in order to better understand how heuristics are embedded in management controllers' decision strategies, but this time using verbal protocols (cf. think-aloud protocols (Ericsson & Simon, 1993)), with n = 17 participants, in the behavioral laboratory of a North American University. The analysis of the protocols indicated that participants relied on phased strategies (H. Lee, Herr, Kardes, & Kim, 1999), using a processing-by-parameter approach (Shields, 1980). This kind of strategy typically involves firstly eliminating some alternatives (in the fashion of elimination-by-aspects (Tversky, 1972)), followed secondly by a more compensatory search and cue weighting process.

In experimental **Study 3** (p. 145ff) the investment scenario, as used in Studies 1 and 2, was also used as the cover story. However, this time, Master's and PhD student participants (n = 31) did not receive all the information immediately. Instead of the full information load used in the other studies, each participant had a fixed budget with which he was able to "buy" KPIs from a consultant. The results indicated that the participants were resistant to spending all the money and (as demonstrated in Study 2) instead used a phased decision strategy. This meant that they reduced the potentially complex decision by focusing (cf. buying) a small subset of information. This small subset was then usually analyzed in a compensatory fashion. The hypothesized effect of a "dependent" decision making style (Scott & Bruce, 1995) causing higher cue acquisition was supported.

In **Study 4** (p. 159ff), a quasi-experimental study (n = 50), using a between-subject design, I find evidence that the acquisition of new information, even if it is noninstrumental, frequently leads to choice reversals (in 2 out of 2 scenarios) or to choice enforcement (in 1 out of 2 scenarios). As expected, participants (graduate students and accounting professionals) extensively engaged in information acquisitiveness, and often weighted the latest information most heavily in conducting a typical management accounting task (e.g. investment decision and fraud detection). This finding is particularly important because information acquisition and evaluation is an activity done by management controllers on a daily basis. Interestingly, the effect is robust both in conditions where the information was free, and where the information was said to be costly. Therefore, it appears that the mere existence of new facts lets participants believe that this information had a higher importance compared to the known facts. The theoretical implications and practical relevance of the results are discussed and integrated into the theoretical framework of dual process theories of reasoning (e.g. Evans & Frankish, 2010).

The qualitative study (**Study 5**) is documented in Chapter 5 (p. 172ff), analyzing the use of heuristics in field settings. The first two themes that emerged out of the analysis of the interviews with the managers and the controllers are the distinction between ideal decision making and rationality assumptions of the interviewees and the applied decision strategies and mechanisms. The interviewees, of the established and the emerging startups in particular, acknowledged that their decision making is strategic; financial decisions are frequently not guided by rationality standards. Rationality to them is typically defined through quantitative data and their precise compensatory analysis.

This thesis concludes with a general discussion of the results (Chapter 6, p. 197ff); including a summary of the theoretical and empirical contribution and a discussion of future research directions.

Figure 3: Outline and content of the thesis

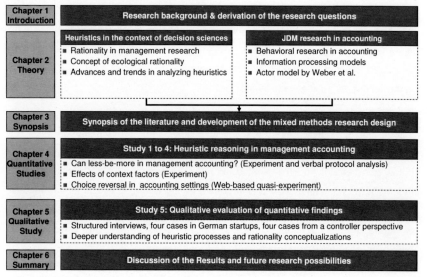

2 JDM and heuristics in (management) accounting

2.1 Rationality in management research[5]

Judgment and decision making[6] topics currently enjoy a high popularity in academia. Interdisciplinary societies such as the *Society for Judgment and Decision Making* (SJDM, formed in 1986) report constantly increasing memberships. Scholars from various management disciplines such as marketing, organizational sciences and management control are interested in accurate descriptive and prescriptive models, in order to understand what are good choices and how to improve decision quality and avoid errors (Bazerman & Moore, 2009).

For most of the twentieth century economics set the benchmark for rationality concepts in management disciplines. However, for the last three decades a strong influence from psychology has been shaping the field in management research as well as in economics (DellaVigna, 2009). Therefore, today most of the theories and models in JDM have a strong emphasis on psychological theories and concepts. This comes as no surprise as, for example, Tetlock (2002, p. 451) highlights that "research on judgment and choice has become psychology's leading intellectual export to the social sciences as to a host of applied fields".

The public also seems to be highly interested in these issues, which can be illustrated with the success stories of popular science books like *The Paradox of Choice* (2004) by Berry Schwartz, *Blink* (2005) by Malcolm Gladwell, *Predictably Irrational* (2008) and *The Upside of Irrationality* (2010) by Dan Ariely or most recently *How we decide* by Jonah Lehrer (2010).

In management research, most notably the research program labeled heuristics and biases (prospect theory), coined by Daniel Kahneman and Amos Tversky

---

[5]   This section and the theoretical framework of this thesis (Chapter 2) are in large parts based on Basel and Brühl (2011).

[6]   According to Bonner (1999, p. 385): "The term judgment typically refers to forming an idea, opinion, or estimate about an object, an event, a state, or another type of phenomenon. Judgments tend to take the form of predictions about the future or an evaluation of a current state of affairs. The term decision refers to making up one's mind about the issue at hand and taking a course of action. Decisions typically follow judgments and involve a choice among various alternatives based on judgments about those alternatives and, possibly, preferences for factors such as risk and money. In other words, judgments reflect one's beliefs, and decisions may reflect both beliefs and preferences."

(1981), had a high impact as in almost all other fields of social sciences (Keren & Teigen, 2004). For an example of its popularity, the famous article "Prospect theory: an analysis of decision under risk" published in *Econometrica*, in 1979 by Kahneman and Tversky, is the most cited article of this journal, with the impressive record of over 1,800 citations until 1996 (Laibson & Zeckhauser, 1998).

A strong reference towards this research program in management studies is often made through the prefix "behavioral"; be it behavioral finance (Thaler, 1993), behavioral accounting (Siegel & Ramanauskas-Marconi, 1989), or behavioral economics[7] in general (Camerer, Loewenstein, & Rabin, 2003; Heukelom, 2007b; Mullainathan & Thaler, 2000). The success of this groundbreaking theory of judgment under uncertainty was crowned with the award of the Nobel Prize for Economics to Daniel Kahneman in 2002.[8] One particular aspect in JDM that attracts increasing (public[9]) popularity is the function of intuition. For example, the hits for the keyword "intuition" using *Factiva* database, even with a conservative search strategy (eliminating duplicates etc.), almost doubled between 2001 and 2009.

The emphasis on decision errors and biases was, however, criticized for missing the point that decisions in the real world do not work according to the laws of logic and that the described norms of the heuristics and biases program are content blind (for early critique see Gigerenzer, 1991; Lopes, 1992). From the viewpoint of programs like natural decision making (Klein, 1993), fast and frugal heuristics (Gigerenzer & Todd, 1999) or evolutionary psychology (Cosmides & Tooby, 1994), it was clear that the ascription of rationality or irrationality should not be left to logic or probability theory and thus these programs open up new research agendas for rationality.

---

[7]   The "behavioral" approach can also be distinguished from experimental economics in that traditional axioms of economics are rejected both positively and normatively (Heukelom, 2007b). Furthermore behavioral economics is not focused on just one single method of experiments (Loewenstein, 1999).

[8]   Amos Tversky died in 1996, thus the prize was only awarded to Daniel Kahneman.

[9]   "Public" interest, because *Factiva* database includes articles from newspapers, popular science magazines etc. It is however an open question if public interest follows academic results or vice-versa.

Figure 4: Increased interest in the role of intuition-based on *Factiva* database

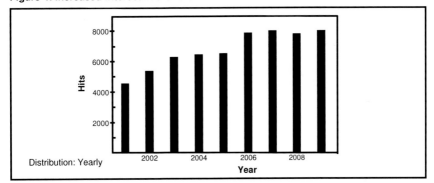

Following the critique on imposing a too high standard of rationality on social actors, the important next step in decision research came in the late nineties with the introduction of a new program by Gerd Gigerenzer and colleagues (Gigerenzer, 2002; Gigerenzer, et al., 1999) called fast and frugal heuristics. This proposal states that under limited resources (e.g. time and money) fast and effective decision strategies can beat complex utility maximization calculations. This concept builds upon the pioneering work of Herbert Simon (1955) on bounded rationality and on concepts that suggest adaptive behavior and simple decision making as successful strategies when making inferences (e.g. Dawes, 1979; Hogarth, 1987; Payne, et al., 1993).

Proclaiming this revolutionary shortcut in JDM, this proposition emphasizes ecological rationality instead of biases, errors and illusions and thus it switches away from logic and probability as normative benchmarks. In summary, studying ecological rationality should reveal "in which environments a given strategy is better than other strategies (better – not best – because in large worlds the optimal strategy is unknown)" (Gigerenzer & Gaissmaier, 2011, p. 456). Goldstein and Gigerenzer (2002) argue that from an ecological rationality point of view, informational structures of the environment are taken into account and these structures are integrated in an adaptive way into bounded decision capabilities.

As a handy metaphor for this program Gigerenzer (e.g. Gigerenzer, 2006) quotes Nobel Prize laureate Herbert Simon, who stresses that "human rational behavior (and the physical behavior of all physical symbol systems) is shaped by a scissors whose blades are the structure of task environments and the computational capabilities of the actor" (Simon, 1990, p. 7). Following this picture, Kahneman and Tversky focus on just one blade, namely our brain, which is indeed not a computer that can work with the principles of unbounded rationality and perfect logic. Thus, the brain is an easy victim to all kinds of biases and lapses. However, scholars who favor the concept of ecological rationality stress analyzing both blades: the cognitive capabilities of human beings and the environment in which they operate.

Advocates of the fast and frugal program argue that, under certain circumstances, these so-called biases (e.g. the reliance on heuristics as mental shortcuts) represent evolved and adaptive mechanisms of human behavior and cognition. Consequently, they can be highly efficient if applied in appropriate situations. In this context Gigerenzer and Todd (1999) and Gigerenzer and Selten (2002) coined the term "the adaptive toolbox", as a metaphor for the human capability to make good and efficient inferences[10] in a fundamentally uncertain world. Thus, broadly speaking this program aims to show in which situations different decision strategies, like fast and frugal heuristics, work to a sufficient degree. As a starting point for the analysis of heuristic reasoning in management accounting, I will provide an overview of the main concepts of rationality in management research. However, I will focus on the concept of bounded rationality. The concept of rationality is deeply rooted in economics and thus this economic interpretation is often taken as a blueprint for how rationality has to work. However, rationality as a concept has many facets and is one of the broadest concepts used in the social sciences. One of the main features of broad concepts is that they lack necessary properties, which is often misinterpreted as being ill-defined. Moreover, its different usage in disciplines like philosophy, economics, sociology and management research adds to the impression of an incoherent concept. One objective of this thesis deals with entangling different strands of rationality and explaining their function in management research.[11]

---

[10]   According to Weber and Johnson (2009) "inferences" are judgments about the world using logic and often imperfect and uncertain information. Because for inferences a unique criterion exists, their accuracy can be evaluated. Preferences address problems without such an external criterion of success (as in matters of taste), thus a calculation of accuracy is not possible in this case. However, since both draw on the same cognitive processes (E. U. Weber & Johnson, 2009) the studies described in this work can be applied for both inferences and preferences.

[11]   One possibility of coping with terminological problems would be to abandon the necessary condition concept and apply concepts like Ludwig Wittgenstein's notion of family resemblance (Wittgenstein, 1953).

The remainder of this thesis is organized in the following manner. I will start with a short introduction as to how, according to the philosophy of social science, we should explain action, which is the core business of social sciences like management research. This will reveal the importance of rationality as a concept in the social sciences. I will then shortly outline unbounded rationality and show its differences to the programs which aim at explicating bounded rationality.

In the next chapter I will analyze and discuss both programs – the heuristics and bias program and the fast and frugal program – which are in the centre of JDM research - and the notion of bounded rationality. Advocates of both programs tend to overestimate differences between them. However, I will conclude this section with a discussion of dual-process theories (e.g. Evans & Frankish, 2010) which offer a promising research agenda to reconcile both programs. Additionally related concepts and relevant factors such as accountability (e.g. Lerner & Tetlock, 1999) or the role of learning and expertise (e.g. Salas, Rosen, & DiazGranados, 2010) are discussed.

This work is an attempt to point out how these new directions in decision research can be a fruitful approach in business studies and in particular in management accounting. To show the diversity of this research program a mixed methods approach was chosen (Creswell & Plano Clark, 2007). The legitimacy of this approach is discussed in Chapter 3 (p. 91ff).

2.2 Explaining social action

Social scientists aim at explaining human action, which is not mere behavior. Central to the explanations of social action are the intentions (objectives) and beliefs of social actors (Rosenberg, 2008). If humans behave purposefully or intentionally[12] scholars coin this behavior "action" (M. Weber, 1947). Therefore, action is a theoretical concept of the social sciences, which I ascribe to social actors. I will use Hempel and Oppenheim's (1965) deductive-nomological-model (DN-model) of explanation to illustrate the role of rationality in explaining social action. A DN-model, which is capable of explaining action, encompasses premises (explanans) and a conclusion (explanandum). There must be several ingredients to a successful explanation.

---

[12]   Intentional processes are not necessarily conscious processes, even goal selection may work unconsciously (Dijksterhuis & Aarts, 2010).

1. Law: A social law as a general rule about the objectives, beliefs and which action to take.

2. Antecedents: objectives and beliefs of the social actors.

3. The action as a consequence.

Figure 5: Explaining action with the DN-model (adapted from Brühl, 2010, p. 53)

Explanans:		
Law (L):		$(O \wedge (O \rightarrow A)) \rightarrow A$
Antecedents:		
- objective of i	Actor i wishes to obtain objective O_i	O_i
- beliefs of i	Actor i beliefs that action A_i is necessary to realize O_i	$O_i \rightarrow A_i$
Explanandum:	Actor i acts A_i	A_i

I will not discuss the feasibility of the DN-model[13], but I will demonstrate why rationality is a central concept in explaining social action. However, I will also discuss why it is a problematic concept. Deductive inferences preserve the truth and if all premises are true then the conclusion will also be true. Central to the DN-model of explanation is the truth of the social law: all actors with the objective (O) and the belief that A is necessary to realize O, will act in accordance with A.

Therefore, our first intuition of rationality is that social actors act intentionally and are able to give reasons as to why they act in the observed manner. Figure 5 exhibits objectives and beliefs of social actors as reasons for their actions. Consequently, the basic notion of rationality is that social actors have reasons (objectives and beliefs) for their actions. Nevertheless, Figure 5 illustrates only a basic scheme as to how to explain action and leaves room for different interpretations of rationality:

I. Rationality as an a priori principle: one interpretation of rationality is that human action is necessary rational (Mises, 1966). Because rationality has the function of an a priori principle it is not possible to empirically falsify it. Logically, the law (L) is a tautology and thus it is analytically true (i.e., it is

---

[13] For a thorough analysis of different approaches to explanation see for instance Salmon (1989); more recent contributions are discussed in Psillos (2007).

true regardless of the true value of A or O). Usually, normative theories, like most economic theories, are based on this notion of rationality.

Economic theories of rationality concentrate on the beliefs of social actors and impose many hypothetical beliefs on them. For instance, they have consistent, stable preferences and are able to rank all alternatives or they have unlimited computational power etc. All this leads to a version of Figure 5 where the beliefs of the actor have to be extended with all the added demands on the preferences of the social actor.

II.   Rationality as a theoretical concept: in this interpretation rationality is a theoretical concept which is embedded in a behavioral theory (on judgment and   decision making) and is linked to empirical concepts (indicators) from which it gains its empirical meaning. Thus, it is empirical research which models the social actors. Psychological research has taken this road and has, for instance, shown that social actors systematically violate assumptions of economic rationality. This is mainly the reason why scholars from psychology have taken alternative routes.

Of course, this dichotomy can be seen as a continuum with both interpretations as opposite poles and a variety of possible concepts of rationality in-between. This can be expressed differently as: there are a variety of models of rationality which varies in the assumptions they make about rational action and in the way they conduct research.

Both interpretations span the discussion in different disciplines, but in the following discussion I will discuss research contributions which mainly focus on the second interpretation. However, I will outline the first interpretation because scholars who engage in behavioral research object to basic assumptions of the economic interpretation of rationality.

2.3 From unbounded- to bounded- to ecological rationality

2.3.1 Money as utility and the origin of modern decision sciences

One tipping point for the social sciences in the twentieth century was the publication of Theory of Games and Economic Behavior in 1944 by John von Neumann and Oskar Morgenstern, because it provided the framework to balance utility, in the description of human preferences, with money. Doing this, von Neumann and Morgenstern extended Daniel Bernoulli's (1738/1954) psycho-physical concept of cardinal utility theory (CUT)[14] and introduced expected utility theory (EUT).This theory states that our decisions are guided by participative value and it is that, not utility, (as laid out by CUT) that is the basis for human (rational) behavior – rather than the maximization of monetary income. Friedman and Savage (1948), for example, were able to explain both risk-seeking and risk-averse behavior referring to an expected utility function; this would not have been possible using only CUT.

This change, in the way individuals base their (economic) decisions, is interpreted by some scholars as the comeback of homo economicus into social sciences (Heukelom, 2005). Thus, using EUT as a yardstick allows for labeling deviations from expected utility as irrational behavior.

The term homo economicus itself (or economic man, homo oeconomicus (Van der Rijt, 2006)) was originally coined by critics of the work of John Stuart Mill in the late nineteenth century (Persky, 1995), and represents the prototype of rational (and self-interested) behavior in classical economic theory.

The principles of rational (economic) behavior stressed by von Neumann and Morgenstern can be summarized in five axioms (Fishburn, 1981), which illustrate the belief system of social actors (acting like homo economicus)[15] in Figure 6 (p. 24).:

i.   If confronted with several options, social actors are able to use a form of pref-
     erence ordering (**order of preferences**).

ii. Preferences of social actors are consistent; no contradictions occur (**transitiv-
     ity of preferences**).

iii. Preferences of social actors are independent from other options or considera-
     tions (**independence of preferences**).

---

[14] Bernoulli stressed in his writings that money has diminishing value. This means that enjoyment does not increase proportionately with increase in wealth (Larrick, 1993). Bernoulli justified this hypothesis by arguing that money gets less valuable, when all basic needs (like food, clothes and a home) have been met. This results in the fact that additional wealth can only add less and less utility, which is also known as the classic concept of diminishing marginal utility in economics (Bell, 1967).

[15] For an elaborated explanation of rationality within EUT see Hastie and Dawes (2010, p. 244 ff.).

iv.   If social actors prefer one option over another, this option is chosen (**choice of preferences**).

v.   Preferences of social actors are not participant to changes no matter how they are presented as long as they are logically equivalent (**invariance of preferences**).

The first question, arising from these assumptions, is how is this normative model of a social actor reached by real human beings? The second question asks, is this normative model an adequate model for social science theories of human decision making? The next sections therefore aim to clarify if these assumptions are maintained and how departures from this ideal model are explained.

For homo economicus, successful decision making is thus closely related to the norms of neo-classical theories of human decision behavior. In other words: unbounded (economic) rationality is fulfilled if all five assumptions are met and this defines a rational action (see Figure 6 on the next page). If we assume however, that rationality can be understood in other forms of successful decision making, and, of course this will highly depend on what counts as successful, different paths can be drawn of how an obviously broad concept of rationality is achieved.

This view, as illustrated in Figure 6, distinguishes between different concepts of rationality. In particular it separates between those models that propagate unbounded rationality and those that rely on bounded rationality (Gigerenzer & Selten, 2002). On the one side, the unbounded rationality concept (the prototype of homo economicus) refers to concepts in which human judgment and decision making incorporate a kind of a microprocessor that calculates the (optimal) outcome.

A caricature of this concept is a description of a super chip driven human agent that knows all the odds and is a perfect Bayesian calculator or as Thaler and Sunstein state: "Homo economicus can think like Albert Einstein, store as much memory as IBM's Big Blue, and exercise the willpower of Mahatma Gandhi" (Thaler & Sunstein, 2008, p. 6). Some models use an optimization under constraints approach, however, that does not change the capabilities of homo economicus.

The optimization under constraints model states that we search for further information until the costs exceed the benefits (for an example see Stigler, 1961). This modification of the unbounded concept however leads to an infinite regress, because all the benefits and costs have to be computed somehow – and how shall a bounded mind conduct such sophisticated estimations? Rieskamp and Otto (2006, p. 207) thus call this symptomatic issue "the recursive homunculi problem of deciding how to decide". The notion of bounded rationality, as introduced by Herbert Simon in the 1940s, is focused on how we deal with the limitations of social actors as human beings (Simon, 1945).

Two paths are depicted in Figure 6 on the next page. First, heuristics and biases deploy norms from the neo-classical approach and benchmark humans with respect to these axioms (Kahneman & Tversky, 2000). Satisficing, a blend of sufficing and satisfying, is concentrated on finding solutions that are good enough and departs from the ideal of optimization (Simon, 1955).

Finally, advocates of fast and frugal heuristics go a step beyond satisficing and point out that under certain circumstances these descriptive models can be seen as a normative standard (Gigerenzer, et al., 1999). Gigerenzer and Gaissmaier (2011, p. 454) define heuristic as "a strategy that ignores part of the information, with the goal of making decisions more quickly, frugally, and/or accurately than more complex methods". This way they make a clear distinction between their view on mental shortcuts and the one provided by Kahneman and Tversky (2000).

In the following section, I will concentrate on the concept of bounded rationality and on the two paths of this concept: satisficing and fast and frugal heuristics.

Figure 6: Visions of rationality (adapted from Gigerenzer, 2002)

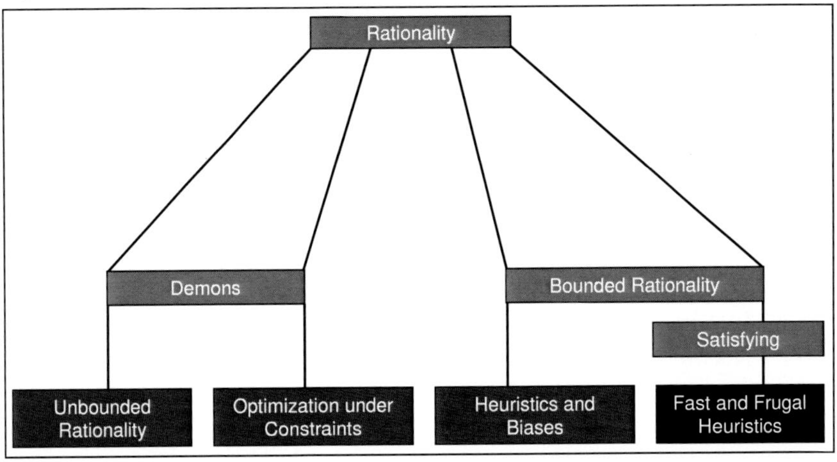

2.3.2 Unbounded rationality and optimization under constraints

The idea of unbounded rationality assumes that people have unlimited computational power, time and knowledge (and from a management perspective you could also include unlimited money, if taken into account that most information in management settings, like benchmark studies, are not available for free). This form of omniscience leads to the final decision that maximizes the expected utility.

Economic models, supposing unbounded rationality are drawn from homo economicus, which is the underlying principle of all neoclassical economic models (M. S. Morgan, 2006): maximizing expected utility and statistical Bayesian models. It seems obvious that the assumption of unbounded rationality is an unrealistic yardstick for human reasoning in the real world.

Contrary to this objection, maybe due to its economic connotation (Becker, 1976), this approach is frequently found when authors in management JDM books use the term bounded rationality (e.g. Bazerman & Moore, 2009; Bonner, 2008). Bazerman and Moore, for instance, provide with their book *Judgment and Managerial Decision making*, (2009, pp. 2-3) a guide for rational decision making. These authors argue that a rational decision maker "will identify all relevant criteria in the decision making process" and that "an optimal search continues only until the cost of the search outweighs the value of the added information". Some of the advice from these authors' even sounds like a description of the concept of unbounded rationality, when they stress: "the rational decision maker carefully assesses the potential consequences on each of the identified criteria of selecting each of the alternative solutions".[16]

However, this is not the meaning of bounded rationality because, as already mentioned, an optimization under constraints approach does not relieve social actors of the heavy burden of homo economicus.

2.3.3 Bounded rationality

Herbert Simon, who primarily studied behavior in organizations, is considered to be the father of the term bounded rationality (Selten, 2002; Simon, 1945). According to Simon (for a summary see Simon, 1993), human agents have only limited information processing capabilities and are therefore not able to perform perfectly rational decisions (in the sense of unbounded rationality). In particular, their knowledge to evaluate consequences and alternatives of possible decisions lacks a deeper understanding of all relevant factors. Simon (1979, p. 502) in particular differentiates between an external uncertain world and our innate bounded cognitive capabilities:

> "Rationality is bounded when it falls short of omniscience. And the failures of omniscience are largely failures of knowing all the alternatives, uncertainty about relevant exogenous events, and inability to calculate consequences."

Furthermore, Simon points out that our cognitive limitations have the consequence that we will not reach optimal decisions; instead we use satisficing decisions as our personal (and more realistic) yardstick. Simon (1997, p. 295) states:

> "A decision maker who chooses the best available alternative according to some criterion is said to optimize; one who chooses an alternative that meets or exceeds specified criteria, but that is not guaranteed to be either unique or in any sense the best, is to satisfice."

Thus, Simon's concept of bounded rationality and satisficing concisely would be the following statement: a perfect and ideal solution might exist for our problems, but

---

[16] In some cases this modification is also compared with Friedman and Savage's (1948) as-if assumption. According to these scholars, people are not actually calculating all odds etc., but they behave as if they would do so and as if they compute somehow a form of expected utility.

because of our bounded mind we are not able to conduct the necessary cognitive steps to reach this goal. Paying respect to this fact, we use satisficing decisions and systematically deviate from ideals of unbounded rationality. With this strategy, we can reach satisfactory but not perfect outcomes.

This approach is supported by the theory of the second best (Lipsey & Lancaster, 1956). According to this classic theory, simply getting closer to an optimization, does not necessarily lead to better overall decisions. Following this theory, it pays if a single condition cannot be reached (e.g. too high costs, lack of skills), to also depart from the other conditions and to reach this way a second-best outcome (i.e. a satisficing outcome).

In Simon's view it is important to recognize that social sciences are always both normative and descriptive, compared to natural sciences that are only descriptive. Thus, we cannot simply describe the decision making of humans without having a normative standard in mind. Simon sees social sciences in the same vein as engineering, where the goal is not only to describe how a bridge is build, but to construct the most efficient bridge possible with the available resources. This fundamentally distinguishes Simon's view from classic economists like Savage (1954), who mainly use normative methods without considering actual human behavior (Heukelom, 2007a).

One of the major credits of Simon's work is that he always insisted that these postulates, like expected utility theory or probability weighting (Baron, 2008), might not fit empirical data. In one of his last publications Simon (2000, p. 25) resumes his research program on bounded rationality:

> "Bounded rationality is simply the idea that the choices people make are determined not only by some consistent overall goal and the properties of the external world, but also by the knowledge that decision makers do and don't have of the world, their ability or inability to evoke that knowledge when it is relevant, to work out the consequences of their actions, to conjure up possible courses of action, to cope with uncertainty (including uncertainty from the possible responses of other actors), and to adjudicate among their many competing wants. Rationality is bounded because these abilities are severely limited. Consequently, rational behaviour in the

real world is as much determined by the "inner environment" of the world people's minds, both their memory contents and their processes, as by the "outer environment" of the world on which they act, and which acts on them."

The tricky part to describing human decision making properly, stems from Simon's (1990) above mentioned scissor metaphor.[17] In line with this picture, the term bounded can be interpreted in two ways. On the one hand management scholars may consider limitations of the environment, like information costs (for example, a survey to find out employee satisfaction can be costly) or the difficulty of even gathering specific information (for example, which products are used by a competitor in order to conduct a benchmark). On the other hand, management scholars may consider cognitive limitations of the human agent, for example limitations in memory storage and imperfect evaluation of statistical information by the management.

However, Simon did not start a research program with empirical research on these issues. As a consequence the concept spread in different research areas with different meanings and different approaches to incorporate bounded rationality into other research programs (Klaes & Sent, 2005). In behavioral economics, for instance, bounded rationality is more in line with mainstream economics as Simon had in mind. Looking at the current state of behavioral economics Sent (2004, p. 750) states: "Simon's ideas are missing from the more recent development". According to Sent (2004) behavioral economics mainly relies on the heuristic and biases program from Kahneman and Tversky.

2.3.4 Heuristics and biases

This program was to a large extent initiated in the late 1970s and early 1980s by the research of Daniel Kahneman and Amos Tversky. They showed that human JDM cannot be accurately described in the terms of unbounded rationality, similar to the computer metaphor, as mentioned in the previous section. The central point of their

---

[17]   Describing the environment as an objective entity, as in Simon's approach, is, for instance, criticized by Weick (1979), who called into question (from an enactment/sense making point of view), that this entity can only be practically comprehended by a decision maker. From a constructivist perspective, he argues that rather decision makers mostly create their own constraints through an constructive process (see also Hodgkinson & Healey, 2008).

position is that our judgments and decisions systematically depart from ideals of logic and probability theory and, thus, from rational behavior. Logic and probability theory laid the ground on which the homo economicus and its prototype of utility maximizer (and EUT) stand and which served as the dominant economic research program until the 1970s (Van der Rijt, 2006). The main thrust of Kahneman and Tversky's research revealed EUT limitations in various scenarios within this approach, however, the axioms of unbounded rationality remained as yardsticks and as a normative frame (for reviews of EUT limitations see e.g. Camerer, 1992; Harless & Camerer, 1994).

Kahneman and Tversky supported their bold hypothesis with a series of experiments, which showed that biases in decisions under risk occur when people estimate participated values and probabilities in the light of gains and losses, and with respect to a participated point of reference. These results can be summarized in two classic graphs, which provide a descriptive picture of judgment under risk[18] and the foundation of what is called prospect theory (see Figure 6, p. 24).

For example, the participated value of a 500.- € win is smaller than the participated value of a 500.- € loss. This bias is not only valid for monetary incentives, consistent with Kahneman and Tversky (2000), it also explains why people fall victim to framing effects and are prone to loss aversive behavior.

Gains and losses, as central reference points (and not final levels of wealth), are key issues when people regularly overestimate small probabilities of potentially positive (e.g. buying lottery tickets) and negative outcomes (e.g. signing an insurance). Compared to these unlikely events (see Thaler & Sunstein, 2008) medium to large probabilities are typically underestimated, as described in the weighting function.

---

[18] In decisions under risk the possible probabilities are known (e.g. the flip of a coin). In decisions under uncertainty the probabilities, however, remain unknown. In the earlier versions prospect theory only addressed decisions under risk, decisions under uncertainty were implemented later into the theory (Kahneman & Tversky, 2000). This is relevant for settings of management decisions, since here risks are often unknown and thus managers face a high level of uncertainty.

Figure 7: Value (a) and weighting function (b) (adapted from Kahneman and Tversky, 1986, p. 259 and p. 264)

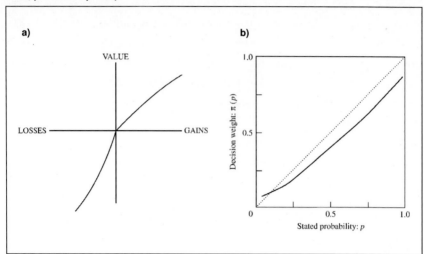

Other than these deviations from rationality axioms, people also fall victim to their limited cognitive capabilities. These limitations lead people in the view of Kahneman and Tversky to use heuristics which, due to their simplifying character, lead to a list of errors in our decision making (see Table 1 on p .32).

Heuristics are, according to Kahneman and Frederick (2002), frequently used shortcuts in which a difficult question is answered by substituting it for a shorter one. One of the first descriptions of heuristics appears in 1972, when Kahneman and Tversky (1972, p. 431) state:

> *"People do not follow the principles of probability theory in judging the likelihood of uncertain events. Apparently, people replace the laws of chance by heuristics."*

In addition to the tendency to overestimate small risks and to underestimate high risks, the most mentioned and cited errors and biases by Kahneman and colleagues are: conjunction fallacy, overconfidence bias, base-rate fallacy (and base-rate neglect), representativeness, availability and anchoring (for a summary see Bazerman

& Moore, 2009; Gilovich & Griffin, 2002; Keren & Teigen, 2004).[19]

The origin of this program is strongly linked with the notion of human beings as intuitive statisticians. This means that in order to maximize certain criteria people do so based on probabilistic information. Thus, the mind represents information in a probabilistic way when making decisions according to this framework. This assumption is important because it allowed Kahneman and Tversky to provide both a normative and a descriptive theory of choice (and its differences); a distinction that was not well-established particularly in economics, where no special attention was given to developing an explicitly descriptive model.

This outline is summarized by Heukelom (2005, p. 7):

> "If man is considered to be an intuitive statistician, and if the world is considered to present itself to the individual in terms of probabilistic information of uncertain events, a decision that deviates from the theoretically optimal decision becomes a failure of the system, or an error of judgment."

The heuristics and biases program[20] claims bounded rationality as well as its proper theoretical foundation (e.g. Camerer, 1998)[21], because this program stresses errors that result from our limited cognitive capacity. Deviations from the ideal of optimization are viewed by proponents of this paradigm as failures that, at least up to a certain level, can be corrected[22] and even must be corrected in order to gain good (and rational) decisions (for prescriptive consequences resulting from heuristics and biases see Thaler & Sunstein, 2008; Tversky & Koehler, 1994).

---

[19] The summary of errors and biases listed here can be easily extended. For instance Eisenfuhr and Weber (2003) list in addition to the above mentioned summary: certainty effects, disappointment effects, illusion of control, mental accounting, regret effects, resolution of uncertainty, splitting-bias, status quo-bias, sunk costs and winner's curse as additional labels for non-rational behavior (see also Koch, 2004 for an overview of biases in auditing). This long list has however raised the critique that research on JDM is reduced to a quest for "the error of the day" (Goldstein, 2010).

[20] This program is also labelled "cognitive illusions program" which is an analogy towards optical illusions like the Müller-Lyer illusion (Kahneman & Tversky, 1996, p. 582).

[21] But it is worth to note that even optimization under constraints is described by some authors as a proper model of bounded rationality (e.g. Arrow, 2004).

[22] The prescriptive principles of this approach are for example manifested in what is called "libertarian paternalism" by Thaler and Sunstein (2003).

Table 1: Some biases resulting from heuristics (Bazerman & Moore, 2009, p. 41)

Bias	Description
Biases emanating from the availability heuristic	
Ease of recall	Individuals judge events that are more easily recalled to be more numerous than events of equal frequency whose instances are less easily recalled.
Retrievability	Individuals are biased in their assessments of the frequency of events based on how their memory structures affect the search process.
Biases emanating from the representativeness heuristic	
Insentivity to base rates	When assessing the likelihood of events, individuals tend to ignore base rates if any other descriptive information is provided – even if it is irrelevant.
Insensitivity to sample size	When assessing the reliability of sample information, individuals frequently fail to appreciate the role of sample size.
Misconceptions of chance	Individuals expect that a sequence of data generated by a random process will look "random", even when the sequence is too short for those expectations.
Regression to the mean	Individuals tend to ignore the fact that extreme events tend to regress to the mean on subsequent trail.
The conjunction fallacy	Individuals falsely judge that conjunctions are more probable than a more global set of occurrences of which the conjunction is a participant.
Biases emanating from the confirmation heuristic	
The confirmation trap	Individuals tend to seek confirmatory information for what they think is true and fail to search for disconfirmatory evidence.
Anchoring	Individuals make estimates for values based upon an initial value and typically make insufficient adjustments from that anchor when establishing a final value.
Con/disjunctive-events bias	Individuals exhibit a bias toward overestimating the probability of conjunctive events and underestimating the probability of disjunctive events.
Overconfidence	Individuals tend to be overconfident of the infallibility of their judgments when answering moderately to extremely difficult questions.
Hindsight and the curse of knowledge	After finding out whether or not an event occurred, individuals tend to overestimate the degree to which they would have predicted the correct outcome. Furthermore, individuals fail to ignore information they possess that others do not when predicting others behavior.

The heuristics and biases program[23] claims bounded rationality as well as its proper theoretical foundation (e.g. Camerer, 1998)[24], because this program stresses errors that result from our limited cognitive capacity. Deviations from the ideal of optimization are viewed by proponents of this paradigm as failures that, at least up to a cer-

---

[23]   This program is also labelled "cognitive illusions program" which is an analogy towards optical illusions like the Müller-Lyer illusion (Kahneman & Tversky, 1996, p. 582).

[24]   But it is worth to note that even optimization under constraints is described by some authors as a proper model of bounded rationality (e.g. Arrow, 2004).

tain level, can be corrected[25] and even must be corrected in order to gain good (and rational) decisions (for prescriptive consequences resulting from heuristics and biases see Thaler & Sunstein, 2008; Tversky & Koehler, 1994).

Overall all the contribution of this program/prospect theory is summarized by Hogarth (1993, p. 409) in *Accounting, Organizations and Society:*

> "*This* [program] *was important for three reasons. First, the model was a constructive attempt to challenge the expected utility model with an alternative that was more descriptively accurate. Second, by being published in a leading economics journal, the paper legitimized efforts to incorporate descriptive elements into economic models in which there is no distinction between normative and descriptive. Third, some elements of the model were derived from basic psychological principles that, although intuitively compelling, lead to logically disturbing behaviors such as reversals in risk attitudes induced by the manner in which questions are worded.*"

2.3.5 Satisficing decisions and what is actually bounded in rationality

After the ideal of unbounded rationality (meaning full rationality and guided by principles of maximizing gains and minimizing errors) was left behind, the current debate tries to clarify which consequences result from these boundaries and how we can deal with them in the best place. The heuristics, resulting from our limited cognitive capabilities, as described by Kahneman and Tversky, are not considered as efficient solutions, rather (in the best case) as second best and "quick-and-dirty" techniques compared to a proper logical analysis.

Many empirical findings corroborate the robustness of these deviations and show that social actors systematically deviate from the standard model of economics (DellaVigna, 2009). However, there is a current debate as to how this program can be put in line with Simon's view of an ecological rationality that includes both cogni-

---

[25] The prescriptive principles of this approach are for example manifested in what is called "libertarian paternalism" by Thaler and Sunstein (2003).

tive and environmental factors (Lopes, 1992; Sen, 2002).[26]

Moreover, some of the so-called errors and illusions are being dispraised for being too imprecise and for lacking a deeper explanation of how and when these errors actually work (Fiedler, 1988; Funder, 1987; Gigerenzer, Hertwig, Hoffrage, & Sedlmeier, 2008). The criticism stresses that heuristics and biases can be understood more as a vague label than as a proper and testable model (Gigerenzer, 1996). Additionally, to classify behavior into categories of rationality or irrationality solely depends on the norms of rationality (L. J. Cohen, 1981). Advocates of the fast and frugal program highlight that using unrealistic yard sticks for human decision making will always lead to a picture of a highly biased and misguided agent (Todd, 2007).[27] With respect to the norms used by the heuristics and biases program McKenzie (2003, p. 405) thus notes: "When a rational model fails to describe behavior, a different rational model, not different behavior, might be called for." By the same token Gigerenzer´s earlier critique (1997, p. 206) of the heuristics and biases program extends this statement by arguing that "it should be clear that the single trenchant conclusion reached by heuristics-and-biases program, namely that people are all too bad at reasoning, is itself, to a large degree, an illusion fostered by all-too-narrow norms of sound reasoning."

Furthermore, some early critics point out that methodological issues play a crucial part, when demonstrating human irrationality (L. J. Cohen, 1981). From a philosophy of science point of view, some of the propositions of this program are questioned for making predictions that explain every possible outcome. For example, the same bias (representativeness) accounts in the hot-hand fallacy and in the gambler's fallacy for two completely different (even contrary) outcomes (Ayton & Fischer, 2004). The

---

[26]   This is a complex task because Simon is author of more than 650 publications (Heukelom, 2007a) and it is obviously easy to misinterpret his writings, mainly for the reason that he contributed to almost every field within organizational studies (Mirowski, 2002).

[27]   With respect to cultural influence factors some researchers like Matsumoto (2007), point out that classical norms for rationality are products of a Western way of thinking. For example self-consistency over an individual's life is not a necessary condition for rationality in some other cultures. A further scholarly reflection of culture and related issues would however be beyond the scope of this work. For an overview of the influence cultural factors on judgment and decision making see Weber and Hsee (2000). Also Staw (2010, p. 413) points out: "What may appear to be universal biases and heuristics, may instead be tendencies that are a product of culture and context."

gambler's fallacy describes the illusion of a player that, for example, in game of rou-lette after a series of black the chances increase for red in the next round. The hot-hand fallacy is the other way round and is used as an explanation, for example, in basketball, arguing that a player who already scored several times is therefore more likely to score the next time. Results like this question the explanatory power of the heuristics and biases program, because using ex-post explanations is neither feasi-ble (Popper, 1959), nor an adequate way for making possible prescriptive conclu-sions and raises the question of "how persuasive is a good fit" (Roberts & Pashler, 2000).

If a certain behavior is rational or not depends of course on the norms you use. Advocates of the fast and frugal approach highlight, that using unrealistic yard sticks for human decision performance will always lead to a picture of a highly biased and misguided agent (Todd, 2007).[28]

In a business context, you can for example easily show that managers act irra-tional, by using a simple between-subject-design, in combination with anchoring. In this thought experiment (adapted from Birnbaum, 1999) you would let two group of managers (between-participant) rate the creativity of a company (measured with the number of patents). The first group finds out that the company has nine patents and should rate the creativity on a 10-point scale. The second group sees 221 patents – however (because of the anchoring effect) the rating of creativity is lower in this case, which leads to the stunning and robust effect of 9 > 221. According to Birn-baum, this effect can be explained by the fact that 9 makes a context of small num-bers more salient (and thus appears large compared to other one digit numbers), whereas 221 is seen in line with other (larger) three digit numbers (like 500, 700, 900).

Proponents of naturalistic decision making (NDM) like Gary Klein (Klein, 1993; Lipshitz, Klein, Orasnu, & Salas, 2001) criticize the heuristic and biases program.

---

[28] With respect to cultural influence factor some researchers like Matsumoto (2007), point out that classical norms for rationality are products of a Western way of thinking. For example self-consistency over an individual's life is not a necessary condition for rationality in some other cultures. A further scholarly reflection of culture and related issues would however be beyond the scope of this work. For an overview of the influence cultural factors on judgment and decision making see Weber and Hsee (2000).

The goal of NDM researchers is to investigate the intuition of experts, using mostly recognition-primed decision techniques, which they also claim is in line with Simon's (1993) suggestions regarding explanations of human behavior. Like Gigerenzer and colleagues, they point out that intuition works as a fruitful way to make decisions. NDM advocates stress that their program is more in line with an ecological view of human behavior, than with an emphasis of biases, as laid out by the heuristics and biases camp. However, it should be noted that the heuristics and bias program revealed important insights in human JDM. We can now see more clearly that cognitive restrictions cause human errors and mistakes. The use of heuristics is a human strategy to reduce cognitive effort and needs to be studied more thoroughly. Moreover, this program stimulated research that tries to show the merits of heuristics in human JDM: the fast and frugal heuristics program.

2.3.6 Fast and frugal heuristics

As an alternative to the heuristics and bias program, and to cope with a highly complex and uncertain environment and with limited time and knowledge, Gigerenzer and colleagues (Gigerenzer, et al., 1999) proposed a number of heuristics as strategies in making inferences.[29] These, by definition simple (Shah & Oppenheimer, 2008), heuristics use evolutionary based skills to adaptively make use of environmental structures. Since their working principles are rooted in the environment, their process follows an ecological rationality rather than an unbounded (economic) rationality. With this move heuristics are shifting away from the negative reputation they earned through much of the behavioral decision research.

This fresh look at heuristics describes their quality depending upon their ability to interact with the environment and is in line with the original Greek meaning of the term heuristic, which can be translated as "serving to find out" (Gigerenzer & Gaissmaier, 2011).[30] Gigerenzer and Gaissmaier (2011, p. 454) define heuristic as "a

---

[29] Cognitive psychologist Myron L. Braunstein already mentions 1976 (in Payne, 1976b, p. 321) that heuristics "produce efficient solutions to difficult problems by restricting the search through the space of possible solutions". However, this early approach does not provide a deeper explanation for the underlying working-principles.

[30] An unprejudiced view on heuristics is also found in the work of early Gestalt psychologist Max Wertheimer (1945), who argues that heuristic methods can be understood as "looking around in order to guide search".

strategy that ignores part of the information, with the goal of making decisions more quickly, frugally, and/or accurately than more complex methods." This concept of judgment and decision making has some typical characteristics:

- It is a **multiple strategy approach** that is searching for different strategies according to the environment, task and cognitive capabilities (adaptive toolbox).

- Heuristics **deliberately ignore information** and this is operationalized by Shah and Oppenheimer (2008, p. 209):

    a) Examining fewer cues.

    b) Reducing the difficulty associated with retrieving and storing cue values.

    c) Simplifying the weighting principles for cues.

    d) Integrating less information.

    e) Examining fewer alternatives.

It is however important to mention that not all five aspects are necessary components of a definition of heuristics, but as a minimum one of the five has to be fulfilled.

Gigerenzer and Gaissmaier (2011) attribute **goal achievement** to heuristics – more quickly, frugally and/or accurately – which is redundant as frugal hints again to information reduction. Moreover, it is problematic to enclose goals into the definition because it does not account for what happens if a strategy does not reach one goal or all three goals.

Consequently, goals of heuristics should be looked at separately and the definition should rely on the criteria by Shah/Opppenheimer. In reference to Figure 6 (p. 25) it is also important to highlight that heuristics in Gigerenzer´s view are neither as-if models of optimization, nor solely descriptions of results – they are rules that describe the (problem-solving) process, in a fast and frugal fashion. They also fundamentally depart from concepts of rationality, like unbounded rationality and optimization under constraints. Furthermore, they go beyond the satisficing heuristics of Simon (1979), because they are not necessarily second best choices – they can even outperform complex calculations under certain circumstances. An example will illustrate how heuristics are seen in this program. One of the heuristics in the adaptive toolbox is the take-the-best heuristic (TTB), coined by Gigerenzer and Goldstein (1996). I can describe this heuristic with five steps:

1. The first step is pure recognition of the cue. For example, if a social actor is asked which company produces more cars out of Volvo or Khodro, she will choose Volvo, simply because she has heard of it.

2. The second step is the search for the values of the cues.

3. The third step uses the discrimination rule. A cue discriminates if one has a positive value and the other has not. This can be illustrated again with the car example: is one type available at carscout24.com (positive cue value) and the other not (negative cue value)?

4. The fourth step is the cue-substitution principle and it states that if the cues do not discriminate go back to step two.

5. The last step is called maximizing rule for choice and it states that if no cue discriminates then choose randomly.

Figure 8: Classic TTB algorithm

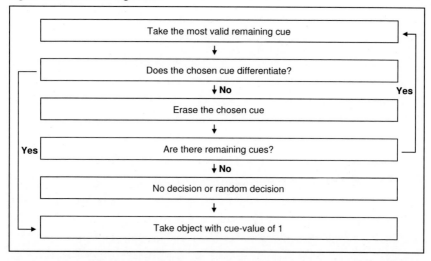

The important point in this lexicographic search strategy is that leaving out information can actually be helpful in making good inferences (compared to algorithms like multiple regression analysis or tallying for example). In order to make accurate predictions and to guide the decision maker, heuristics necessarily have three elements: a search rule, a stopping rule and a decision rule.

The ideal environmental structure to make simple heuristics like TTB work in terms of efficiency and robustness, is mathematically described by Martignon and Hoffrage (1999). This environment is characterized by non-compensatory information. This means that the cue weights (meaning how high the validity of the cue is) exponentially decrease, for example from 1.0 to 0.5 to 0.25 to 0.125 (…). In such an environment no other algorithm (like "Dawes's rule"[31] or "Minimalist") can outperform the TTB heuristic.

Figure 9: Accuracy of the TTB heuristic (Gigerenzer & Goldstein, 1999)

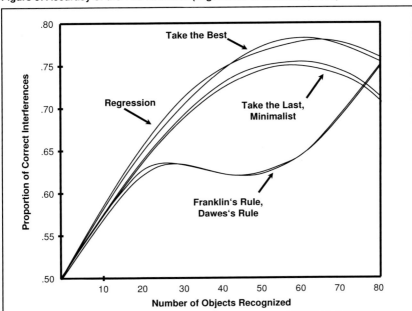

The next crucial feature of heuristics is the distinction between fitting and predicting. It is obvious that in order to explain the past ex post (fitting), it is helpful to use as many cues as possible. This may be the reason why we have got better at understanding the causes of the recent financial crisis; besides all the ad-hoc/post-hoc

---

[31] Dawes rule (adapted from Robyn Dawes' "improper linear models" [Dawes, 1979]), is a compensatory strategy where the positive cue values are added and negative ones are subtracted. Franklin's rule multiplies each cue value by its weight and sums the total (Hogarth, 1987). The minimalist heuristic only relies on the direction of the cues. It takes the last heuristic and remembers the last successful application and uses the same strategy again.

explanations that are not of any use. Despite all the good explanations of the past, there are serious problems to using these explanations to predict the next big crash ex-ante. One reason for this is called "noise" by cognitive scientists and refers to information that is either redundant or that has no predictable value at all (nevertheless it can be expensive in terms of time and money). The danger of including too many informational cues of this type is called over-fitting.

Figure 10: Fitting versus predicting

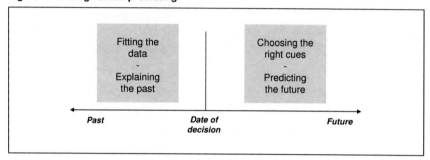

Other heuristics, which are supposed to be included in the adaptive toolbox and that are empirically supported are: recognition heuristic, default heuristic and earlier heuristics such as tallying, tit-for-tat, imitate the successful (for an overview of different heuristics including empirical findings see Gigerenzer & Brighton, 2009).

The efficiency of heuristics is not a brand new participant for all fields of study and is, for instance, well documented in social contexts, where tit-for-tat as a fast and frugal strategy was shown to be highly efficient (Axelrod, 1984), as well as simple rules (clearly evolutionary based) like imitate-the-majority (Boyd & Richardson, 2005) or imitate-the-successful (Boyd & Richardson, 2005). These social heuristics use evolved and learned capabilities and are reduced to a minimalist set of building blocks.[32]

2.3.7 Bounded minds and ecological rationality

Why do some heuristics work efficiently? According to Gigerenzer and Todd the working principle (that also accounts for the less-is-more effect) behind efficient heu-

---

[32] This is in line with evolutionary psychology, which states that humans have "neurocognitive adaptions designed for social exchange" (Cosmides & Tooby, 2005, p. 590).

ristics is ecological rationality (Gigerenzer & Todd, 2008; Todd & Gigerenzer, 2003). In line with Berg (2010) a decision or judgment is rational from a ecological perspective when it can exploit structures of the environment. This exploitation works systematically and, thus, it is not a random process. In addition, the simplicity of the heuristic structure guarantees its robustness, which is shown in the ability to generalize dynamic and uncertain environments. This is of interest to management research because we have to keep in mind that the use of heuristics is not intended to fit a data set of the past. Contrary, heuristics are used to make predictions in a highly uncertain world. Nevertheless, is ecological rationality different from bounded rationality?Chase, Hertwig and Gigerenzer (1998, p. 212) describe ecological rationality and bounded rationality as separate constructs:

> *"We argue that to discover how the mind works, and how well, we need to understand how the mind functions under its own constraints – its bounded rationality – and how it exploits the structure of the social and physical environments in which it must reach its goals – its ecological rationality."*

Hoffrage and Reimer (2004, p. 442) use the same distinction and add to this approach that "Models of ecological rationality describe the structure and the representation of information in actual environments and their match with mental strategies, such as bounded rational heuristics." The interaction of adaptive minds with an uncertain environment (as the core element of ecological rationality) is also mentioned by Vernon Smith (2003, p. 470), who points out in his Nobel Memorial Lecture in 2002:

> *"Ecological rationality uses reason – to examine the behavior of individuals based on their experience and folk knowledge, who are 'naïve' in their ability to apply constructivist tools to the decisions they make; to understand the emergent order in human cultures; to discover the possible intelligence embodied in the rules, norms, and institutions of our cultural and biological heritage that are created from human interactions not by deliberate human design. People follow rules without being able to articulate them, but they can be discovered."*

In line with this argumentation, it can be concluded that our bounded cognitive capacities/computational limits (cf. bounded rationality), paired with a matching environment can lead to rational decisions from an ecological angle. Bounded rationality is thus a necessary precondition for modeling ecological rational behavior. This distinction is also opined by Stevens (2010, p. 100), according to whom, "Ecological rationality appeals to the evolutionary idea that adaptations match the environment in which they evolved. Therefore, decision mechanisms should not be universal and domain general but specifically tailored to the environment in which they operate."

The fruitful interplay of cognition and environment may also be illustrated by what is called situated cognition (Robbins & Aydede, 2009; and for a discussion of situated cognition in management research see Wrona, 2008). Followers of this program, which is widely used in organizational sciences, point out that the context (respectively environment) is not a passive entity that is perceived by social actors. Rather, situated cognition is embedded in the context and, especially in social contexts, it is described as a reciprocal interaction with individual cognition.

Scholars of ecological rationality and those of situated cognition agree that context may influence cognitive processes and that these processes definitely use elements of the context. Another aspect of agreement is that situated cognition has a broad definition of what constitutes context, which is in line with ecological rationality. For example, both see social behavior as relevant context (Hertwig & Herzog, 2009).

However, compared to ecological rationality, approaches of situated cognition do not tell us how individual minds exploit the structures of the context. The cognitive structures described by situated cognition-oriented scholars are seen to be directly influenced by the context. For ecological rationality this is not the case, because the cognitive structures (e.g. working memory) are rooted in an evolutionary development and thus do not object to a direct transformation. Compared to ecological rationality, situated cognition however does not tell us anything about how individual minds exploit the structures of the context. The cognitive structures described by situated cognition-oriented researchers also are seen to be directly influenced by the context. Ecological rationality and situated cognition researchers agree however that context can influence cognitive processes and that these processes can vise-versa use elements of the context. That situated cognition has a broad definition of what constitutes context, is also in line with ecological rationality. For example both can see social behavior as a relevant context (Hertwig, Hoffrage, & the ABC Research Group, in press).

2.3.8 Critique of fast and frugal decision strategies

The fast and frugal heuristics program has been established as an alternative to the heuristics and bias program. However, despite the many studies for the use of fast and frugal heuristics in real life and laboratory settings, and a trend towards more evolutionary descriptions of human judgment and decision making, there are several doubts regarding this program.

For example, Oppenheimer (2003) points to the fact that actual decision making involves usually far more calculations, than the simple mechanism described by Gigerenzer and colleagues. This finding is also picked up by Hilbig and Richter (2010), who argue that within the description of fast and frugal heuristics, it remains unclear how adaptive heuristics are selected (the so-called strategy selection problem). In addition, they present empirical evidence that the recognition heuristic is only one applied strategy among many. Thus, Gigerenzer and Brighton's (2009, p. 134) claim that "a majority of participants consistently followed the recognition heuristic" is not fully empirically supported.[33] Hilbig (2010) furthermore highlights in a paper titled "homo heuristicus outnumbered" that the adaptive toolbox needs to be more précised on the process level of reasoning and that even more complex mechanisms do not enforce severe information costs.

Secchi and Bardone (2010) even suggest that the idea of bounded rationality in general needs an update, because new technologies and social resources were not integrated in this concept, when it was coined by Herbert Simon in the 1940s and 1950s. These authors propose that scholars should switch to a new approach called "extendable rationality", which would allow for integrating technological advances into our concept of rationality. Moreover, because ecological rationality requires some implicit learning function, how exactly this learning (of heuristics) can be measured, or even improved, remains vague.

---

[33]   The same result, that not a majority of participants used fast and frugal heuristic when making inferences, was also stressed in another study by Newell, Weston and Shanks (2003) that took a closer look at the TTB heuristic.

This is true in particular for settings that are more complex like organizations and elaborate decision issues, for example mergers and acquisitions. Because most empirical studies of heuristics focus on small scale problems and well defined issues, future research should bear this in mind and aim to increase external validity by investigating real scenarios (Salas, et al., 2010).

This is also why another problem with the ecological rationality approach is that it is mainly outcome oriented. However, this focus is not fully in line with Simon's original notion of (psychological) procedural rationality that he distinguishes from (economic) substantive rationality in his descriptions of bounded rationality. According to Simon (1976, p. 131): "Behavior is procedurally rational when it is the outcome of appropriate deliberations. Its procedural rationality depends on the process that generated it."

This view on rationality also takes into account a means ends relationship that is missing if only the outcome is compared to another yardstick. Additionally, the analysis of ecological rationality might be limited to either artificial computational models (in the fashion of Adaptive Control of Thought-Rational theory (ACT-R)) or simple (dichotomies such as win-loss scenarios) like soccer matches. In more complex business settings a focus on more procedural characteristics (for an overview of processing tracing methods in JDM see Payne & Venkatraman, 2011) could thus be more fruitful than the endless search for appropriate benchmarks (see also section 6.3, p. 203ff of this thesis for more suggestions regarding the focus on procedural aspects) .

Also Simon (1986, p. 210) suggests that JDM processes shall be seen in light of available knowledge and computational means, but without emphasizing the direct outcome:

> "The rational person of neoclassical economics always reaches the decision that is objectively, or substantively, best in terms of the given utility function. The rational person of cognitive psychology goes about making his or her decisions in a way that is procedurally reasonable in the light of the available knowledge and means of computation."

To conclude the different aspects of this critique, the challenges for fast and frugal heuristics and ecological rationality can be summarized into three categories:

- The first addresses the nature of heuristics itself: How many types exist? Are individual differences important (Stanovich & West, 2000)? For example, Scott and Bruce (1995, p. 820) state that "decision style is not a personality trait but a habit based propensity to react in a certain way in a specific decision context." Are some people more ecological rational and thus more successful than others? Is this, for example, one of the reasons why Apple is so successful, because managers of the company constantly adapt their products to a complex changing environment, where simple and intuitive rules are preferred over complex calculations?

- The second challenge concerns the application of fast and frugal heuristics and is of special interest for management research. Are there normative/prescriptive consequences from working principles, like less-is-more, and how do management scholars have to rethink their assumptions regarding rationality and optimal decisions?

- The third issue addresses Simon's (1976) notion of procedural rationality, that he distinguishes from substantive (economic) rationality. The challenge for fast and frugal heuristics and ecological rationality (as a working principle) is that they are mainly outcome oriented. This focus often leads to artificial (ACT-R) or simple (Wimbledon results) scenarios for testing these models. Do business scholars thus need to implement ecological rationality in their models, or is a simple focus on bounded rationality (understood as a precondition, see the previous section) sufficient for analyzing JDM in more complex business settings?

Gigerenzer (2007) stresses that the fast and frugal program describes how real people solve real problems. Therefore, it seems important to collect as many empirical examples of applications in real management contexts. However, until now there have not been many studies of this kind. One of the few studies is that of Wübben and Wangenheim (2008), who showed that in retail marketing fast and frugal heuristics, predicting non-active consumers, can be more efficient than complex binomial distribution models. In a recent finance study by DeMiguel, Garlappi and Uppal (2009) they showed that a naïve 1/N rule of portfolio selection is not outperformed by more sophisticated methods.

Nevertheless, the most important insight from the large existing body of research on bounded rationality is, to be successful, managers sometimes have no other choice than to rely on their adaptive capabilities in thinking and deciding. There is growing evidence that the human mind is equipped with efficient strategies for this search which stems from our evolutionary past (Cosmides & Tooby, 1994; Tooby & Cosmides, 2005). Thus, the central issue is if heuristics represent efficient tools in dealing with daily challenges (Astebro & Elhedhli, 2006). For example it has been shown in several studies that our ability to make accurate forecasts is far from being accurate (e.g. Hsee & Zhang, 2004) and it seems promising to compare heuristic estimations against these (more elaborate) forecasts.

Table 2: Summary of critique of the fast and frugal heuristics/ecological rationality approach

o   How is decided which heuristic should be selected (strategy selection problem)?
o   How are heuristics combined with other decision algorithms (evidence for phased strategies)?
o   Are there individual differences that moderate the use of heuristic reasoning?
o   How are task and environmental characteristics, like accountability, related regarding the use of heuristics?
o   How can the external validity of the existing research on heuristic reasoning be extended?
o   Is the whole concept of bounded rationality to vague as a research objective?
o   Is the approach of ecological rationality too outcome oriented and misses the point of procedural rationality (Simon, 1976)?

2.4 Development of behavioral research in accounting

In order to understand JDM research in accounting (and heuristic reasoning in accounting) it is important to know how "behavioral" aspects were introduced into the accounting community. This way, research lines and major issues in the last five decades of behavioral accounting research can be identified and current topics and concepts from a broader cognitive context, like ecological rationality and heuristic reasoning, can be linked with this tradition. This section provides just a short sketch of the most important milestones in the research field of behavioral accounting research. For a more detailed overview see Birnberg and Shields (1989), Burgstrahler and Sunden (1989) or for a more recently published work, refer to Shields (2009) personal perspective on behavioral accounting research.

The book Accounting and its Behavioral Implications (1969) by William Bruns and Don DeCoster, and the article of the same name that was published in 1970 in *The Accounting Review,* are widely considered to be the foundation of behavioral accounting research (Lord, 1989; Shields, 2009). This new focus on behavioral aspects in accounting issues should, however, be understood within the context of a tradition of earlier works by scholars such as Argyris (1953),[34] Devine (1960), Stedry (1960), Benston (1963), and Dyckman (1964), all of whom paved the way for Bruns and De-Coster to introduce a crisp, behavioral perspective on accounting. They refer, for example, to such established theories as aspiration theory (Stedry, 1960), and cognitive dissonance theory (Festinger, 1962; Foran & Don, 1974).

These pioneering authors were interested mostly in issues pertaining either to the influence of budgeting on behavior or to the responsibility of the companies accounting system for motivating their members. But they were also the first papers published to address the issue of how (different) accounting information is communicated and understood by managers and accountants (e.g. Fertakis, 1969). Based on the many seminal pieces of work published between 1960 and 1970, this period has been labeled as a "decade of awakening" (Lord, 1989, p. 127) for behavioral accounting research.

The first concise definition of what actually constitutes behavioral accounting research was provided by Hofstedt and Kinard (1970, p. 43), who define it as "the study of the behavior of accountants or the behavior of non-accountants as they are influenced by accounting functions and reports." This definition was re-used by the next generation of behavioral accounting researchers (such as Dickhaut (1973), Ashton (1974b), and Libby (1975)), who used innovative methods, such as lab experiments, to address these matters. These scholars explicitly quote research and theories applied in cognitive and social psychology. Referring to famous behavioral researchers such as Egon Brunswick and Herbert Simon (who, for example was the doctoral supervisor of Andrew Stedry), they introduce the first interdisciplinary approaches to behavioral accounting research (for a review of psychological theory in

---

[34]   According to Lord (1989), this was the first published work to investigate the behavioral effects of accounting information.

management accounting see also Birnberg, Luft, & Shields, 2007). The growing interest of behavioral accounting research during this time is also reflected in the foundation of the journal *Accounting, Organizations, and Society* (AOS) in 1976. This journal acted as a catalyst for high quality behavioral accounting research (Lord, 1989) and also allowed for the publication of various methodological approaches such as experiments, case studies, and survey data.

In the early 1980s, scholars in behavioral accounting research increasingly referenced Tversky's and Kahneman's research (1973, 1974), which is now known as the heuristics and biases program. Libby (1981) suggested that behavioral accounting research should concentrate on this approach towards behavioral decision theory. The impact of this is documented by Snowball (1986), who found that the seminal 1974 *Science* paper "*Judgments under uncertainty: heuristics and biases*", by Tversky and Kahneman, is the most cited article within behavioral accounting research. Later in the decade, behavioral accounting research received the status of a "mature and accepted accounting research area" (Lord, 1989, p. 139). Like the heuristics and biases program, limitations of the individual decision maker became the subject of various studies (e.g. Libby, 1981; 1985; Shields, 1980).

For example, Shields (1980, p. 430) was one of the first to demonstrate that increased complexity of performance reports leads to the tendency of managers "to minimize, or at least reduce, cognitive strain when they search and process information". This study can be seen as a fruitful extension of the work of Ashton (1974a) ("*Behavioral implications of information overload in managerial accounting reports*"), who introduced the issue of an individual's cognitive capabilities in accounting reports. These two pieces of work are of particular interest to behavioral accounting research, as they provide a more precise description of the (heuristic) decision processes. For instance they integrate the elimination-by-aspects (EBA) concept of Tversky (1972) or other (normative) decision strategies such as weighted additive rule (WADD) and equal weight rule (EQW)[35] (for a detailed describtion of decision

---

[35]   In Tversky's original writing (1972, p. 1) EBA working principle is described in the following way: "At each stage in the process, an aspect is selected (with probability proportional to its weight), and all the alternatives that do not include the selected aspect are eliminated. The process continues until all alternatives but 1 are eliminated." According to Bettmann and colleagues (1991, p. 41), WADD rule simply "considers the values of each alternative on all the relative

strategies see also Bettmann, Johnson, & Payne, 1991; Payne, 1976b). This seminal approach allows for a more accurate description of what constitutes bounded rationality in managerial decision making.

According to Kotchetova and Salterio (2004, p. 549), the 1990s represented the "era of expertise:" it gave particular attention to the conditions in which expertise leads to successful behavior in accounting, and what sort of learning mechanism is used in its acquisition. This research differed from earlier studies, insofar as the precision with which descriptions of how and when expertise can lead to better decisions were made (Libby & Luft, 1993; J. F. Smith & Kida, 1991). They gave particular analytical focus to more complex interactions of environment, ability, and experience.

This distinguished the research from the earlier work of scholars such as Wright (1988), who used years of experience as a proxy for expertise, and who did not find that this proxy (expertise) reduced bias in a substantial way (see also Section 2.2.4, p. 46ff, for a more complete discussion on expertise in JDM research). The fact that behavioral accounting research scholars were better able to judge the quality of decisions in the assigned tasks, is considered by Kotchetova and Salterio (2004, p. 550) as a "critical breakthrough" and a "competitive advantage" over other disciplines such as psychology, and a true contribution to the field of behavioral oriented research.

New themes emerging in the 2000s in behavioral accounting research are highlighted in Table 3 on the next page and can be characterized in a broader diversification and specialization of behavioral accounting research topics, for instance team (multi-person) decision making in accounting contexts (Owhoso, Messier, & Lynch, 2002) or behavioral negotiation issues (Fisher, Frederickson, & Peffer, 2006; Gibbons, Salterio, & Webb, 2001) in addition to emerging issues in the area of informal control mechanisms (e.g. the effect of an ethical environment) (Booth & Schulz, 2004). As in most other disciplines engaging in JDM research typical frontiers and boarders between disciplines begin to disappear (Goldstein, 2010).

---

importance of the attributes." EQW is the application of Dawes' improper linear models (1979), in which all information should be balanced equally (no beta-weights).

Table 3: Development of behavioral research in accounting in the last 50 years

Period	Main Topics	Selective Publications
1960 – 70 *"Introduction of behavioral research in accounting"*	o The influence of control and budgeting on behavior o Incentive functions, motivation in accounting o Communication and understanding of accounting information by managers/accountants *"The influence of management control systems on the behavior of organizational participants, the influence of accounting information on internal and external users, and the behavior of accountants themselves"* (Ashton, 2010, p. 5)	o Benston (1963) o Bruns & DeCoster (1969) o Fertakis (1969)
1970 – 80 *"Decade of awakening"*	o Research on models influencing the individual decision maker, relative expertise and limited self-insight o Cognitive and social psychology research on accounting (experimental methods), information processing, and Brunswick lens model applications *"Questions researchers in the 1970s were asking included: how information should be provided, for example, level of aggregation; what type of information should be provided, for example, opportunity cost and feedback; and how much information should be provided to address or avoid problems such as functional fixation and cognitive overload"* (Trotman, et al., 2011, p. 325)	o Hofstedt & Kinard (1970) o Dickhaut (Dickhaut, 1973) o Ashton (1974a, 1974b) o Libby (1975)
1980 – 90 *"Maturity and acceptance"*	o Limitations of the individual decision maker o Heuristics and biases in behavioral accounting research, and debiasing techniques *"Researchers were acknowledging* (in the 1980s) *that individuals possessed bounded rationality, which had implications for information search and information processing behaviors (…)."* (Trotman, et al., 2011, p. 329)	o Shields (1980) o Libby (1981, 1985) o Wright & Anderson (1989)
1990 – 2000 *"Era of expertise research"*	o Learning functions (expertise) o Decision support systems o Psychological variables (e.g. fairness, trust etc.) *"The focus (…) was still on investigating how accounting impacts individual decision making behavior, and through this, identifying how the predictions of economic models might be improved."* (Trotman, et al., 2011, p. 330)	o Luckett & Eggleton (1991) o Bamber (1993) o Luft (1997)
2000 – *Diversification and specification*	o Hindsight bias and outcome effects, o Knowledge structures (mental models) o Behavioral (budgeting) negotiation issues	o Cloyd & Spilker (2000) o Vera-Muñoz et al. (2007) o Fischer et al. (2006)

2.5 JDM and cognitive aspects in behavioral accounting research

The importance of JDM[36] research in the context of behavioral accounting was recognized at an early stage. Davidson and Trueblood (1961, p. 577), for instance, stress that, "the challenges that accounting faces today and in the future [...] may be characterized as accounting for decision making". Decision making in behavioral accounting research mostly relies on psychological theories and emerged from the behavioral accounting research in the 1960s.

Trotman and colleagues (2011, p. 279), referring to Libby (1981), point out that within accounting the goals of JDM research are typically found in the following areas (in a broader sense): "evaluating the quality of the judgments of auditors, prepares and users of accounting reports; describing how the judgments are made; determining which factors impact these judgments and why; developing and testing theories of the underlying cognitive processes by which judgments are made; and improving the judgments of auditors, preparers and users of accounting information."

According to Birnberg, Luft and Shields (2007, p. 114), three psychological disciplines are in particular relevant for behavioral accounting research.[37] These disciplines are:

- **Cognitive psychology** – the study of processes that influence human thinking (e.g. prospect theory (Kahneman & Tversky, 1979), mental models (Johnson-Laird, 1983)).[38]

---

[36]   According to Trotman et al. (2011, p. 279) judgment and decision are often confused in behavioral accounting research research. They highlight that: "judgment usually refers to the process of estimating outcomes and their consequences (e.g. likelihood of a material misstatement, risk assessment, estimate of an account balance, estimate of future cash flows), while decision making involves an evaluation of these consequences which leads to a choice among the alternatives (e.g. quality/not qualify audit report, invest/not invest). Judgments are an important input for decisions."

[37]   These disciplines are however not completely mutually exclusive. Also the mentioned theories can frequently not be separated accurately.

[38]   Accounting scholars interested in this area adopted psychological models such as the lens model (Brunswick, 1957), probabilistic judgments, cognitive style and pre-decisional behavior at an early stage in the 1960s (Birnberg, et al., 2007).

- **Motivation psychology** – the study of processes that influence behavior and effort (e.g. attribution theory (Weiner, 1985), cognitive dissonance theory (Festinger, 1962)).

- **Social psychology** – the study of how other people influence individuals' minds and behavior (e.g. role theory (Deutsch & Krauss, 1965), social comparison theory (Shaw & Constanzo, 1982)).

This thesis mostly focuses on cognitive psychological theories, concepts and topics such as dual process models, decision making style or intuition. To some minor degree, social psychological theories are also involved in describing decision making behavior. An example of the social psychological component would be for instance the role of accountability and research in the field of self-other JDM. Birnberg et al. (2007) also point out that findings from existing research on the implementation of psychological theories in behavioral accounting research can be organized into two main categories. The first addresses informational effects, for example the limitations of decision makers due to the effects of bounded rationality. The second concerns motivational effects, for instance the effect of a belief in fairness in budgeting scenarios.

Snowball (1986) argues that the strongest connection between psychological models and concepts in behavioral accounting research in general and decision making in particular, can be seen within the field of human information processing. However, "information processing" as a general description could work in all dominant disciplines. For instance, both cognitive and social psychologies address the processing of information: it is only the context that varies. Whereas cognitive aspects frequently deal with cues or chunks of information (Simon, 1972), social aspects consider more interpretative pieces of information, such as social accounts (Brehm, et al., 2002). Kotchetova and Salterio (2004, p. 550ff) also analyzed the nine leading journals in accounting[39] from 1995 to 2002 and still found that information processing was by far the most popular topic, accounting for 87.1% (230 of 264 in

---

[39]   These journals are, according to Kotchetova and Salterio authors referring to Brown and Huefner (1994): *Journal of Accounting Research; The Accounting Review; Contemporary Accounting Research; Accounting, Organizations and Society; Auditing: Journal of Practice & Theory; Journal of American Taxation Association; Journal of Information Systems, Journal of Management Accounting Research;* and *Behavioral Research in Accounting.*

total) of all published JDM articles, followed by research on heuristics and biases with 13.6% (36 of 264 in total). Other former popular topics, such as Brunswick's lens model approach practically disappeared from JDM research in accounting, appearing in only 1.1% of the articles (3 of 264 in total).

Table 4: JDM accounting articles by JDM approach: 1995-2002 (Kotchetova & Salterio, 2004, p. 551)

JDM approach	JDM accounting articles	
	Total	(%)
Information processing	230	87.1
Heuristics and biases	36	13.6
Bounded rationality/satisfying	14	5.3
Rational actor models	7	2.7
Computational modeling	4	1.5
Rationality and the normative descriptive distinction	3	1.1
Brunswick's lens model approach	3	1.1
Einhorn and Hogarth's ambiguity model	1	0.4
Total JDM accounting articles[40]	**264**	

Birnberg (2009) argues that the objectives of current behavioral accounting research can be separated into four main strands of research: individuals, groups, organizations, and environmental conditions. He points out that the role of individuals in particular, is the object of various studies, enjoying the most popularity. Individual choice and strategic issues (from an individual perspective) constitute other notable current topics in this area. This thesis also investigates decision making from an individual perspective; however some organizational elements are included in the qualitative approach.

---

[40] According to these authors, some articles combined various approaches, thus the total number of reported approaches was estimated to be 298.

Figure 11: Dominant psychological disciplines in behavioral accounting research

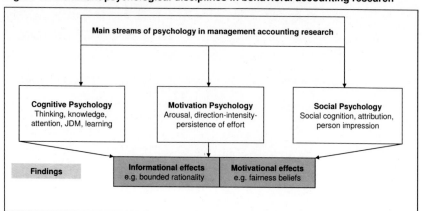

2.5.1 Information processing in the context of behavioral accounting

Whereas general JDM research (at least under this label) is a rather new development in accounting research (Ashton & Ashton, 1995; for an overview see Bonner, 2008; Hogarth, 1991 for an earlier summary; Kotchetova & Salterio, 2004; Sprinkle, 2003 for management accounting in particular),[41] there is a history, starting in the late 1960s,[42] of research that investigates the processing of accounting information (Schick, Gordon, & Haka, 1990). Heuristic reasoning can be seen in line with this body of research that frequently analyzes the issue of information overload (see San Miguel, 1976 for an early study of this issue).

From this perspective, the use of heuristics reflects a reaction to an overwhelming supply of data, or an information overload. For instance, Schick and colleagues (1990) speak of "simplifying strategies," rather than heuristics.

Another issue within this information processing perspective is the frequent attempts by organizations to avoid risks by acquiring large quantities of information. As

---

[41]   According to Kotchetova and Salterio (2004), the publication of the two *Journal of Accounting Research* articles by Ashton (1974b) and Libby (1975), using a form of Brunswick's lens model, marked the starting point for accounting JDM research.

[42]   This period interestingly also marks the systematic introduction of IT-based decision support systems in organizations (Eppler & Mengis, 2004).

Thompson (1967, p. 13) has argued, "the central problem for complex organizations is one of coping with uncertainty." In this framework two factors are commonly distinguished. The first is the information load (IL) that an actor faces; the second is the information processing capacity (IPC) that the actor can compute. Within this distinction, most accounting research follows a process perspective, focusing on one or more of the following aspects: decision to search for data/information, information processing, and information analysis/evaluation.[43]

Fertakis (1969), in an early paper on information processing, discusses whether more (accounting) information might also lead to better financial reporting (externally, at least). Even at this relatively early stage, Fertakis specifies the crucial factors in determining the optimal information load to be the information needs, and the IPCs, of the external information users. According to this author, to ignore these two factors would increase the risk of information overload.

Miller (1972) furthers this discussion on individual IPC in an accounting setting. He suggests that increasing the individual's conceptual level might also lead to more efficient information processing (but see Wilson, 1973 for critical comments on this paper).

Ashton (1974a), another seminal critic in behavioral accounting research, argues that an increase in the quantity of accounting information (in managerial accounting reports) does not necessarily propagate decision making quality. It can even have contrary effects – for example, information overload can lead to reduced decision effectiveness. A classical framework, that is still valid for analyzing information processing and JDM in accounting, was presented in 1977 in *Accounting, Organizations and Society* by Libby and Lewis.

These scholars argue that this area can be best analyzed using an input-process-output model. Within this model the information set (cues) work as an input, the judge (decision maker) represents the process section and the output is analyzed through the judgment (prediction or decision). Most of the behavioral accounting research until today (including this thesis) fits into this classification model. It repre-

---

[43] The above-discussed psychological aspects can be implemented in all three stages. Also, although it not consistently used through a variety of studies, the term "overload" can be found in all three stages of the information processing process (Schick, et al., 1990).

sents a valuable tool for pinning down research questions and for identifying open issues.[44]

Figure 12: Classification of human information processing based on Libby and Lewis (1977)

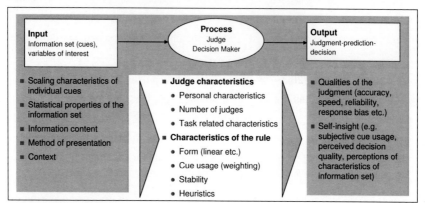

According to Schick et al. (1990), empirical studies (in leading accounting journals such as *The Accounting Review* or *Accounting, Organizations and Society*) on this matter were first published in the early 1980s. Casey (1980, 1982), for instance, demonstrates (in a task where bank loan officers had to predict bankruptcy) that more information can lead to longer evaluation periods but not necessarily raise accuracy. Snowball (1980), in his study, analyzed the influence of higher information loads in accounting settings. He finds that a rise in information leads to more confident, but (surprisingly) less heterogeneous, predictions. Shields (1980, 1983) also presents elaborate empirical descriptions of how information load affects management controller's analysis of performance reports. As suggested by a huge body of psychological research (see Chapter 2 of this thesis, p. 15ff), his results indicate that the accuracy of accountant's judgments resembles an inverted u-shaped function of the information load: there is evidence that suggests the occurrence of information overload. Shield's study, in its proclamation that "more" information is not always beneficial, and particularly as it appears so early in accounting research, is a very

---

[44] Critique of such information processing models however frequently highlight that these kinds of models lack situational influences, are to focused on elementary processes and not sufficient for understanding the complexity of the process (too much focus on "how") (Funke, 2003).

notable piece of work. The role of learning and expertise has also appeared repeatedly as a topic of discussion in these earlier studies (see section 2.7.4, p. 79ff). Iselin (1988) substantiates her claim that more experienced accountants need less time, even when they face a greater information load. Thus, as discussed in a psychological context in section 2.7.4 (p. 79ff), learning and expertise have strong effects when trying to cope with an increased complexity.

A more recent literature review on information overload was conducted by Eppler and Mengis (2004, p. 326). The authors analyzed the research on information overload in various disciplines, and among them was accounting. They conclude that:

> *"Researchers across various disciplines have found that that the performance of an individual correlates positively up to a certain point. If further information is provided beyond this point, the performance of the individual will rapidly decline."*

This review revealed that the main causes of information overload could be organized into the following five categories: personal factors, information characteristics, task and process parameters (e.g. time pressure, or an overabundance of accounting standards), organizational design, and information technology. The resulting symptoms of information overload, similarly, can be categorized into four main fields: limited information search and retrieval strategies, arbitrary information analysis and organization, suboptimal decisions, and strenuous personal situation. Using key words such as "information (over)load" and "cognitive (over)load" in the *EBSCOhost* database, they identify 19 relevant peer-reviewed articles in the field of accounting research on this topic from 1970 onwards. It is interesting to note, however, that among these 19 articles, only four (Iselin, 1993; Simnet, 1996; Swain & Haka, 2000; Tuttle & Burton, 1999) were published after 1990 – i.e. after the publication of the accounting specific literature review by Schick et al. (1990).[45] Other articles that focus on this topic are mostly the "classic" articles from the early 1980s, as discussed in the previous paragraph.

---

[45] For a recent article on information load from the German accounting community see Volnhals and Hirsch (2009).

In light of this, it appears that this issue, currently speaking, is of little interest in the field of behavioral accounting research. Thus, the introduction of state of the art research on bounded and ecological rationality could provide some fresh insights into this rather stagnant topic. Most articles in this area do not state precisely whether or not more information would actually improve the decision making process. This finding, that more information does not always lead to greater accuracy, is particularly relevant to the making of forecasts and predictions (see also the distinction between fitting and predicting on p.39ff of this work). Also, many of the papers discussed by Eppler and Mengis (2004) contribute just marginally new insights to this issue; they frequently replicate Miller's (1956) classic findings on the limits of the human capacity to process information, simply in different contexts or disciplines. From this perspective it appears to be particularly important to distinguish the benefits of adding more information from the "computational" limits of actors in organizations. Particularly when making prescriptive recommendations, it appears important to make the distinction suggested by Milkman, Chugh and Bazerman (2009) between bounded rationality, which can not be improved, and bounded judgments, that can be improved.

2.5.2　Research on heuristics in accounting research

In an early *Journal of Accounting Research* article on behavioral decision theory (in accounting), Einhorn and Hogarth already point out (1981, p. 6) that "heuristics exist because they serve useful functions and their benefits outweigh their costs." In (behavioral) accounting research however most research rather investigated the downsides of heuristics in the tradition of the heuristics and biases program analyzing popular concepts such as representativeness, availability or the anchoring heuristic (e.g. W. B. Johnson, 1983; Libby, 1985; Wright & Anderson, 1989). This may be due to the fact that it took behavioral scientists longer to demonstrate their effectiveness versus the easier to demonstrate robustness of deviations from economic standards (Einhorn & Hogarth, 1981).[46]

In order to analyze heuristics as a general topic in (behavioral) accounting research an extensive database research was conducted using Science Direct and

---

[46]　But see Tversky (1972) or Thorngate (1980) for early exceptions.

Business Source Premier. In these databases abstracts and titles of all publications were screened for the keywords: heuristic, bias, representativeness, availability. The period for the search was limited from 1980 to 2010 as this marks the starting point were the heuristics and biases program was adopted by accounting research (Kotchetova & Salterio, 2004). Based on Brown and Huefner (1994) and Kotchetova and Salterio (2004) the analysis concentrated on the nine most influential journals in accounting. According to Kotchetova and Salterio (2004, p. 550) these nine journals "include the top four journals defined by Brown and Huefner (1994) and Trotman and colleagues (2011) (JAR, TAR, CAR, AOS) as well as the five journals of the various interest groups in the American Accounting Association." These are: *Journal of Accounting Research (JAR); The Accounting Review (TAR); Contemporary Accounting Research (CAR); Accounting, Organizations and Society (AOS); Auditing: Journal of Practice & Theory (AJPT); Journal of American Taxation Association (JATA); Journal of Information Systems (JIS), Journal of Management Accounting Research (JMAR); and Behavioral Research in Accounting (BRIA)*.

Interestingly only 38 publications in total were found, which have the above-mentioned keywords in the title or appearing in the abstract. This is insofar surprising as the inclusion of a single word in the abstract is a rather soft criterion for being included. Consequently, many approaches towards heuristics are not just from a behavioral perspective (e.g. formal analytic models and including auditing, financial accounting and managerial accounting research) are included in these 38 publications.

Among these publications only 10 (approximately 25%) had one of the key words in the title (as an indicator for the main research question of the paper). Analyzing the timeline of the publications regarding heuristics and the related key words in title or abstract, indicate a pike between 1987 and 1997 with around 50% of the publications (18). Research on heuristics is found in three out the four top journals.

Surprisingly *Behavioral Research in Accounting* as a specialized journal in behavioral topic was not found to publish much research within this field. It has however to be added that as a limitation this keyword search is not perfectly proof against misses in the analysis. If for instance the keyword has been gut feeling or rule-of-thumb then it would not have been included in the list. Also the recent research on ecological models of rationality (for a summary of rationality concepts in business research see also Basel & Brühl, 2011; Rieskamp & Reimer, 2007) and the potentially resulting adaptive character of heuristics (Gigerenzer, 2002) have not been a research subject in behavioral accounting research until now.[47] Overall, it seems that the issue of heuristic reasoning in behavioral accounting research pops up from time to time, also in the leading journals like *The Accounting Review* or *Contemporary Accounting Research*. However, what is missing is a constant stream of research, or similar research questions that have been picked up in various publications. This is maybe due to the lack of a theoretical foundation or to the vague nature of some of the described heuristics that can post-hoc account for a wide range of behavior (Gigerenzer, 1996). Consequently, the particular value of the concept of ecological rationality is that it allows a more solid theoretical framework for analyzing heuristic reasoning also in accounting settings.

Table 5: Heuristics as a research topic in major accounting publications*

Journal	1980s	1990s	2000s	Total
JAR	1 (1)	0	0	1 (1)
TAR	3 (2)	3	3(1)	9 (3)
CAR	2	3 (1)	1	6
AOS	2 (1)	2 (1)	2	6 (2)
BRIA	-**	2 (1)	2	4 (1)
JMAR	0	2 (1)	3 (2)	5 (3)
JIS	0	1	3	4
AJPT	0	0	2	2
JATA	1	0	0	1
Total	9 (4)	13 (4)	16 (3)	38 (10)

* Numbers in brackets indicate that publication includes keyword(s) in the title of the article.

** BRIA was initially founded in 1989.

---

[47]   For an exception see the study by Bedard and Wright (1994) published in BRIA that deals with the functionality of heuristics in an auditing setting, but without refering to concepts of adaptive decision making). Additionally the impact of this study analyzing *Google Scholar* only is rather limited.

To get a more complete picture of behavioral accounting research, this keyword search (as illustrated in Table 7) can be compared with a recent study by Trotman, Tan and Ang (2011), screening for the publications of JDM experiments in the four leading accounting journals (AOS,CAR, JAR and TAR) from 1970 until 2009.

As experiments represent one major tool in heuristic reasoning, it is of interest to compare these two numbers. Focusing on management accounting shows that there is a constant rate of experimental publications since the 1980s with an increase in the 2000s. In particular, *The Accounting Review* seems to be more open for experimental research in management accounting, indicating a raising interest for this kind of behavioral accounting research.

Table 6: Publication of JDM experiments in accounting (Trotman, et al., 2011, p. 281)

Discipline	Journal	1970s	1980s	1990s	2000s	Total
Audit	AOS	3	23	21	11	58
	CAR	0	3	22	22	47
	JAR	8	54	28	8	98
	TAR	5	29	38	28	100
	Total	16	109	109	69	303
Financial accounting	AOS	5	18	7	1	31
	CAR	0	0	2	5	7
	JAR	14	11	9	5	39
	TAR	14	11	3	20	48
	Total	33	40	21	31	125
Management accounting	AOS	1	12	14	17	44
	CAR	0	3	6	16	25
	JAR	10	12	1	4	27
	TAR	4	12	9	26	51
	Total	15	39	30	63	147
All Disciplines	Total	64	188	160	163	575

Despite this documented constant stream of published research on JDM and heuristics in behavioral accounting research there are some gaps in research that shall be addressed in this thesis. The first area concerns the frequently observed focus of accounting scholars to rely on rather static, mathematic models of human decision making that are typically based exclusively on economic theory (e.g. Balakrishnan & Sivaramakrishnan, 2002). Closely linked to this issue is the lack of process-oriented models (see Payne & Venkatraman, 2011) in behavioral accounting research that incorporate state of the art concepts and models from psychological (JDM) research (for an overview see Baron, 2008).

This is insofar relevant for management accounting, as a focus on subjective decisions (using psychological models) is more likely to lead to a better understanding (instead of mimicking heuristics and biases studies (following Kahneman & Tversky, 2000)) and most importantly improving accounting related decisions (Luft, 2011; Milkman, et al., 2009). On the other hand, a list of optimizing models as suggested for instance by Balakrishnan and Sivaramakrishnan (2002) (concerning capacity planning and cost-based pricing) explains little to nothing regarding the processes an individual decision maker faces. Additionally (as already discussed in detail in section 2.3.2, p. 25ff) these economic models frequently assume that decision makers act like "hyper-rational maximizers of utility from wealth (and leisure)" (Luft, 2011).

Within this thesis, this research gap (the lack of process models within behavioral accounting research, using current JDM models and concepts) is approached by the analysis of heuristic reasoning. The existence of heuristic mechanisms within accounting settings is an established norm (Einhorn & Hogarth, 1981; Shields, 1980), however the integration of multiple psychological concepts and models (as discussed in the following sections, including new perspectives regarding the rationality debate) is a novel contribution regarding this issue.

The research gap, as summarized here, is closed by using multiple methods for better approaching process characteristics of heuristic reasoning in management accounting. This approach yields fruitful outcomes JDM research in accounting in general, due to the solid theoretical foundation.

2.6 Excursus: Assuring rationality – a German perspective

One important distinction between the Anglo-Saxon and the German-speaking (management) accounting community is that in the latter, management accounting is frequently described, in particular by Weber and colleagues (e.g. Dyckhoff & Ahn, 2001; Schäffer, 2002; J. Weber, 2011a; J. Weber & Schäffer, 2008a; J. Weber & Schäffer, 2008b),[48] to function as a way to assure the rationality of the management. Their concept is based on the premise that within organizations bounded rational agents suffer from various limitations and thus an assuring function is needed and fulfilled by management controllers.

This theoretical conceptualization of accounting is of particular interest to this thesis for its specific focus on concepts of rationality in business research (see Chapter 2 in this thesis, p. 15ff). The Anglo-Saxon perspective appears less optimistic concerning the role and the capabilities of management controllers. Their starting point is frequently that all agents within organizations (including accountants) depart from (perfectly) rational decisions. For instance Sprinkle (2003, p. 288), with respect to JDM within organizations, highlights that: "Despite the perfect rationality assumption governing agency models and most models of economic behavior, ample evidence indicates that the judgments and decisions of both producers and users of information are not of the highest quality."[49]

Weber and colleagues (J. Weber & Schäffer, 2008b; J. Weber, Schäffer, & Langenbach, 1999) explicitly state both the cognitive limitations and the opportunism risks of management to be the main challenges of management controllers in their function as a "critical counterpart," and as a consultant of the management.[50] Rationality is also not understood in absolute terms (an impossible feat, according to these scholars); rather it is constructed through a community of social actors. Assuring rationality is not meant to be a form of anticipation or realization through particular actions. Rather it is passive, with a clear focus on the assuring function (Schäffer & Weber, 2001). The goal of rationality itself is (in line with classic economic concep-

---

[48] But see Brändle (2007) for some critique on this controlling function.

[49] For other examples from an Anglo-Saxon perspective see for example Bonner (2008).

[50] For an elaborate summary of definitions of management accounting (and the German counterpart "controlling" respectively, see also Horváth (2009, pp. 49ff.,73ff.).

tualizations see Chapter 2 of this thesis, p. 15ff) to maximize utility, including a weighting of goals and sub-goals. This approach explicitly excludes effectual and emotional components from their view on rationality, as they do not allow for the optimal allocation of resources with respect to means-ends relationships.

In contrast, the popular Anglo-Saxon textbook Management Control Systems by Anthony and Govindarajan (2001, p. 71) is more neutral, outlining the main tasks to be "preparing and analyzing performance reports, [and] interpreting these reports for managers." They also add to this the task of recommending actions to the management, and another of implementing management decisions. They neglect, however, any discussion of why some decisions of the management might by flawed. Also, the brief definition provided by Kotchetova and Salterio (2004, p. 548), deriving from a more behavioral background, that stresses that "accounting can be broadly thought of as the measurement and the communication of relevant economic information to decision makers," is rather neutral and avoids any notions of rationality. Drury (1997, p. 4), on an only slightly more prescriptive note, argues that, "management accounting is concerned with the provision of information to people within the organization to help them make better decisions." With respect to the limited capabilities of organizational actors, he highlights that, "business people are content to find a plan that provides satisfactory profits rather than to maximize profits."

The JDM responsibility of accountants within organizations is also stressed by the German community (e.g. Beckmann & Huch, 2002; Kappler, 2002). Here, the assuring of what is labeled instrumental rationality ("Zweckrationalität", which is the optimal decision balancing reflection and intuition (Schäffer, 2002, p. 99)) also plays an essential part of the decision making process of management controllers.

The issue here, of how to improve the functional rationality (meaning an optimal allocation of resources with respect to means/ends relations) of organizational/management decisions, is also an important landmark in the definition of management accounting (cf. "controlling" in the German community) as an academic discipline. Furthermore, the concept of instrumental rationality is itself not invented or exclusively used by (German) accounting research. For instance, both Tribe (1973) and Brown (1978) analyze this means to an ends efficiency – respectively from a law and a philosophical perspective, explicitly taking into account the "goodness" of the goals.[51]

2.6.1 The actor model by Weber and colleagues

Consistent with this framework, Weber and colleagues (e.g. 2011b) suggest an actor model that uses the limitations of will and ability to describe the role of management controllers within an organization. Assuring the rationality of the management, as in previous studies, takes central focus in their approach. The assumption that will power is limited by cognitive constraints, but that ability could be potentially improved up to a certain point, allows proposing a multi-theoretical framework for management accounting research.

One important starting point for this particular actor model is the subjectivism proposed by von Hayek (1937). This proposal can be distinguished from holistic and collectivistic ones, as its main focus is the explanation of social phenomena explicitly as a function of individual actions, developments and decisions. For von Hayek (1979, p. 60), it is particularly important to stress the potential explanations given by the social sciences, highlighting that "the social sciences no less than the natural sciences aim at revising the popular concepts which men have formed about the objects of their study, and replacing them by more appropriate ones."

These "appropriate" concepts are, for von Hayek, observed in individual actions rather than in imprecise, collectivistic models. This position is in line with the methodological individualism suggested by Popper (1967). The conclusion drawn from these perspectives, that conflicting views and actions can be integrated in one organizational setting, is seen by Meyer (2005) as an important contribution for principal agent models.

The other theoretical foundation of the Weber et al. actor model is the economic approach, developed by Becker (1976). From this scholar's work, the model adopts its underlying rationality assumptions.

---

[51] But as Einhorn and Hogarth point out (1981), the goals themselves are difficult to evaluate from this perspective. They stress that a time horizon must always be added, as otherwise, short- and long-term goals may stand in conflict with each other.

These are:[52]

  a) Utility maximizing behavior.

  b) Stable preferences.

  c) The existence of market equilibrium.

These assumptions are, in Becker's perspective, the central criteria to consider when explaining human action through the conditions the actors face. Within this framework, Meyer (2005) stresses that the explanation of a single (and unique) action is not the goal of this framework; rather, it works towards an aggregate model.[53] Consequently, homo economicus (equivalent to rational actions and self-interest guided behavior) is also an important reference for the actor model, as is a strong reference towards an "open" understanding of what constitutes utility. All personal interests of actors can designate themselves as utilitarian from this perspective.

Thus, both monetary and altruistic preferences can have a utilitarian value for the actor.[54] This aspect of the model is important insofar as this view of utility allows for an explanation of differing interests within an organization that could potentially be in conflict with the organization's goals (a danger of opportunism). Assuring rationality, in this case, means securing the organization's higher goals. In other words, the explanation of action in this model (see Figure 13 on the next page) allows management controllers to identify any underlying conditions and intentions, which can then be challenged for their functional rationality with reference to the organization's goals. Meyer (2005) stresses that homo economicus works similarly to a micro hypothesis. Anomalies on the macro level have to be traced back to the micro level.[55]

---

[52] See section 2.3 (p. 22ff) of this thesis, for other normative models of rationality and a discussion of these concepts.

[53] Interestingly, Meyer (2005) points out that single actions apart from aggregate models can be better explained through other disciplines, such as psychology. In this view, micro phenomena (e.g. single actors and their actions) are integrated into a larger scope but the goals for explanations are on a macro level (e.g. the progression of the inflation rate). However, "social laws" in the fashion of historicism are clearly avoided in this approach.

[54] This view of utility is, however, frequently criticized for being a post-hoc explanation that is ultimately a universal proposition with little scientific value (e.g. N. Berg, 2010).

[55] Here, Meyer (2005, p. 15) refers to "behavioral decision theory" (Einhorn & Hogarth, 1981), which in this case can be seen as a synonym for the heuristics and biases program.

Figure 13: Explaining social action within the actor model (adapted from Meyer, 2005)

Explanans:	Explanandum:	Reference
Action conditions + rationality assumptions	→ *Actions and consequences*	Becker's (1976) homo economicus model
Abstract situational elements + rationality principles	→ *Actions of (social) actors*	Popper's (1967) situational analysis

2.7 Toward a theoretical framework of heuristic reasoning in management accounting

2.7.1 Advances and trends in analyzing heuristics

In this work the definition of heuristics as effort reduction mechanism by Shah and Oppenheimer (2008) is adopted (see p. 34). This approach allows integrating both fast and frugal heuristics and heuristics and biases. According to Gigerenzer and Gaissmeier (2011) there is no strict dichotomy between heuristic and non heuristic. Thus, this suggestion by Shah and Oppenheimer (2008) is in particular useful, because it allows sufficient freedom to describe heuristics not only from a strict dichotomy perspective.

Of course, this is not the only existing definition of heuristic reasoning. As illustrated in Table 7 (see next page) there are various other approaches in disciplines, such as artificial intelligence/computer science or cognitive sciences providing definitions of heuristics in their particular field.

Table 7: Various approaches and definitions of heuristic reasoning

Authors	Definition / Approach
Artificial intelligence/Computer sciences and Operations research	
Feigenbaum and Feldman (1963, p. 6)	A heuristic (heuristic rule, heuristic method) is a rule of thumb, strategy, trick, simplification, or any other kind of device that drastically limits search for solutions in large problem spaces. Heuristics do not guarantee optimal solutions; in fact they do not guarantee any solution at all; all that can be said for a useful heuristic is that it offers solutions which are good enough most of the time."
Lenat (1982, p. 190)	A piece of knowledge capable of suggesting plausible actions to follow or implausible ones to avoid. For a body of heuristics to be effective (useful for guiding rather than merely for rationalizing in hindsight) each heuristic must specify a situation or context in which its actions are especially appropriate or inappropriate.
Streim (1975, p. 151)	Heuristics are non-arbitrary action plans that structure and control solution processes. Heuristics can be distinguished from arbitrary methods since a justification of their use can be provided in an inductive or deductive manner. The central characterization of heuristic reasoning is complexity reduction.
Cognitive sciences/Psychology	
Shah and Oppenheimer (2008, p. 209)	All heuristics rely on one or more of the following methods for efford-reduction: examining fewer cues; reducing the difficulty associated with retrieving and storing cue values; simplifying the weighting principles for cues; integrating less information; examining fewer alternatives.
Todd, Neil and Paul (2001, p. 6676)	Heuristics are approximate strategies or "rules of thumb" for decision making and problem solving that do not guarantee a correct solution but that typically yield a reasonable solution or bring one closer to hand. As such, they stand in contrast to algorithms that will produce a correct solution given complete and correct inputs. More specifically, heuristics are usually thought of as shortcuts that allow decisions or solutions to be reached more rapidly and in conditions of incomplete or uncertain information – often because they do not process all the available information.
Business studies	
Krabuanrat and Phelps (1998, p. 85)	Heuristics are intentionally ignoring aspects of the decision in order to reduce cognitive load. They are identifying similar past cases/similar decisions (taken by others) and using their decision outcomes as guides. They are searching for an acceptable solution rather than the optimal one, only generating alternatives of the first possibility is rejected. Heuristics are forms of pooling knowledge, carrying out small-scale experiments.
Powalla (2010, p. 18)	A heuristic is a non-arbitrary method to make reasonable conclusions from incomplete information. Heuristics operate based on a reduction of the problem solving effort. Heuristic reasoning does not guarantee a solution.

In this section I want to frame the different programs and show their commonalities. Therefore, I do not stress their differences, but show how they might reasonably be linked.[56] However, I will focus on the concepts of bounded rationality and will not elaborate on the link to unbounded rationality, concepts which exist for instance, in economics.[57]

Starting with the distinction made by Chase, Hertwig and Gigerenzer (1998) between bounded and ecological rationality, I illustrate the main component of ecological rationality with Figure 6 (p. 25) and Figure 14 (p. 70). As already stressed, within ecological rationality it is of utmost importance to look at how the environment influences the tasks (c) and how the environment shapes and has shaped the cognitive capacities of social actors (b) (Elio, 2002). The key critique on the heuristics and bias program is its main reliance on the relationship between tasks and cognitive capacities of social actors (a).

However, in my view both programs show us not only the pitfalls, but also the merits of human reasoning. Humans do not constantly err, because they use biased heuristics, nor do humans constantly engage in efficiently exploiting their environment – because they use fast and frugal heuristics. A more realistic picture looks like this: humans have an evolutionary past in which they constantly learned and adapted to their biological and social environment and this shaped their cognitive capacities. For instance, they learned to detect cheaters in social exchange situations which indicates a special heuristic for this important task in a social environment (Cosmides & Tooby, 2005). In addition, humans are not error free and, even more importantly; they face a wide range of tasks in a modern technological environment. Research shows that if humans are not familiar with those tasks they make errors when trying to solve them but, if they were tutored a lot of those problems disappeared. Eventually, both programs could profit from a wider framework of reasoning which I will illustrate next.

---

[56] See the reviews of this dispute as well as amendments in line with my suggestions in Samuels, Stich and Bishop (2002) and Samuels and Stich (2004).

[57] Since Simon's original publications of bounded rationality many suggestions have been discussed as to how to integrate bounded rationality in social and economic analysis, see for example contributions by Williamson (1985), Lindenberg (1992), Conlisk (1996), or by Smith (2003) and a short overview in Bendor (2001).

Figure 14: Simon's scissors explicated

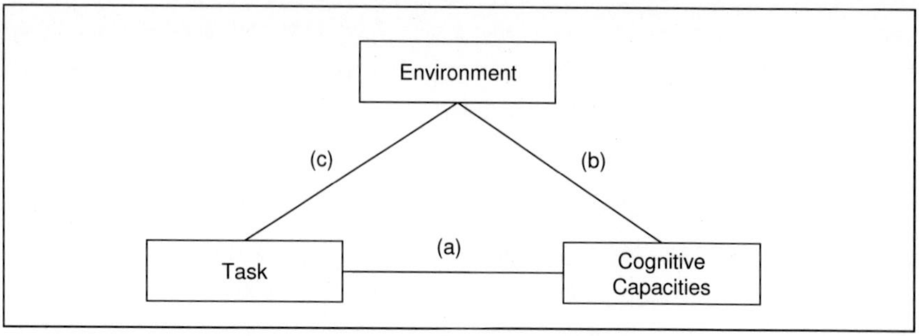

2.7.2 Dual process models as a unifying approach

According to Stanovich and West (2000) our judgment and decision making is partitioned into two main categories labeled System 1 (intuitive) and System 2 (reflective) (see Table 8, p. 72).[58] On the one side, System 1 is characterized by automatic, effortless and associative processes and is particularly relevant in affective contexts. The System 2 working principle on the other side is best described as controlled, deductive and dominated by serial processing. Both are working concurrently and it is important to acknowledge that the reliance of System 1 on automatic processes does not necessarily mean that this System is less capable than System 2.

Concerning a general description of dual process models, it is important to note that among cognitive scientists there are many different (sometimes even conflicting) dual process models with different taxonomies. For instance Stanovich (2004), lists over 20 different dual process models. For simplicity sake, this work will focus on the most central aspects with the most agreement among decision making scholars (Evans & Frankish, 2010). I will use the labels System 1 and System 2 for the overall distinction and focus on process and content characteristics (see Table 8, p. 72), excluding a lengthy philosophical (for a philosophical point of view see Frankish, 2010) and an in-depth neuroscience oriented discussion (for a discussion focussing on findings from neuroscience see Rugg & Yonelinas, 2003).

---

[58] There is an on-going discussion about the components of the mind (Keren & Schul, 2009). Here I only differentiate between dual-process and dual-systems approaches with the latter being the more comprehensive component of the mind (Frankish, 2010).

As an example of the power of System 1 Sloman (1996) mentions chess grandmasters, who are able to conduct perfect moves after a short glimpse on the board. Despite the reflective nature of System 2, this system can lead to wrong decisions as well, for the reason that people simply apply the wrong rules.[59]

In order to integrate the fast and frugal heuristics view by Gigerenzer and his research group[60] into this model, Kahneman and Frederick (2002) suggest that these heuristics fall into System 2. However, they suggest a dynamic relationship. First, heuristics are spontaneously initiated by System 1 and then later adopted by System 2 (as they are seen as a deliberate strategy). Biases, like the conjunction fallacy, occur when System 2 does not correct intuitive errors by System 1. In line with this explanation the approach of Gigerenzer (1991) of letting "cognitive illusions disappear", can be attributed to System 2 that in these cases used the salience of some cues to correct the biases of System 1. The issue of how heuristics shall be integrated into a dual process framework is also picked up by Frederick (2002), who distinguished between heuristics that fit into System 1 ("automated, heuristics", e.g. affect based heuristics) and heuristics that fit into System 2 ("deliberate choice heuristics").

This approach can be considered as a possible solution to integrate the competing views on intuitive judgments and the usefulness of heuristics. This view is also favored by Kahneman (2000, p. 682), who highlights that: "Tversky and I always thought of the heuristics and biases approach as a two-process theory." (see also Kahneman, 2011 for a more recent integration of the heuristics and biases program into a dual process framework).

---

[59] Sloman (1996, p. 11 ff) lists various examples from different research contexts. For instance the occurrence of simultaneous contradictory beliefs, like the famous "Linda" conjunction fallacy (Kahneman & Tversky, 2000). According to Sloman people often report, when confronted with the evidence that it is less likely that Linda is both a lawyer and a feminist (compared to the single condition): "I know it is less likely but it feels so wrong just to choose one single condition".

[60] However, is has to be highlighted that Gigerenzer (and most of his research group) (e.g. Kruglanski & Gigerenzer, 2011) personally prefers a unified theoretical approach (unimodel) to human reasoning and criticizes dual process approaches, for instance for not having well-defined cut-off points between the two systems (the so-called continuity vs. dichotomy problem).

Table 8: Characterization of Systems 1 and 2 (based on Kahneman & Frederick, 2002)

System 1 (intuitive)	System 2 (reflective)
Process characteristics	
Automatic	Controlled
Effortless	Effortful
Associative	Deductive
Rapid, parallel	Slow, serial
Process opaque	Self-aware
Skilled action	Rule application
Content	
Affective	Neutral
Causal propensities	Abstract
Prototypes	Sets
Concrete, specific	Abstract

Still, I have to clarify the role of ecological rationality in this dual-process model of reasoning. This is relevant, because obviously both systems can lead to successful decisions and it is challenging to infer descriptive implications from this model.[61] One possible option is to refer to the experience of social actors. Exploiting the environment (i.e. to behave ecological rational) is not synonymous with learning, rather, learning is a pre-condition to exploiting the information of the environment. I guess that only experienced social actors will be able to decide if a heuristic will be satisfying and when to switch to more effortful rule-based reasoning.

If this account is true, then the idea of ecological rationality is another way to explore under which circumstances experienced managers (in marketing or manage-

---

[61] Although Gigerenzer and Regier (1996) and more recently Kruglanski and Gigerenzer (2011) express serious doubts about the integration of fast and frugal heuristics into the broader perspective of dual process models of reasoning (as suggested for example by Chaiken & Trope, 1999; Epstein, 1994; Sloman, 1996). The differences between the views of Gigerenzer and colleagues on the one side and Kahneman on the other side can be classified in terms of degree and not as two mutually exclusive views of human decision making (Frey & Benz, 2004).

ment control) make efficient decisions and recommendations, and under which circumstances they also commit biases (Kahneman & Klein, 2009). This could be used to explain when heuristics are useful (Gigerenzer & Brighton, 2009) and when they might mislead the decision maker (Kahneman & Tversky, 2000). One promising avenue of research is in clarifying how System 1 and System 2 interact and when System 2 processes override processes of System 1 (Stanovich, 2010).[62] As I have outlined in this thesis, management scholars should pay attention to cognitive processes of social actors. This could contribute in practice towards knowing how to create an environment that encourages social actors to freely express and act according to managers' "gut feelings" and heuristics (in line with this suggestion see also the results of study 6, p. 157ff).

Furthermore, for management research, it would be interesting to discover if heuristics represent efficient tools in dealing with daily challenges and how they are actually used (Astebro & Elhedhli, 2006). For example, it has been shown in several studies that our ability to make accurate (effective) forecasts is inadequate (e.g. Hsee & Zhang, 2004) and it seems promising to compare heuristic estimations against these (more elaborate) forecasts. In a dual-process setting this research could contribute to the interplay of heuristics and effortful reasoning in realistic management settings.

As in any growing field of research, there is a lack of coherence between the labels of dual-processes or dual-systems (see for instance tables 1 and 2 in Evans, 2008, p. 257). For instance, the model from Table 8 (on the previous page) provides no deeper explanation of how the underlying cognitive processes work (it is not a process model) and how one system merges into another (Keren & Schul, 2009). In this case, a further explication is necessary of how heuristics (as System 1 mechanisms) co-exist and co-work with more rule-based systems (System 2). This is of crucial importance for the research on dual process models, as critics like Keren and Schul (2009, p. 544) argue that these models "lack of any predictive power and the tendency [of scholars] to employ them as an after-the-fact explanations."

---

[62] Evans theorizes on a more general two mind hypothesis and argues against a chief executive model of the mind, however, he also distinguishes between a reflective and an intuitive mind (Evans, 2010).

Further research will show if dual-process theories yield enough progressive energy to fuel this research program of judgment and decision making in management. That a two system approach is also common in business studies can be seen for instance in Weber, Schäffer and Langenbach's (1999) description of the function of management controllers. They stress that management decisions are often lead by intuitive and irrational reasoning, therefore management controllers are needed in order to assure the rationality. Thus, the accountants can be seen as System 2 agents, working rule oriented and effortful, which counterbalance potential biases made by the management as System 1 agents.[63]

This model, however, excludes any connotations about decision processes and utilities and probabilities. These represent important starting points for the heuristics and biases approach, whereas the ecological rationality concept explicitly excludes utilities and probabilities from its theoretical framework of human decision making – in this view there is no room for any form of intuitive statistician homunculus in the adaptive toolbox.

Furthermore, dual process models tell you per se little about when a more tacit strategy should be preferred over a deliberate one and how this approach could be fueled with ecological rationality. Consider for example the following scenario (adapted from Epstein, Lipson, Holstein, & Huh, 1992), which could work as a demonstration for dual process mechanisms but not for ecological principles: Two companies (together with others) are in a bidding contest regarding the acquisition of an emerging biotech firm. After the contest is over, one company learns that their offer was rejected and that they paid 20 million less than the winner did. The other company is told that they suffered a close loss – they only offered 1 million less than the winner did. Which CEO would be more annoyed after this news? Participative ratings would argue that the CEO of the second company would be more annoyed because they were closer to winning the auction. On the one hand from a rational point of view (at least according to Epstein, et al., 1992) both should feel the same way because they both "lost" the competition – the final outcome is for both the same. An

---

[63]   However, this description departs from Slomans (1996) view on dual processes because it strongly   focuses on the errors made by System 1 dominated managers and does not take into account possible positive outcomes of System 1.

interpretation from an ecological rational perspective would be that the second company should feel more annoyed and treat this reaction as a feedback mechanism for
future auctions and place a higher bid next time.

2.7.3 Clarifying some claims about intuition

Daniel Kahneman and Amos Tversky start their book, *Choices, Values and Frames*
with the famous line "making decisions is like speaking prose – people do it all the
time, knowingly or unknowingly" (2000, p. 1). Considering the widespread popularity
of JDM topics in business studies, it appears that this often cited quote (e.g.
Connolly, Arkes, & Hammond, 2000) rings true. Furthermore, this issue is also of
interest from the dual process perspective, as discussed in the previous section. According to most scholars (e.g. Evans, 2008) System 1 relies on automatic (and intuitive) processes that happen without (or with little) awareness.

The function of intuition - "the unknowingly" aspect of JDM - is investigated particularly frequently by scholars in business studies, going back even to the early work
of social scientists like Herbert Simon (1945) and Chester Barnard (1938). Whereas
Simon in most cases considers the function of intuition in the exclusive context of
bounded rationality, Barnard uses the distinction between logical and non-logical
processes as a starting point for his analysis of managerial JDM. He claims that if we
are not aware making it, the decision, as it lacks deep reflection, must not be logical.

The relevance of intuition can be seen not only by its increasing appearance in the
surrounding research, buy also by its practical applicability: various studies have
shown that intuitive strategies are frequently used by managers (Agor, 1990;
Gigerenzer, 2007; Isenberg, 1984; Parikh, Neubauer, & Lank, 1994). Despite the
popularity of issues related to unconscious or intuitive JDM topics in business studies, there is surprisingly little consensus within the scientific community regarding
two fundamental questions: First, what constitutes intuition and unconsciousness in
business related judgments? And second, what role does heuristics play within this
field (see on this issue also Frederick, 2002)? The second question includes not just
complicated issues such as, when these mental shortcuts are used and under what
circumstances they are most efficient (see, e.g., Gigerenzer, et al., 1999; Kahneman
& Tversky, 1983), but also much more fundamental concepts, such as the formation
of a workable definition of the term "heuristic," both of which appear to be absent in
the various studies (cf. Shah & Oppenheimer, 2008).

A proper scientific investigation of intuition and its related concepts requires first of all a stringent definition of the terms (Carnap, 1960). On the one hand, early works in business studies such as Barnard (1938) have made the simple distinction between intuition and rationality. This argument implies that anything that simply pops into our mind is intuitive, thus, not subject to deliberate considerations and therefore non-logical. The problem with this approach (to define intuition against rationality) is that it is tautological. I might reword the argument to read: The decision is irrational because it is intuitive, and irrational because it uses intuition. The absence of any form of intuition, or so the argument goes, is a necessary but not a sufficient prerequisite for a rational decision.

On the other hand, several decades later Miller and Ireland point out that intuition can no longer be seen as the opposite of rationality: "intuition," they state, "corresponds to thoughts, conclusions, or choices produced largely or in part through "subconscious mental processes" (C. C. Miller & Ireland, 2005, p. 251). This kind approach, however, leaves open the questions, what actually constitutes intuition, and what are the underlying processes. To stress such terms as "subconscious mental processes," leads to the danger of perceiving intuition as a mysterious participant in the decision making process. Additionally, the use of the term "subconscious" is misleading in a managerial context because this term is linked to (Freudian) psychoanalysis. From a modern scientific point of view, terms like "non-conscious" or "unconscious" are preferable. These examples highlight the difficulties that business scholars face in trying to arrive at a consensus over elemental terms and concepts.

That business administration scholars use vague labels for intuition and sometimes even deny a deeper understanding of the underlying processes, is because they do not integrate up-to-date results and concepts from other disciplines into their models of managerial JDM. In particular, cognitive and social psychologists have tried to overcome any form of black-box-thinking[64] by focusing specifically on the underlying processes of thinking, memory, and intuition. Betsch (2008, p. 4), for example, defines intuition from a more process-oriented perspective:

---

[64]   At least after the so-called cognitive revolution, which started in the late 1950s and by the end of the 1970s replaced the existing paradigm of behaviorism, which claimed that (psychological) research can not access the black-box of the human mind (Pinker, 2002).

> *"The input to this process is mostly provided by knowledge stored in long-term memory that has been primarily acquired via associative learning. The input is processed automatically and without conscious awareness. The output of the process is a feeling that can serve as a basis for judgments and decisions."*

Even if automatic and unconscious steps are mentioned, as they are here, this definition includes references to two well-studied concepts (long-term-memory and associative learning) and thus creates a solid basis for the research. It is interesting to compare the psychological approach undertaken by Betsch with Rowan (1990), who uses a (widely cited) definition of intuition from a managerial perspective. Rowan's study highlights firstly how narrow some crucial labels like rationality can be, and secondly, delineates some sources of misunderstandings of intuition in the business context. According to Rowan (1990, p. 195):

> *"Intuition is knowledge gained without rational thought. And since it comes from some stratum of awareness just below the conscious level, it is slippery and elusive, to say the least (...). New ideas spring from a mind that organizes experiences, facts, and relationships to discern a path that has not been taken before."*

This definition is problematic on two counts. Firstly, like Bertrand, he contrasts intuition with rational thought. This argument suggests that any deliberate thinking processes should be preferred over non-deliberate ones. However, various empirical evidence suggests that even enhanced awareness (or sometimes particularly enhanced deliberation), can in some cases lead to non-optimal and even non-rational outcome (for examples see Dijksterhuis, Bos, Nordgren, & van Baaren, 2006; J. G. Johnson & Raab, 2003). This finding is labeled by Dijksterhuis and his colleagues (2006; 2006) the "deliberation-without-attention effect." In a series of studies they showed that unconscious thought, in a complex consumer choice situation (e.g. which house or car to buy), could outperform a more conscious evaluation of the factors. Secondly, the emphasis of a "path that has not been taken before," conflicts with the frequent notion of expertise in intuition (e.g. Salas, et al., 2010) and associative learning. Here intuition must be differentiated from terms like creativity (which by definition produce something new (Sternberg, O'Hara, & Lubart, 1997)). Furthermore, the research of Betsch (2008) and other psychologists (e.g. Seligman & Kahana, 2009) highlights associative learning as one building block of intuition, and points to the significance of learned patterns. Thus, in a particular situation the (adaptive) decision maker can rely on various kinds of learned patterns or strategies that might be released in a non-conscious manner.

Khatri and Ng (2000, p. 59) emphasize that intuition is a complex concept that is not easily accessible in business studies. However, they also clearly state that intuition is neither the opposite of rationality, nor a random process of guessing. These authors highlight the learned foundation of intuition by arguing:

> "It is a sophisticated form of reasoning based on chunking that an expert hones over years of job-specific experience (...). To the extent that the lessons of experience are logical and well-founded, so is intuition."

Heuristics appears to be somewhere in-between conscious and unconscious decision making. Whilst some titles of monographs and articles focus on the latter end of this spectrum (e.g. "the intelligence of the unconscious" by Gigerenzer, 2007), others focus more on the conscious application of heuristics (Hilbig, Scholl, & Pohl, 2010). The stand that this thesis takes is that heuristics can indeed be both. The "learning" aspect is of particular importance to this dissertation. As with well learned processes, like driving a car, for example, we can not always describe exactly the kind of actions we accomplish in various tasks (Baddeley, Eysenck, & Anderson, 2009).

Heuristics may thus work with a combination of pure intuition, and conscious decision making (e.g. consciously relying on the recognition heuristic (Gigerenzer & Gaissmaier, 2011)). In this framework, the efficiency of a heuristic process is determined by its ability to be adaptive regarding task and environment, and not by the level of attention the decision maker allocates to it. It is, however, assumed that most heuristics are frequently intuitive strategies (at least when they are developed); because their working mechanism has to be observed several times before they can be articulated. Moreover, this distinction allows for the integration of dual process theories into a model for heuristic reasoning. The role of affect, which is highlighted in intuitive managerial decision making (Dane & Pratt, 2007), can be easily integrated into this concept (heuristics from a process perspective). The connection of intuition and heuristics is illustrated in the following diagram (Figure 15).

Figure 15: Heuristic reasoning and its reliance on intuition

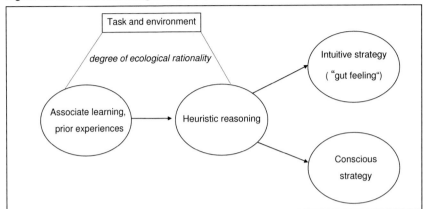

2.7.4 The function of learning and expertise

A crucial factor in the analysis of JDM and in particular heuristic reasoning is the function of learning and expertise.[65] Especially when it comes to the filtering of ecological rationality out of multi-stage decision processes, it appears important to stress that "without learning the decision making cannot be adaptive" (Krabuanrat & Phelps, 1998, p. 85). This provokes two important areas for debate:

Firstly, how heuristic reasoning is learned, and what kind of learning environment could strengthen such a development. Secondly, what function is played by expertise; do the heuristics used by experts (and/or more experienced participants) somehow have a superior quality; and do experts perform badly when they rely on heuristic reasoning (see Ericsson, et al., 2006).

Regarding the first question, Rieskamp and Otto (2008; 2006) suggest a strategy selection theory (SSL), that tries to overcome the often cited "strategy selection problem". This theory describes a process model of the learning mechanisms behind

---

[65] As mentioned before, the term expertise is used here not in a very strict sense as laid out by other authors (e.g. Ericsson, et al., 2006; Ericsson, et al., 2007; J. F. Smith & Kida, 1991). In this thesis expertise is used rather on a continuum, having novices on one side and highly skilled experts on the other. Thus with respect to business studies, it is basically assumed that some people have more experience (for various reasons) in making business related decisions than others. This can be seen as a necessary but not sufficient condition for expertise.

heuristic reasoning that are used when inductive inferences are made.[66] To agree with these authors, it is clear that a meta-strategy (cf. making tradeoffs of costs and benefits) would not be the best explanation for strategy selection. Rather, people build up a repertoire strategies (such as heuristics) through learning. They point out that instead of simple stimulus-response (S-R) associations, unobservable cognitive strategies are used. These cognitive mechanisms are then reinforced through feedback mechanisms, with the strategies "expectancies" as yardsticks of their success.

The strategy selection model implies further that as a first step, a decision maker sets an expectancy level and an appropriate strategy. After the strategy is used, the success or failure of the strategy is evaluated and the expectancy is updated. After this feedback mechanism, strategies are selected proportional to the updated expectancies. According to strategy selection theory, through this simple feedback loop, we know what we can reach (and with what kind of strategy) in a particular environment and we thus become adaptive decision makers through this learning function. Rieskamp and Otto (2006) tested empirically their predictions of their theory. They found that strategy selection theory (compared with other models), explains best how people select heuristic mechanisms in accordance with the adaptive toolbox (as suggested by Gigerenzer, 2002) in changing environments.

Figure 16: SSL theory (simplified version of Rieskamp and Otto, 2006)

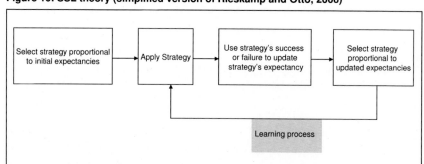

---

[66]   Inductive inference is the task of making an informed guess about the future, using observations of the past.

It appears reasonable to add to strategy selection theory what Hogarth (1987, 2002) labels *kind* and *wicked* environments. In *kind* environments, feedback is provided in an easy and reliable way. *Wicked* environments are characterized by a lot of noise and non-timely and non-veridical feedback mechanisms. With respect to SSL the crucial feedback aspect is the success or failure rate of the applied heuristic. If feedback is of poor quality or too noisy, there is less chance within SSL to update expectancies and thus to select the most successful (i.e. adaptive) heuristic.

If feedback and learning, as demonstrated by strategy selection theory, play such a crucial role, it appears important to question in the next step if constant learning changes the way heuristics are used. In other words: if experience and expertise influence the way when and how we rely on heuristics.

Shanteau (1992) for instance stresses that experienced people face the same (cognitive) limits as naïve decision makers. This author concludes, considering the results of multiple studies, that experts do not differ in the amount of cues they use; but they do differ in what kind of cues they actually consider. This observation fits nicely with the concept of ecological rationality. Despite our limited cognitive abilities, we have the potential to make good decisions within these boundaries. Experts have thus learned (in a kind environment) to evaluate cue validities and to engage in heuristic reasoning without major tradeoffs.

Slovic (1969) shows in a classic study that business professionals, as experts, have a natural preference for frugal decision models. In this study, he found that professional stockbrokers relied on only six to seven cues when making inferences. In auditing, Ettenson et al. (1987) found that partners, managers and students did not differ significantly in how many cues they considered to evaluate a proposed account adjustment. What differed, however, was the cue weight between the groups. Interestingly, professionals (in this study) frequently used strategies that put heavy weight on a single cue, which outnumbered this way most of the others, when evaluating the decision quality. Altman (1968) shows already in the 1960s that limited cue selections indeed can also be successful (as a hint for ecological rationality), demonstrating that up to three cues can be enough for predicting bankruptcy.

Baylor (2001) points out that expertise and intuition (see Section 2.3.3, p.26ff) can be linked, and suggests a u-shaped developmental progression of intuitive thinking. It can be assumed, following this argumentation, that intuition is just as well reflected when only a few cues are considered. Thus, both novices and experts rely on their intuition, but only experts can identify the ecological rationality of the cues, or engage in what Baylor (2001) labels as "mature intuition."[67] Empirical evidence of the recognition heuristic demonstrates for example that increased decision quality is not a linear function of more knowledge. Rather, decision quality increases with the acquisition of a little knowledge, and then decreases with an intermediate level of knowledge, peaking at the point where all relevant cues and criteria are known (see Gigerenzer et al., 1999).

This kind of framework can also explain why Smith and Kida (1991, p. 485), analyzing heuristics and biases in an auditing setting, conclude: "Biases found readily in other research are not evident in the judgments of professional auditors." This concept of mature intuition and the possible link to ecological rationality, shell be illustrated in a simplified way in the Figure 17.

Figure 17: U-shaped progression of intuitive thinking in relation to expertise

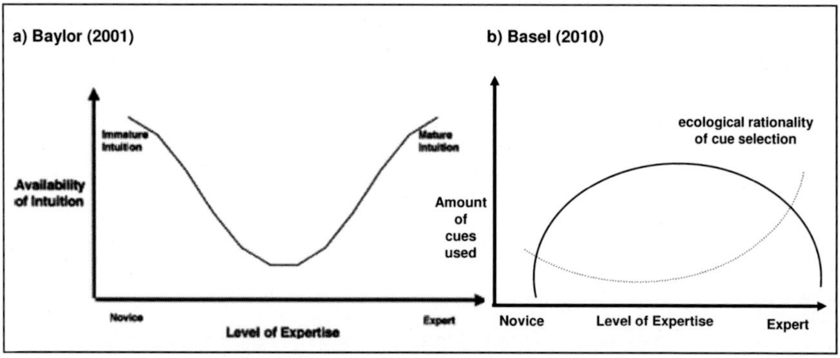

2.7.5 The role of accountability and self-protection

The effects of accountability are well documented, both in general JDM (for an overview see Lerner & Tetlock, 1999), and in more specific business research (e.g. Cronshaw & Alexander, 1985). Accountability manipulation is commonly regarded as

---

[67]   Note that ecological rationality is slightly higher for novices than for people with some expertise, but not for experts. This can be explained by the fact that people with some experience cannot rely on pure recognition because they know too many of the cues and thus consider too much (redundant) information (see Gigerenzer, 2007).

a multidimensional concept: it can be divided into the following "sub-manipulations": "the mere presence of another," "identifiability," "evaluation," and "reason-giving" (Lerner & Tetlock, 1999). These manipulations themselves can be moderated by biases such as the false-consensus effect, a bias that results in the impression that others hold opinions similar to your own (Ross, Greene, & House, 1977).

Hence the working mechanisms behind accountability are often more complex and subtle than common sense reasoning would expect. Lerner and Tetlock (1999), evaluating a huge body of existing research, suggest that the key working principle of accountability on people's JDM be integrated into a flexible contingency model. They point out that accountability leads to an effortful and self-critical search for cues when making a decision or a judgment. Lerner and Tetlock (1999, p. 263), with respect to cue selection in JDM, conclude:

> "This search leads participants to a) survey a wider range of conceivable relevant cues; b) pay greater attention to the cues they use; c) anticipate counter arguments, weight their merits relatively impartially, and factor those that pass some threshold of plausibility into their overall opinion or assessment of the situation; and d) gain greater awareness of their cognitive processes by regularly monitoring the cues that are allowed to influence judgment and choice."

Following this conclusion it will be less likely for individuals to engage in heuristic reasoning (understood as an efford reduction approach as suggested by Shah and Oppenheimer (2008)), when raising the level of accountability. This can be explained by the fact that heuristics could be harder to justify, and people want to avoid appearing foolish in front of others, as documented in various studies (e.g. Shafir, Simonson, & Tversky, 1993; Tetlock, Skitka, & Boettger, 1989).

The undoubted influence of accountability is confirmed by various studies. McAllister and his colleagues (1979), for example, found that accountability decreased the likelihood that people will use a simple weighting formula (as opposed to a more complex calculation); Weldon and Gargano (1988) observed less cognitive loafing when accountability was high; and Kahn and Baron (1995) demonstrated that in high accountability situations participants adopted more complex, non-compensatory decision strategies. However, what has remained unanswered in the surrounding research is whether there can be delineated a clear switch from a well-defined heuristic (such as TTB), to a more cognitive demanding tactic in situations related to accountability.

As previously stressed (see Section 2.1, p.15ff) considering all the available cues and using complex compensatory strategies is not necessarily the best way to achieve an optimal decision. With regards to accountability, some scholars agree. Simonson (1989; 1998), for instance, showed that accountability could lead to higher compromise and attraction effects, and to an increase in ambiguity aversion.[68] Tetlock and colleagues (1994; 1996) also point out that accountability in general raises the chances of integrating all available information, regardless of its actual relevance.

Of course, there are also numerous studies that emphasize the benefits and positive outcomes of accountability. For example participants in a study by Simonson and Nye (1992) were more willing to write off sunk costs when accountability was high. However, this effect was only observed for participants that had experienced some training on smart investment decisions. Thus, the positive effects of accountability depend on what kind of learning mechanisms are involved (see here also the previous sections on learning and expertise) and what kind of expertise the audience (as a reviewer of the action) has. This desire, to fulfill the expectations of one's audience, is also documented in a study by Lord (1992), who found that auditors matched their post-decision statements (for instance number of justifications, excuses etc.) to the expectations of the audience.

An important issue addressed by Lerner and Tetlock (1999) is the question of whether accountability alters how people think or what people say they think. For example, when in a high accountability environment, people may use a heuristic strategy, and just report that the strategy they used was more complex (as it is easier to justify). This issue should be understood alongside research on the role of self-

---

[68]   Compromise effect is the tendency of a choice option to appear more attractive, simply because it is presented in the middle of others. Attraction effect refers to the attractiveness of a relatively inferior alternative, when it is added to a group of closely competing options.

protection in JDM (March & Shapira, 1987).[69] Simonson (1989), for instance, showed that people, when they have to make a difficult choice between two alternatives, prefer the one that is most justifiable.

Larrick (1993) suggests that affective and motivational factors should be integrated into decision theories. Such variables have not been included in universal theories such as cardinal utility theory, expected utility theory or prospect theory. According to this author (1993, p. 442), these theories are elegant because they "propose that a single, hardwired mechanism guides the decisions of all people." However, he maintains that, "the approach may be too general and too basic. The psychophysical approach to decision making fails to capture some of the more human aspects of decision making." In order to avoid this problem, Larrick (1993) emphasizes the importance of regret when making a decision. His assumption is based on the findings of the classical motivational theories of Atkinson (1957) and, more recently, Lopes (1987). He refers in particular to the concept of "need for achievement,"[70] coined by Atkinson and McClelland (1976; 1951) and adopts Lopes's idea of combining the level of aspiration with the need for security. Need for achievement appears to be of special interest to business studies: McClelland (1964) found that business executives, compared with other professionals of comparable social and economic status (like university professors), score significantly higher on this concept (see also Mook, 1996, p. 543). This aspect is interesting as it stresses the relevancy not just of pure outcomes, but also of the importance of the decision maker's self-evaluation, assuming that is, that he wants to be perceived as a competent and intelligent person (as would be the case in most social contexts). Larrick (1993, p. 448) summarizes his findings on self-protection in JDM:

> *"People focus on two goals when they make decisions. One goal is to maximize their expected outcomes; the other goal is to maintain a positive self-image."*

---

[69] For a general discussion of the role of affect in JDM see for example Loewenstein and Lerner (2003). An in depth discussion of all affective factors that possible could influence decision making and heuristic reasoning would however be beyond the scope of this work.

[70] Geen (1995, p. 145) defines need for achievement as: "The tendency to approach success that is equal to the perceived expectancy of success on the task multiplied by the value of success [...]. Expectancy and value are not independent; as one increases the other decreases."

Heuristic reasoning can be integrated into these findings insofar as it represents a successful strategy and thus can maximize expected outcomes (this connection could also be enforced through learning). Nevertheless, how the use of heuristics influences the self-image remains an open question. It could be speculated that high accountability lowers the satisfaction gained from heuristic strategies and thus leads to more complex decision modes, thus functioning as a self-protective mechanism.

2.7.6 Self-other decision making

An important emerging feature in recent JDM research is the distinction between decisions made for yourself against those made for others (often labeled "self-other decision making") (for a review see Bonaccio & Dalal, 2006). For management controllers this issue is of crucial importance as they work as advice givers within the organization (Anthony & Govindarajan, 2001; Byrne & Pierce, 2007; J. Weber, 2011a). A huge body of research demonstrates the practical relevancy of this distinction, and highlights that people choose different strategies for themselves compared to those as advice givers (e.g Jonas, Schulz-Hardt, & Frey, 2005; Polman, 2010; Stone, Yates, & Caruthers, 2002).

For example, Kray (2000) found that proxy decision makers base their choices on the prominence of cues, compared to personal decision makers, who weighed cues equally. Furthermore proxy decision makers seek for more cues than personal decision makers (Jonas, et al., 2005). According to Polman (2010), this can explained by the fact that proxy decision makers face more pre-decisional information distortion than personal decision makers. Information distortion is the tendency to bias decision-relevant information to support a valued belief or preference (Gilovich, 1991). Thus, in pre-decisional distortion, "there is a strong tendency to bias information to support a developing preference in the process of making a decision" (Polman, 2010, p. 433).

Regardless of how advice is provided, it is also important to consider how the management (as recipient) reacts upon being given advice by other parties. For instance Tost, Gino and Larrick (2010) found that feelings of power, mediated by feelings of competitiveness and confidence, can lead individuals to listen less to the advice of others. This finding was supported in examples of both novice and expert advice. Whilst it appears obvious that advice by novices may be neglected, it is surprising to note that expert advice was also ignored. The authors suggest that in such a case, (high expertise) advice is experienced as a threat to status (in particular when feelings of power and competitiveness were high). In an other related study, Gino (2008) showed that more expensive advice tends to be given more weight by decision makers regarding the use of heuristics in management accounting, this may explain why there are more reports of complex (and thus costly) strategies being used than simple decision algorithms.

These findings can also be interpreted from another perspective, i.e. by considering the reciprocal relationships of management controllers within a company. Because they also receive information and cues by others, it can be concluded that the aforementioned processes also apply to accountants. Hence, heuristic reasoning could be explained by the fact that an accountant ignores some cues, as they are presented to him as advice.

This tendency, labeled by Yaniv (2004) as "egocentric advice discounting," [71] is a robust finding in self-other decision making (Bonaccio & Dalal, 2006). The research in this area shows that internal states have a high impact on which advice (presented in various forms) is considered, and which advice is ignored. Moreover, asking for advice can be seen as a sign of incompetence and uncertainty.

2.7.7 Précis of theoretical framework regarding the application in management accounting

Considering the eclectic streams within the research on heuristic reasoning, a modified and updated version of Libby and Lewis' (1977) (see Figure 12, p. 56) model of information processing is presented in this thesis. This means that a theoretical framework of heuristic reasoning in management accounting can be drawn, focusing on input, output and, in particular, the process characteristics (Payne & Venkatraman, 2011) of heuristics reasoning. This distinction reduces the complexity within this field of research towards a model which can be approached both experimentally (searching for cause--and-effect relations (Bortz & Döring, 2006)) and through the use of qualitative methods (with the objective to better describe the ac-

---

[71]   An early explanation of this tendency (seen in line with the effectiveness of ecological rationality) is the effect of diminishing marginal returns (Hogarth, 1978). This is the effect that in a judgment the advice received first is of a far higher value than the advice received second, third etc.

tual process (Brühl, Horch, & Orth, 2008) of how heuristics are implemented into JDM in "large worlds" (Savage, 1954) and what constitutes rationality in these worlds):

- **Input characteristics:** these include not only classical manipulations of independent variables such as statistical properties of cues or the method of presentation, but also the broader context. For instance, the distinction between the "small world" of the experimental setting and the "large world" of the qualitative approach is also manifest in this dimension. This includes also the notion of accountability, which represents one key dimension of social context factors, which is not displayed in the information set (cue) qualities: research.

- **Process characteristics** generally include two dimensions. On the one hand the specification of the decision maker/judge (e.g. decision making style) and on the other hand, the underlying characteristics of the (decision) rule. If heuristics are clearly defined through an effort reduction approach (Shah & Oppenheimer, 2008) or through precise search and stop rules, like in the fast and frugal approach (Gigerenzer, et al., 1999), they represent precise decision rules that can be compared (from a process perspective) to rational rules like weighted additive or equal weights (Payne, 1976a). These two elements are linked by the theoretical approach of dual process models (Evans & Frankish, 2010; Kahneman & Frederick, 2002). Using this model can account for both the use of compensatory and non-compensatory rules.

- **Output characteristics** are typically external criteria to evaluate the decision. But also self-insight and post decision questionnaires or subjective cue usage can assess this dimension.

This framework considers bounded rationality as a precondition of human JDM. Thus, the limitations can manifest both in limited cognitive capacities and in limited available information. From this point of view, bounded rationality is explicitly concerned with the input and process dimensions. Ecological rationality, on the other hand, only manifests in the output dimension. As this thesis deals mostly with input characteristics (e.g. accountability) and process descriptions (e.g. through verbal protocols), ecological rationality is not the central reference point here (see also section 2.3.8 (p. 43ff) for the summary of the critique of fast and frugal models/ecological rationality).

This framework also allows for the integration of the existing empirical evidence of the different visions of rationality (unbounded-, bounded- and ecological rationality, see Figure 6, p. 25), whereas unbounded rationality is typically "tested" in formal analytical models, assuming that stable choices and preferences can be mathematically described (for an example from an accounting perspective regarding this issue see Balakrishnan & Sivaramakrishnan, 2002; Friedman & Savage, 1948 for a classic). This economic perspective, which excludes process descriptions (Payne & Venkatraman, 2011), is particularly concerned with the mathematical analysis of input and output characteristics of the decision problem. Nevertheless, some research on models of bounded rationality is rather input-output driven. For instance, Luce (2000) summarizes various approaches that deal with the utility of gains and losses exclusively from an input-output perspective. Empirical studies that address the process dimension from a bounded rationality framework are, for instance, the classic verbal protocol studies by Ericsson and Simon (1993).

In line with this argumentation, it can be concluded that our bounded cognitive capacities/computational limits (cf. bounded rationality), paired with a matching environment can lead to ecological rational decisions. Bounded rationality is thus a necessary precondition for modeling ecological rational behavior. This distinction is also advocated by Stevens (2010, p. 100), according to whom: "Ecological rationality appeals to the evolutionary idea that adaptations match the environment in which they evolved. Therefore, decision mechanisms should not be universal and domain general but specifically tailored to the environment in which they operate"

This suggested model allows an approach to the research gap specified in section 2.5.2 (the lack of process descriptions within behavioral accounting research, using current JDM models and concepts, p. 58ff) and an analysis of the research questions as stated in Chapter 1 (see p. 3ff) of this thesis. Combining various methods and considering multiple concepts and models is the key factor in closing the research gap identified. The studies (and if appropriate their hypotheses) presented in Chapter 4 and 5 are docking into this model at various stages. Taken together they form a more complete picture of heuristic reasoning in management accounting.

Figure 18: Towards a theoretical framework of heuristics in management accounting

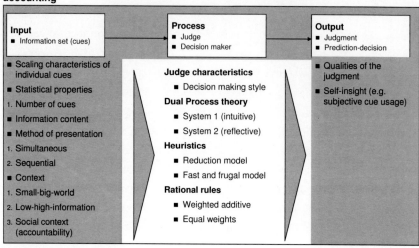

3 Synopsis and research design

3.1 Synopsis toward the empirical research design

Combining quantitative and qualitative methods into a single mixed methods re-search design is a relatively new technique in the social sciences. Creswell and Plano Clark (2007, p. 5) suggest the following definition, which shall also be followed in this thesis:

> *"Mixed methods research is the type of research with philosophical assumptions as well as methods of inquiry. As a methodology, it involves philosophical assumptions that guide the direction of the collection and analysis of data and the mixture of qualitative and quantitative approaches in many phases in the research process. As a method, it focuses on data collection, analyzing, and mixing both quantitative and qualitative data in a single study or series of studies. Its central premise is that the use of quantitative and qualitative approaches in combination provides better understanding of research problems than either approach alone."*

Johnson, Onwuegbuzie and Turner (2007, p. 123), in their definition of mixed meth-ods, also stress the goal of better understanding the research problem, and point out that mixed methods are adequate "for the broad purposes of breadth and depth of understanding and corroboration." However, there is no perfect agreement amongst authors as to: a) where and when such an approach is appropriate in general b) how ("weighting decision"; cf. equal or unequal combination of the qualitative or quantita-tive approach), when ("timing decision") and at which stage ("mixing decision") each of the elements should be combined (Creswell, 2003; D. L. Morgan, 2007; Morse, 2003; Steckler, McLeroy, Goodman, Bird, & McCormick, 1992) . For instance, in the *Handbook of Mixed Methods in Social and Behavioral Research*, edited by Tashak-kori and Teddlie (2003), various combinations and concepts of mixed methods mod-els are presented.

Scholars agree that mixed methods can be distinguished from multi-method ap-proaches, because the latter only combine various techniques within one single paradigm (e.g. experiments combined with questionnaire surveys within a purely quantitative design). Thus, this thesis could be described as a mixed methods work containing multi-method elements, because the quantitative part includes classical experiments in combination with web-based experiments and verbal protocols (which could be seen as a naturally mixed methods approach).

The reason that a combination of quantitative and qualitative elements is a relatively new phenomenon within social sciences (for an overview of some notable exceptions see Greene, Caracelli, & Graham, 1989; Kelle, 2007), can be traced back to the "paradigm debates" (sometimes materialistically labeled "paradigm wars" (for a review see Jackson & Carter, 1993)), which occurred in the period between the 1970s and the 1990s. In these debates, purists who favored either quantitative (taking a (post-) positivist point of view) or qualitative (taking a constructivist or hermeneutic one) research models, highlighted the so-called incommensurability thesis. This thesis entails that quantitative and qualitative methods could not (and should not) be combined (and all attempts to do so necessarily lead to failure), for the reason that they represent two fundamentally different (and thus incommensurable) worldviews[72] (see M. L. Smith, 1994).

The use of mixed methods is frequently justified, relying on the philosophy of pragmatism (e.g. Maxcy, 2003; D. L. Morgan, 2007; Newman & Benz, 1998). Pragmatists, such as Peirce (1960) or Dewey (1938) and, more recently, Rorty (1986) and Putnam (1974), stress that practical relevance should guide scientific work and research. They argue that one (if not *the*) major goal of research is to address practical issues and reflect on whether the relevant theoretical discourses actually matter, with respect to a practical context (for an overview of pragmatism as a research paradigm in a mixed method context see Feilzer, 2010; for classic definitions of pragmatism see Hookway, 2008; Thayer, 1967).

Pragmatists reject the incommensurability thesis and promote the use of both quantitative and qualitative methods (Tashakkori & Teddlie, 1998). The pragmatists' point of view is summarized by Tashakkori and Teddlie (1998, p. 30): "Study what interests and is of value to you, study it in the different ways that you deem appropriate, and utilize the results in ways that can bring about positive consequences within

---

[72]   Sieber (1973, p. 1335) sums up the main differences between the two research paradigms as "one stressing the superiority of deep, rich observational data and the other virtues of hard, generalizable data."

your value system." Patton (1990) calls this the "paradigm of choices". This approach suggests that methodological orthodoxy is obsolete and instead argues for methodological appropriateness as the key criterion for the evaluation of methodological quality.

Another justification for combining quantitative and qualitative methods is suggested by Brühl (2010), referring to an action based model which links the concepts of "explaining" and "understanding" (Dilthey, 1977). Brühl argues that the central difficulty from a pragmatist point of view in justifying mixed method research is its diversity, which makes it difficult to integrate "explaining" and "understanding" into one framework. As an alternative, Brühl proposes three statements for overcoming the claimed incommensurability (Lincoln & Guba, 1985):

1. The complexity of the social reality and our human perception of this reality prevent us from developing a unifying theory that can fully describe, understand and explain.

2. The complexity of the social reality and our human perception of this reality prevent us from fully describing, understanding and explaining this reality with one single method.

3. The social reality itself is coined by social actors, who operate within the social system, relying on their own values and norms in their actions. Methods of the social sciences shall thus allow to understand and explain the intentions and the rationality of the actors.

For this thesis, the last statement is particularly relevant. The research question (see section 1.2, p. 3ff): how do management controllers cope with the challenge of increasingly complex tasks and when do they rely on heuristics in order to reduce complexity can be best approached when the function of heuristics is explained and their use is better understood.

Other scholars, such as Greene and Caracelli (2003; 1989) point out that different worldviews can be integrated into one study. Hence, they also reject any absolute choice between the two traditional paradigms. In line with these authors, it can be, under certain circumstances, necessary to include both paradigms in research in order to grasp the complexities of (social) reality.

Another stand on mixed methods is that different paradigms should be used, depending on the chosen research design (Creswell, Plano Clark, Gutmann, & Hanson, 2003). Creswell and his colleagues (2003), for example, propose six different possible research designs and argue that no single paradigm could be sufficient for all of these. Overall, mixed methods designs represent a non-dogmatic approach which aims to better understand and explain our complex (social) reality.

That mixed methods approaches enjoy increasing popularity in business studies was recently shown by Molina-Azoìn (2011). This author used a citation analysis to show that articles using mixed methods have a significantly higher impact factor compared to mono-method articles and review articles. In his sample (within the field of management and entrepreneurship), he also found that a dominant/sequential design is the most common characteristic of the published mixed methods studies.

The objective of realistically describing heuristic processes is also central to this thesis and the foremost reason for choosing a mixed methods design. This work is guided by the idea that a pure investigation into behavioral accounting only makes sense if the results of experiments are reflected in the real decisions and judgments of management controllers and managers. It is therefore also the aim of this study to increase the external validity of the quantitative studies, by combining them with structured interviews.

Prescriptive recommendations in business studies appear to be useful only if they take into account both the "small worlds" of the labs and the "big worlds" of complex real life scenarios (Savage, 1954). Of course, as is frequently stressed by behavioral researchers (e.g. Loewenstein, 1999), as explicatory power goes up, so does the number of new, open questions.

With respect to causal linkages, authors like Tashakkori and Teddlie (1998, p. 23) argue that: "There may be causal relationships, but we will never be able to pin them down." This view can also be demonstrated by combining inductive (from the qualitative approach) and deductive (from the quantitative approach) logic. In a mixed methods approach, therefore, both objective and subjective points of view are taken into account. Recently, Ahrens and Chapman (2007, p. 314) in the *Handbook of Management Accounting Research* also pointed out that:

> "*We see this mutual misunderstanding and suspicion across the methodological divide as unhelpful for the field. Positivistic and*

qualitative studies deserve each other. Without the specifics of qualitative studies, the general assertions of positivistic research would be hollow. The specific investigations of qualitative research question and refine the general statements of positivistic studies".

The are numerous ways in which to conduct mixed methods research (for a recent summary of concepts and design see Horch, 2009). The two central issues a researcher faces when doing mixed methods research are the "weighting decision" and the "timing" decision (Creswell, 2003; Creswell & Plano Clark, 2007). The first of these involves the question of whether one element (the quantitative or qualitative) has any priority in the research process. The second addresses when and in what order the two methods are combined.

In this thesis, a so-called explanative design (Creswell & Plano Clark, 2007) is used, in which the quantitative part takes the lead (QUAN → qual design). The conducted experiments (quantitative study) build the foundation for the whole thesis and serve as the basis for the interview study (qualitative study). This kind of order is symbolized as QUAN → qual (the arrow indicates a sequential design, capital letters indicate that this method has the lead) (B. R. Johnson, et al., 2007). This particular combination, in which the quantitative study is conducted first, followed by the qualitative one (in order to better explain the quantitative findings), is suggested by various scholars. Steckler and his colleagues (1992), for instance, call this course of action "Model 3 – quantitative methods to embellish qualitative findings". In the description given by Morse (2003), this procedure is called Model 8, which means that a quantitative method is used sequentially with an deductive theoretical drive.

The purpose of the mixed methods approach within this thesis is, ideally, to achieve complementary results. However, other purposes of this type of research, as laid out by Greene, Caracelli and Graham (1989, p. 270), can also be reflected in this thesis. Nevertheless, a classic triangulation, which is the search for confirmation of the results through a second method, with respect to this thesis, is difficult because various experiments (which practically represent a multi-method approach within the mixed methods framework) are contrasted with only one single interview study. In general, concerning this thesis, the author concurs with Hoetger (2005, p. 84), who states: "The combination of qualitative and quantitative methods allows me to capture a more complete, holistic, and contextual portrayal of the phenomenon".

This way complementarity, which is the search for explanation through a second method, is one main objective for using a mixed methods design in analyzing heuristic reasoning in management accounting. Finally, expansion, which is the attempt to broaden scope and depth of research body is another advantage.

3.2 Specifications of research design and research gap

3.2.1 Specification of the quantitative approach

Researchers with a behavioral focus are frequently methodological eclectics. Therefore, the key element in such research is mostly (social and/or cognitive) psychological theory, rather than a specific type of method (for a comparison of behavioral and experimental economics, see Loewenstein, 1999). Nevertheless, experimental methods, in particular, have become increasingly important tools in addressing current behavioral issues (Plott & Smith, 2008; Shadish, Cook, & Campbell, 2002). Experimental methods allow the researcher to isolate and manipulate a small group of independent variables (e.g. information load) and to measure a dependent variable (e.g. the number of cues used as a proxy for heuristic reasoning). This classic approach to experimental investigation was originally adopted from the natural sciences and enables the researcher to make inferences about any possible underlying causal relationships (see Kempf, 2006 for the transfer of methods of natural sciences into social sciences like psychology). Ariely (2010, p. 6) summarizes the meaning of experiments in the social sciences as follows:

> *"For social scientists, experiments are like microscopes or strobe lights, magnifying and illuminating the complex, multiple forces that simultaneously exert their influences on us. They help us slow human behavior to a frame-by-frame narration of events, isolate individual forces, and examine them carefully and in more detail. They let us test directly and unambiguously what makes human beings tick and provide a deeper understanding of the features and nuances of our own biases. Sometimes experiments reveal surprising, counterintuitive findings; at other times, they confirm intuitions most of us already have. But intuition is not the same as evidence; and only by conducting careful experimentation can we discover whether our hunches about a certain human foible are right or wrong."*

The use of statistics, which is typically involved in analyzing experimental results, allows for a high degree of objectivity and a variety of possible ways by which to determine reliability, as well as enabling other researchers to replicate any findings (Bortz, 2005; Welkowitz, Ewen, & Cohen, 2002). The key feature of any research is its external and internal validity (V. L. Smith, 1994). According to Loewenstein (1999, p. F26), internal validity refers "to the ability to draw confident causal conclusions from one's research. External validity refers to the ability to generalize from the research context to the settings that the research is intended to approximate." Unsurprisingly, some tension exists between these two aspects. The more the researcher controls the internal validity of an experiment, the more artificial the setting becomes and, consequently, the lower the external validity.

For example, in experimental accounting research, when striving for high external validity, the aim is typically to identify tasks and processes that closely resemble those faced by accountants and managers in their daily jobs (Sprinkle, 2003). The limitation of this approach is that experiments necessarily include only a small extract of a complex reality. Using combinations of various studies and mixed methods approaches is necessary but not sufficient to overcome this restriction. It has to be stressed that the "big world" complexity can only implemented using qualitative methods. Cause and effect models represent they key feature of experimental approaches. Consequently a series of quantitative study might demonstrate the robustness of some effects but is not necessarily an indicator of an higher external validity.

In this thesis, a combination of multiple experiments and quasi-experiments is used in order to shed some light on which factors influence heuristic reasoning in management accounting. Classic paper-pencil experiments, under controlled conditions, are used, along with web-based quasi-experimental approaches ("quasi", because in web-based experiments no perfect control of all conditions (e.g. temperature etc.) is usually possible; see Birnbaum, 2000).

3.2.2 Specification of the qualitative approach

Typically, most research on heuristic reasoning is based on quantitative, experimental research. This is true both for the classical heuristics and biases studies by Kahneman and Tversky (e.g. 1981), as well for more recent studies of lapses and errors in people's judgments and decisions (e.g. Camerer, et al., 2003). In addition, the contrasting paradigm of fast and frugal heuristics operates mainly with the same methods (e.g. Gigerenzer, et al., 1999) usually focusing on experiments, cognitive modeling (e.g. ACT-R) and only in rare cases on questionnaire-based studies. Only older studies in JDM, published in high ranked journals, use purely qualitative methods (e.g. Slovic, 1969).

However, critics, especially of the fast and frugal approach (e.g. Hilbig, 2010; Hilbig & Richter, 2010; Oppenheimer, 2003), stress that such models of heuristics lack external validity and are not adequate models of how decisions are made in reality (interestingly, however, these arguments are made by using the same methods these authors criticize).

When adapting the concept of fast and frugal heuristics into business settings, one major problem is that existing research mainly concentrates on clearly-defined problems with well-known ex-post outcomes, like Wimbledon tennis matches or past stock market returns (Gigerenzer, et al., 1999; Ortmann, Gigerenzer, Borges, & Goldstein, 2008). These accurate yardsticks are needed to evaluate the efficiency and robustness of fast and frugal heuristics. However, the transfer and implementation of these findings into the more complex dynamics of large-scale business decisions appears difficult for several reasons. One major reason is, of course, that you can not easily find ex-post yardsticks with which to measure the success of single decisions in these dynamic environments. With thousands of decisions happening each day, it seems impossible to track the impact of simple heuristics through the bundle of influences that shapes the outcome. Furthermore, most scenarios lack the counterpart necessary to evaluate the efficiency of the chosen decision. For example, in most cases of M&A decisions, it is impossible to know how things would have turned out if you had chosen another company for the merger.

This point is not only valid in relation to fast and frugal heuristics; it also is of interest when investigating the general use of heuristics in business settings (Krabuanrat & Phelps, 1998). To date, research on heuristic reasoning in business settings has not provided a deeper understanding of how heuristics are part of the organizational decision making process. This issue even relates to basic questions, such as, how and when are heuristics used in the dynamic field of real business tasks? What sorts of heuristics are used? Do they resemble existing models? How does the organizational culture and its hierarchies affect the use of heuristics? Are heuristics only popular in individual decisions or can they also observed in group decisions (Reimer,

Hoffrage, & Katsikopoulos, 2007)? Matters like these represent a true research gap and offer potentially fruitful insights regarding the application of heuristic in contexts that are more open.

The issue of unavailable yardsticks can be solved by focusing more on a descriptive approach of heuristics in accounting settings together with an analysis of the underlying rationality assumptions. This focus is also stressed by Simon (1976) in his approach of procedural rationality. According to Simon (1986, p. 210): "The judgment that certain behavior is rational or reasonable can be reached only by viewing the behavior in the context of a set of premises or givens. These givens include the situation in which the behavior takes place, the goals it is aimed at realizing, and the computational means available for determining how the goals can be attained."

Consequently, a process oriented framework focusing on the situation, goals and means can solve the yardstick issue. As one key feature of qualitative research is indeed, the process description (for a summary of features of qualitative research see also Brühl, et al., 2008), (compared to quantitative research , which rather outcome oriented) it fits nicely into a more process oriented model of heuristic reasoning. The process orientation is also documented in the overall framework in Figure 18 (see p. 90). As stressed in the introduction of this thesis (see section 1.2, p. 3ff), the open questions can be summed up in five main areas of interest:

- How do management controllers **cope with the complexity of** "**large worlds**"?

- When do they **rely on heuristics** in order to reduce complexity?

- Is there **evidence of the adaptive character/ecological rationality** of the decisions made by management controllers?

- What kinds of **search strategies** do management controllers use?

- What kind of role is played by **individual differences,** and to what degree is the task itself and its characteristics, such as accountability, responsible for the decision strategy?

These issues are particularly of interest for management controllers, because they are often portrayed as agents who should assure the rationality of the (top) management (J. Weber & Schäffer, 2008b) and (at least from a classical point of view on rationality) should therefore not use any form of heuristics (J. Weber, 2011b). However, this assumption conflicts with empirical findings, that heuristics (both effective ones and the ones leading to biases) are used by experts in various domains (Kahneman & Klein, 2009). In addition, the role of management controllers as advice givers to the management is of interest and it would be a worthwhile subject of study, if heuristics can be traced in vertical as well as horizontal dialogues.

Taking this into account, it appears promising not only to conduct quantitative studies regarding heuristic reasoning in management accounting, but also to extend the social sciences' understanding of their application in dynamic settings. Issues arising from this perspective are not only limited to what kind of heuristics are used. Do they, for example, resemble the precise fast and frugal models suggested by Gigerenzer et al. (1999) and are there signs of an underlying ecological rationality (for instance referring to the learning function) in the way management controllers use heuristics? A qualitative approach could be used to bridge the gap between the fast and frugal and the heuristics and biases approaches. Qualitative findings could also be aligned with the concept of dual process models (Kahneman & Frederick, 2002; Sloman, 1996), allowing for a theory-based evaluation of the results.

An additional advantage of conducting qualitative research in JDM in accounting is that it allows for the possibility of introducing complementarity (Heath, 2001) as a model for cross-validating existing results of heuristics research. For example, it is possible, using this method, to further analyze the principles of why management accounts leave out information under certain circumstances in some decisions, as has been documented in quantitative studies (e.g. Basel, 2010). From a pragmatic perspective, the possibility of conflicting results can be viewed as an opportunity to formulate a new hypothesis, rather than as a true handicap resulting from the combining of different methods.

The openness of the qualitative approach, with no specific ex-ante hypothesis but with a strong theoretical foundation (Flick, 2006), fits with a research field in which many (quantitative) puzzle parts have not yet been integrated into a more complex and dynamic whole. Single-influence factors are therefore probably not sufficient to enable a complete understanding of JDM in accounting. Various degrees of accountability and task complexity (Lerner & Tetlock, 1999) are almost impossible to isolate in demanding quantitative models.

3.2.3 Qualitative research in management accounting

According to Lee and Humphrey (2006), accounting is "more than a numbers game". These authors stress that despite the need to capture more social and organizational aspects in (management) accounting through qualitative research, this discipline remains mostly quantitative and economics-based. This tendency appears to be particularly true for the North American accounting community and for leading North American journals such as *The Accounting Review* (TAR) or *Contemporary Accounting Research* (CAR) (see Merchant, 2011).

That qualitative research does not enjoy the same popularity as quantitative study (e.g. large scale surveys or archival studies) may be due to the fact that qualitative research represents a "profoundly theoretical activity" (Ahrens & Chapman, 2007, p. 299). This does not mean that statistical analysis is per se less embedded into a theoretical framework, but that the potential of qualitative research is closer linked to its theoretical argumentation. For example, on the one hand it is possible to conduct a properly structured equation model without a solid theoretical basis.[73] On the other hand it is impossible to reach a satisfactory conclusion in analyzing interview data without a link towards existing theories. For instance, Ahrens and Chapman (2007, p. 306) highlight:

> "For qualitative field researchers, the field as a social reality can be made sense of if it is defined with reference to theories that can illuminate its activities. It is not an objective reality out there and ready to be portrayed in the best (most faithful) way."

Another reason for the difficulty in achieving (and publishing) high-standard qualitative research in management accounting is that explanations and results tend to more complex. For example, models in field studies usually cannot be described in terms of easy-to-grasp dependent and independent variables (Libby, 1981; Luft & Shields, 2003). This issue has the consequence that the results of qualitative studies are more difficult to present in formats that require a more condensed way of presentation (e.g. paper abstracts or conference proceedings). Consequently the attention

---

[73] For a critical comment on mindless testing for significance levels and statistical rituals in the social sciences see also Sedlmeier (2009) or Sanabria and Killeen (2007).

rates for qualitative research are harder to capture through these traditional sources, as compared to crisp quantitative results stressing multi-star p-values, effect sizes and causal relationships.

That qualitative research in management accounting, despite the "innate" complexity of theoretical models and results, offers various opportunities and benefits is summarized by Vaivio (2008, p. 65) in three points:

- First, qualitative research **takes us beyond a narrow and functionalist view** of the management accounting phenomenon.

- Second, qualitative research **protects us against a scientific imperialism**, which reduces management accounting to an issue of mere economic choices.

- Third, qualitative research **critically scrutinizes normative prescriptions** for improving management accounting.

These aspects are particularly relevant for this piece of work. Furthermore, with respect to the general topic of this thesis (under the label JDM research in management accounting), Vaivio (2008, p. 66) concludes:

> *"Decision processes are rarely rational and linear. Rather, they are complex bundles of interconnected, loosely coupled events that bounce back and forth. They involve many actors who represent diverse opinions, interests, biases, hidden agendas and competencies. Decision making often gets interrupted, marginalized, diverted, restarted or merged with another stream of urgent concerns. Moreover, rational control – on closer empirical examination – is also an illusion. What the officially sealed decision in fact suggests in terms of concrete operational action cannot be articulated with precision. Targets are imperfect approximations of what the organization seeks and are interpreted in different ways by biased local agents."*

That (behavioral) economic models offer only limited insight into how decisions are made, is also stressed by proponents of ecological rationality like Berg and Gigerenzer (2010). These authors argue that more process models are needed to improve understanding of JDM processes. For instance, with respect to the tendency of some (economic) models to explain human behavior with additional free parameters, Berg and Gigerenzer (2010, p. 138) argue that "this approach almost surely fails at bringing improved psychological insight about the manner in which social variables systematically influence choice in real-world settings."

However, these scholars do not consider qualitative methods (or mixed method approaches) in their suggestions for overcoming these limitations and improving explanations of human decision making behavior (Hertwig, et al., in press). According to Flick (2005) or Kelle et al. (1993), this is not an unusual tendency in the social sciences and frequently, qualitative methodologies like interviews and case studies are only seen as a possible first step in a larger quantitative design.

In this view, qualitative approaches are rejected due to their limited sample size and are only seen as first impulses for the next step in the research process. That qualitative studies also achieve some form of generalization is however stressed by Lukka and Kasanen (1995). In their view, the particular strength of qualitative research is that this paradigm allows for elaborating in detail the strengths and weaknesses of the theories used. Furthermore, they highlight that qualitative research is in particular suitable for modifying theories.

That new influencing factors or characteristics can be identified through qualitative methods is also stressed by Wrona (2005). This author in particular refers to the possibility to "unfreeze thinking" that represents one key element of qualitative approaches. Take into account that a (real organizational) decision process in management accounting has multiple degrees of freedom and, due to that, a serious amount of complexity, qualitative methods would seem even more suitable than classic quantitative approaches. However, Wrona (2005) adds that representativeness (not understood as the bias/heuristic by Kahneman and Tversky), is clearly not possible with qualitative approaches (but this is also not the central focus of this approach).

3.2.4 Limitations of the applied mixed methods design

Besides several clear arguments in favor of mixed methods research (as described above), there are also some limitations and weaknesses to this approach. Firstly, a mixed methods design is expensive, in relation to both time and money. Additionally, working with mixed methods requires double skills, in qualitative methods and in statistics. However, these issues do not affect any validity of results gained out of mixed methods studies per se. Rather, these challenges are important in the planning process and in the development of a research framework.

More fundamental is the critique that triangulation and complementarity, using the qualitative study after the quantitative study (Greene, et al., 1989), could entail an enhanced likelihood for an interviewer bias, resembling a classic Rosenthal effect (Rosenthal, 1966)[74], just as in an interview setting. The interviewer could be less open and more likely to lead and interpret the interview towards his desired outcomes (which would ideally replicate the results of the quantitative study, or at least allow a stringent complementarity). This is one reason why purists argue that researchers should work within one paradigm.

Another weakness of mixed methods designs is that this paradigm, being relatively recent, does not explain in a specific way how to cope with mixed findings (Kelle, 2007; Wrona & Fandel, 2010). For example, if your experiments clearly show that people trust their neighbor in a buying decision more than any expert, yet all qualitative data points in the opposite direction, does this falsify your results? Can qualitative data in a mixed methods design falsify results? Open questions like this should be seen as a limitation of the mixed methods approach and call for further development of the philosophical and methodological foundations of mixed methods research.

3.3 Mixed methods in the context of testing theories

As highlighted in the previous section, several authors have stressed the limitations of focusing purely on either quantitative or on qualitative research methods (for an overview of the debate see D. L. Morgan, 2007; Sale, 2002). Outside of these dogmatic positions, some scholars within management research, such as Christensen and Sundahl (2001) or Carlile and Christensen (2004), have proposed that a combination of both quantitative and qualitative methods is actually essential to the full process of theory building. In doing so, they combine positions from Karl Popper

---

[74] The classic Rosenthal effect is an observer-expectancy effect in which the expectations of the experimenter (or in case of this thesis of the interviewer) unconsciously bias the responses (answers) of the participant (interviewee) towards the desired direction. This tendency thus threatens the internal validity of studies in the behavioral sciences (Kempf, 2006). Strategies to control this sort of effect are typically double-blind research designs. However, this approach is rather difficult for qualitative studies.

(1959) and Thomas Kuhn (1972) in a pragmatic way. In their view, both deductive and inductive principles are necessary in order to construct theories[75] in a sound way.

From Popper and his school of critical rationalism, these theorists adopt the idea that a scientific theory must be falsifiable. This criteria is extended by Christensen and Sundahl (2001), in that a theory must also be capable of yielding to anomalies. This concept is adapted from Kuhn (1972), according to whom research exists within a particular paradigm, in which these anomalies play the role of challengers for existing standards and beliefs. In the view of Kuhn (1972), these anomalies must be overcome in order to justify the existing paradigm. For Christensen and Sundahl (2001), anomalies are the key elements for theory improvement and they are found through observation, description and measurement of phenomena. In their model, deductive processes enable a prediction of the phenomena. Inductive processes (as a possible second step) can be used in order to confirm the predicted results. Furthermore, within the inductive process there is also the possibility of discovering anomalies, when the observed phenomena are classified.

This model of combing quantitative and qualitative methods fits with the research process utilized in this thesis. Assumptions based on bounded rationality and the derived concept of ecological rationality are used in experimental studies to predict the judgment and decision making behavior of management controllers. As a second step, these findings are classified and then some anomalies which have occurred are investigated in the structured interview studies.

---

[75] As a clipped and precise definition for theory, Christensen and Sundahl (2001, p. 15) propose that a theory: "Is a statement of what causes what, and why, and under what circumstances."

Figure 19: Theoretical embeddedness of the research design (adapted from Buss, 1995; Christensen & Sundahl, 2001)

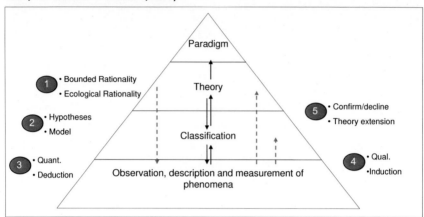

The above course of action seems especially appropriate to this study because eco-logical rationality is a model or a concept, rather than a fully developed theory with clear cause and effect relations. From a "paradigm" point of view, it is possible to argue that neo-classicism stumbled over the anomalies discovered by the fathers of prospect theory and now the approach of ecological rationality has delivered a few new anomalies that cannot sufficiently be explained by the notion of a highly biased mind.

With respect to the research presented in this work, it is however necessary to add a few remarks on the model proposed above and to switch from strict falsifica-tions in the sense of Popper (1959), towards a Lakatosian concept of philosophy of science (Lakatos, Worrall, & Currie, 1978). The paradigm behind this work can be seen in the adaptation of classic evolutionary theory, as laid out by Charles Darwin in the nineteenth century (see Bowler, 2009 on Darwin in general; Darwin, 1872 for a classic; Pinker, 1997 for a more recent discussion of evolutionary theories), into modern social sciences. One key issue surrounding evolutionary approaches in the social sciences is the assumption that, while our environment (mostly because of technological innovations) has changed a lot, our psychological mechanisms for making decisions have not (Fasolo, McClelland, & Todd, 2007).

Following this line of reasoning, a direct conclusion of evolutionary explanations is also the notion of bounded rationality. However, as shown in previous chapters, there are competing models of what actually constitutes bounded rationality and what the resulting consequences are, both on a descriptive and prescriptive level. These competing models are not competing paradigms; rather, they can be labeled as what Lakatos (1970; 1978) called middle-level theories. In this way, social scientists doing research in this field do not aim to falsify the "hard core" of the meta-theoretical research program;[76] instead, they focus on providing hypotheses and specific predictions within this general paradigm. In this fashion, they compete for the "best" explanations within an agreed field of axioms or starting points.

Figure 20: The hierarchical structure of evolutionary explanations (based on Ketelaar & Ellis, 2000)

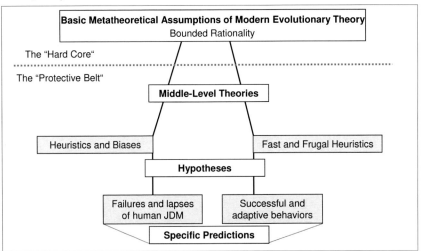

That strict falsifications are not possible in this model seems obvious. No theory is immune to criticism in its early stages and even regarding well-established theories, some antagonisms or open questions frequently remain (for a similar argument see also Putnam, 1974). Additionally, a link of two binary oppositions (e.g. the nature-nurture debate) would not be possible if one of the middle-level theories had to be removed after one falsification. Thus, the approach of Lakatos appears, especially

---

[76]   This, however, does not imply that a meta-theory is not testable at all. Nevertheless, a paradigm is not falsified in the classical sense; instead, it tends to fade over time (Kuhn, 1972).

for the matter of evolutionary explanations, as a more fruitful one. As Newell (1990, p. 14) puts it:

> "(...) we are not living in the world of Popper, as far as I'm concerned, we are living in the world of Lakatos. Working with theories is not like skeet shooting – where theories are lofted up and bang, they are shot down with a falsification, and that is the end of the story. Theories are more like graduate students – once admitted you try hard to avoid flunking them out.... Theories are things to be nurtured and changed and built up. One is happy to change them to make them more useful."

Using Lakatos can also enable a refutation of the claim that evolutionary explanations are unfalsifiable and immature (for a critical comment on the explanatory power of evolutionary approaches see Buller, 2005; Horgan, 1995). Most critiques point out that evolutionary theory can explain post-hoc almost everything in the social sciences. Any form of cooperation can be explained with altruism and if any mistakes were made it is because those involved are limited by their bounded rationality. As Ketelaar and Ellis (2000, p. 10) stress, this argument would only be true if vaguely labeled and as not testable (middle-level) theories were used, as such models "that do not have testable consequences represent poor science no matter what theoretical perspective they come from".

Moreover, this critique can only address the "hard core" of this theory, if the theory does not allow for precise predictions. That theories require a complex system of inter-causal relations that can be empirically tested and developed seems obvious (Gigerenzer, 1998). Following this line of reasoning, Ketelaar and Ellis deduce (2000, p. 1) that: "Modern evolutionary theory meets the Lakatosian criterion of "progressivity", based on its ability to digest apparent anomalies and generate novel predictions and explanations."

4 Step I: Experimental studies

4.1 Study: 1 can "less-be-more" in management accounting[77]

4.1.1 Introduction – heuristic reasoning in an investment decision

Imagine you are the CFO of a major player in the consumer goods industry and, after carefully analyzing an attractive foreign market, you are planning to enter it with a strategic acquisition. How would you choose the possible candidate for this process, and how many factors do you take into account?

The possible number of performance indicators that can be considered is typically very large and ranges from hard facts like sales numbers to more soft factors like employee satisfaction. But even fashionable decision aids from investment gurus and textbook recommendations do not reduce the complexity to zero, and at some point you have to decide which company makes the best investment. This can become especially tricky if you take into account that most information (for example, that gained from benchmarks and/or through the help of management consultants), comes at a cost, and that, in addition, you do not have unlimited time to make a decision in such a dynamic environment.

Regarding this issue, Krabuanrat and Phelps (1998) suggest, in an explorative approach, that in strategic decisions heuristics represent a frequently-used decision mechanism. This is in line with the findings of Gigerenzer (2007), who states that a majority of executives in his sample report using their gut feelings (as a synonym for heuristics) at least 50% of the time (see also the results of a survey conducted by Accenture, 2008).[78] Heuristics itself can be understood, according to Shah and Oppenheimer (2008), as effort reduction mechanisms, that work for instance by examining fewer cues or by simplifying the weighting of cues. However, there are several open research questions that arise from this, when it comes to the use of heuristics in business settings (see also Section 2.7 p. 67ff):

---

[77] I kindly thank Florian Dost and Jens Sievert for their support in evaluating the data sets of this study.

[78] That such a strategy is nevertheless acceptable in practice has recently been highlighted by a increasing number of practitioners like Plaschke et al. (2011, p. 6), who recommends that practitioners "shift away from precise forecasting" and proposes more adaptive ways of making strategic decisions.

The first of these open research questions addresses the antecedents of the use of heuristics. Explicitly put: How do CFOs (and controllers) cope with the complexity of an almost unlimited supply of information? And when do they rely on heuristics, as effort reduction mechanisms, in order to reduce complexity?

Most (neo-) classical literature on business decisions assumes rational behavior (independent from factors such as individual differences) and even though researchers on heuristics such as Krabuanrat and Phelps (1998) report the use of some heuristics, they also find decision processes, such as investment decisions, that are at least reported to be dominated by rational behavior. This finding is also supported by Nutt (1998). Analyzing 317 business decisions in a field study, he finds that intuitive tactics (such as heuristics) are rarely used (and successful).

However, it is expected that participants will use heuristics, as an effort reduction mechanism (Shah & Oppenheimer, 2008), which can potentially be an adaptive decision strategy (Gigerenzer, et al., 1999). This is in line with the results of numerous previous studies on heuristic reasoning in management accounting (e.g. the classic study by Shields, 1980), (cognitive) psychology in general (e.g. Payne, 2011; Payne, et al., 1993) and (surprisingly) the reports of the decision strategies used by business analytics practitioners (see the results of the study conducted by Accenture, 2008). This effort reduction preference will hold true even in a strictly experimental setting, where an economically sound investment decision is to be made, using the advice of a particular calculation mechanism and even if all participants are familiar with the used stimulus material (here, the analysis of KPIs). The prescriptive rule that works as a benchmark in this study is the equal weight rule (EQW), which is for instance described by Payne et al. (1991). As suggested in the theoretical framework in section 2.7 on p. 67ff of this thesis(see also Figure 18, p. 90), this strategy, as a compensatory rule, is classified as a rational rule, even if beta-weights are missing (compared to a weighted additive model). The stunning efficiency of this rule is for instance documented by Dawes' (1979) improper linear models approach. This assumption is being tested in the following hypothesis:

H1: Participants will ignore advice to decide rationally (in the sense of strictly following the instructions of the equal weights rule) and will use heuristics in an ostensibly rational decision task.

Relevant to the use of heuristics is the assumption that information itself is precious and in particular, in investment decisions usually comes at a cost. In line with the research of accountability (H. Lee, et al., 1999; Lerner & Tetlock, 1999) as a social influence factor (see also Figure 18, p. 90), participants will at least consider more information, if a higher amount of cues is available. However, considering does not necessarily mean that participants actually use the information for making the requested decision (and thus following the equal weights rule). For instance if a participant analyzes 8 out of 10 cues (e.g. by circling the numbers), but bases his decision upon a single cue (e.g. if he writes, "I just base my decision on ROI and rank the companies regarding the investment decision accordingly"), he considered 8 cues but only used 1 cue in his final decision. This distinction between cue use and cue consideration, is in line with the differentiation of relevant and instrumental information (Bastardi & Shafir, 1998). Whereas relevant information might be of interest for the participant, only instrumental information can influence the actual decision.[79] Furthermore this distinction is in line with finding that experts and non-experts do not differ in amount of cues they use, but usually differ in sets they consider (Shanteau, 1992).

This results in a general need to consider given information, so that:

H2: The more information cues available, the more information cues will be considered in making a decision.

However, due to the assumption of bounded rationality, the participants' capability or willingness to process more information decreases, while the use of heuristics increases, leading to the third hypothesis:

H3: The more information cues available in a decision, the less information is used relative to the full information set.

---

[79] This issue of different information types in an accounting setting is subject of an empirical analysis in Study 4 of this thesis (see p. 158ff).

The potential influence of personality shows the relevance of this to human resource management, where a principal decides what kind of agent would be most suitable for making sustainable decisions (Barber, 1998). For example, management controllers are often portrayed as pure rational agents who prevent the management from making decisions based purely on their gut feelings see section 2.6 (see p. 63ff) and 2.6.1 (see p. 66ff) (J. Weber & Schäffer, 1999).

Following this theoretical concept, accountants should be less likely to exclude available information from their judgments, and will instead utilize heuristic reasoning.[80] That a rational thinking style (referring to the "thinking" dimension within using Myers-Briggs type indicator) also leads to a better accounting performance (at least in the classroom), is also documented in an analysis by Oswick and Barber (1998).

Scott and Bruce (1995) suggest a measure that distinguishes between five styles of decision making (rational, avoidant, intuitive, spontaneous, dependent). In line with this distinction, a manager with an intuitive style would prefer the use of heuristics, unlike an executive with a more rational style. In line with research on personality characteristics in accounting, it is important to note that there is an open debate as to whether decision making styles can be identified independently from stable personality traits (Gul, 1984; Mischel, Shoda, & Smith, 2007). According to Zimbardo et al. (2004, p. 601), personality represents the "unique psychological characteristics of an individual". However the researchers who developed the GDMS (see Appendix p. 211ff) Scott and Bruce (1995, p. 820) clearly separate personality and its associated traits from the concept of a decision making style. These scholars highlight that:

> *"Drawing on the theory presented, decision making style is defined here as the learned, habitual response pattern exhibited by an individual when confronted with a decision situation. It is not a personality trait, but a habit-based propensity to react in a certain way in a specific decision context. Whereas personality traits have long been embroiled in the cross-situational consistency argument*

---

[80] However, in one of the few empirical studies on differences between managers and accountants Helliar and colleagues (2002) find only little differences between these two groups, analyzing their risk perception in various scenarios. These authors also stress that both groups fall victim of the same sort of biases like framing and react similarly with respect to loss aversion.

opened by Mischel (1968) the decision-style literature generally acknowledges that situations can affect the choice of decision style."

Following the argument by Scott and Bruce (1995) that decision style is influenced by a "specific decision context", I hypothesize:

H4: Participants with a rational decision style use more information cues than participants with an intuitive decision style.

The second area of open research questions addresses the quality of decisions made by heuristic reasoning. In relation to this, some recent research indicates that within business settings, heuristics can lead to successful outcomes. For example, Borges, Goldstein, Ortmann and Gigerenzer (1999) showed that a simple heuristic, based purely on brand recognition, could be an excellent predictor for a brand's performance on the stock market. Wübben and von Wangenheim (2008) recently demonstrated that a frugal heuristic is sufficient to distinguish active from non-active consumers. These results stand in sharp contrast with the research program of heuristics and biases, mostly developed by Kahneman and Tversky (2000; 1986), in which errors and lapses stemming from the use of heuristics are emphasized.

The examples of successful fast and frugal heuristics, as suggested by Gigerenzer and colleagues (Gigerenzer, 2006; Gigerenzer & Brighton, 2009), are mostly from areas where a clear normative criterion exists against which the heuristics can be evaluated. In this study the prescriptive criteria of equal weights (Bettmann, et al., 1991) is used a benchmark. In line with the suggested framework of heuristic reasoning (see Figure 18, p. 90), this part of the study analyzes the output of the process, referring to the quality of the decision process.

Regarding the availability of information, I therefore pose that:

H5: The more information cues available, the better the participant's decision quality.

However, to support the notion of successful heuristics I hope to falsify the following hypothesis (in line with the frequently quoted less-is-more effect (Gigerenzer & Brighton, 2009)):

> *H6: The more information cues used by a participant, the better the quality of the participant's decision.*

These short examples demonstrate that several points regarding heuristic reasoning in business settings still need clarification. As a starting point, it appears reasonable to take a closer look at how heuristics are used in well-defined business settings.

4.1.2 Method

An appropriate method by which to investigate heuristic reasoning in business set-tings is that of looking at investment decisions, based on the evaluation of perform-ance indicators (Volnhals & Hirsch, 2009). As within the widely used Balanced Scorecard (Kaplan & Norton, 1992), performance indicators from financial (e.g. sales in €), customer (e.g. customer satisfaction), internal processes (HR qualification costs in €) and innovation and learning (e.g. number of new patents) are presented to the participants as a possible basis for their decision. Investment decisions are also particularly interesting because, according to Krabuanrat and Phelps (1998), these kinds of generic management tasks are not typically solved by heuristic rea-soning.

Participants[81] and procedure

In total, n = 212 undergraduate and graduate students, from one European and one American university, participated in the between-subject-design[82] study. All of them had finished at least one management accounting class, which ensured that they

---

[81]   In line with APA (American Psychological Association, 1974) guidelines, the term "participants" is used instead of "subjects" in all studies included in this thesis.

[82]   For the validity of students as surrogates for professionals in business studies see Remus (1986) and also Ashton and Kramer (1980) for limitations in accounting settings. With respect to the use of students as surrogates in this thesis (see also Study 2, 3 and to some degree 4 of this thesis), I argue that my research interest is mainly to analyze cognitive processes underlying accounting tasks. As I assume a similar cognitive architecture for both accounting students and professionals, I only see minor limitations with respect to this fact.

were familiar with typical performance indicators such as ROI. As a reward, each participant received one candy bar and the chance to win additional *Amazon* vouchers[83] in return for "a good and economically wise decision", as an additional incentive to select their strategy carefully.

The participants were limited to 20 minutes, as a proxy for time pressure. A pre-test, without any time pressure, indicated that this is sufficient time to balance all the available cues and to calculate the order of the possible decisions according to the instructions. I collected data using a paper and pencil questionnaire because I assumed that I would gain further insight about participants' decision making processes by analyzing the notes taken. In addition, participants were asked to explain how they decided on the relative attractiveness of the investment options presented to them. The cover story was presented to the subjects in the following way:

Dear student,

In the following task we ask you to make an investment decision in the brewery sector. Imagine you work in the accounting department of a large, multinational brewery called Nicebrew. This company wishes to enter the highly competitive German market with a strategic acquisition and authorizes your team to make recommendations to the CFO.

After analysing the German market you come to the conclusion that six traditional breweries from various regions are of particular interest for Nicebrew:

- o *Prinzenbräu (Bavaria)*

- o *Südbacher (Hesse)*

- o *Lupaner (Baden-Württemberg)*

- o *Grafenbräu (North Rhine-Westphalia)*

- o *Niedritzer (Saxony)*

- o *Fritzbräu (Berlin)*

As a next step, you engage the top-consulting company McLinsey to screen the breweries, so that you can work out a ranking for your presentation to the CFO of Nicebrew Dr. Till Tiberenzer. On the next page you'll find the results of McLinsey in an accounting report style. They, however, were quite late in delivering these results and

---

[83]   For the limited effects of financial incentives, see Camerer and Hogarth (1999)

> you have only a few minutes left before the board meeting starts. Your job now is to make a final ranking of the six possible candidates in this short period of time. The consulting company claims that they were balanced in finding out both numbers and percentages of each performance indicator (PI). According to the book The Intelligent Investor (2003) by Benjamin Graham all information should be balanced. Then please fill in the attached questionnaire. Work alone   and do not disturb your neighbour. With a good and economic wise decision you'll have the   chance to win one of three   attractive prices. Thank you very much for your participation.

After the participants had ranked all the companies, they were asked to fill out the General Decision making Style developed by Scott and Bruce (1995), which includes 25 items on a 5-point Likert scale (see Appendix p. 211ff for the full GDMS scale). In addition to the GDMS, the participants were asked to rate their management accounting skills and their general academic performance as control variables (CV). Three researchers separately analyzed the open questions that described the decision making process of the participants, as well as the notes taken on the questionnaire. A careful missing value and data consistency analysis lead to the exclusion of 42 participants. The remaining 170 students represent the main sample used for data analysis. The mean age of the remaining respondents was 21.2 years (SD = 2.6), with a gender distribution of 41.2% female and 58.8% male. The sample consisted of 88.8% students from an American university and 11.2% from a European university.

4.1.3 Results

> H1: Participants will ignore advice to decide rationally (in the sense of strictly following the instructions of the equal weights rule) and will use heuristics in an ostensibly rational decision task.

As stated in the discussion of H1, I expected the respondents to use heuristics even in situations that are predisposed to use a rational decision making process. This hypothesis (H1) is supported by the analysis of the data. The level to which the participants used heuristics, as opposed to following the instructions (by balancing all information given), was determined by an analysis of the amount of information used by the students. Three researchers separately analyzed the decision comments and notes taken by the respondents, resulting in three measures made with a Cronbach's α of 0.936.

After this first step, a discussion led to the use of a single item to provide information about the cues used in the investment decision. By analyzing the information used by participants, I was able to demonstrate that, on average, only 39.6% of the information given was used. A t-test against the value of 100% (which means that participants followed instructions and used all information), resulted in a highly significant (t = -25.95, p < 0.001) rejection of the null hypothesis, indicating that only a subset of the information provided was used to process the data. Therefore, the respondents chose not to follow the instructions and instead used heuristics. In fact, only 14.1% of the respondents used all the information given in the experiment.

H2: The more information cues available, the more information cues will be used in a decision.

The underlying assumption of this hypothesis is that information itself is precious and comes at a cost, leading to a need for information usage. This hypothesis (H2) is partially supported analyzing the data set. When looking at the information actually used by participants, I observed relatively constant values (Table 9), indicating that the use of heuristics is relatively independent from the amount of information available.

Table 9: Absolute number of information used depending on amount of cues presented

Absolute cues presented	Absolute cues used		
	Mean	SD	N
5	3.20	1.39	45
10	4.96	3.15	44
20	4.14	3.06	81

Nevertheless, an ANOVA revealed that the amount of information given had a significant impact (F = 4.5, p < 0.05) on the absolute number of information cues used by participants. There seems to be a tendency to use more information if more information is available, even if a paired t-test shows that this effect is mainly driven by the highest value of 4.96 cues used in the 10-cues setting.

H3: The more information cues available in a decision, the less information will be used relative to the full information set.

Whereas the absolute amount of used information shows a significant but only minor absolute difference between the experimental groups, it seems reasonable to assume that people are neither willing nor capable of processing more information. This can be clearly observed in Table 10, which shows a decreasing usage of information relative to increases in the amount of information given and thus supports my hypothesis (H3).

Table 10: Percentage of cues used depending on amount of cues presented

Absolute cues presented	Percentage of cues used		
	%	SD	N
5	64.0%	27.8	45
10	49.5%	31.5	44
20	20.7%	15.3	81

This was again checked by an ANOVA ($F = 52.7$, $p < 0.001$), which revealed that the amount of information given had a highly significant impact on relative information usage. Furthermore, I assessed the size of the impact that the amount of information given had on the usage of heuristics by recoding and building groups based on the measure of relative cues used. The following crosstab exposes the dependence between the amount of information given and the relative usage of it.

Table 11: Crosstab – Relative cues used depending on absolute cues presented

			Relative cues used (grouped)			Total
			< = .20	.21 - .40	.41+	< = .20
Absolute cues presented	5.00	Count	4	13	28	45
		Expected Count	18.3	13.5	13.2	45.0
	10.00	Count	9	17	18	44
		Expected Count	17.9	13.2	12.9	44.0
	20.00	Count	56	21	4	81
		Expected Count	32.9	24.3	23.8	81.0
Total		Count	69	51	50	170
		Expected Count	69.0	51.0	50.0	170.0

Kendall's tau-b = -0.561, p< 0.001
Kendall's tau-c = -0.545, p< 0.001

The measure of Kendall's tau shows a moderate and highly significant negative effect, supporting our third hypothesis.[84]

H4: Participants with a rational decision style use more information cues than participants with an intuitive decision style.

This hypothesis (H4) regarding the influence of individual differences was not supported by the results.

I used the General Decision making Style (GDMS), designed by Scott and Bruce (1995), to control for personality traits that might influence the way participants decide on investment alternatives. This scale was recently tested for its validity and reliability by de Bruin, Fischhoff and Parker (2007), with good overall results. The total scale consists of 25 items distinguishing five styles of decision making, which are described as rational, avoidant, intuitive, spontaneous and dependent (see Appendix p. 211ff).

To check the applicability of this scale, I tested whether the items belonging to a specific decision making style resulted in a uni-dimensional solution when performing a factor analysis. This was the case for all five factors. To test H4, I calculated factor scores and used them as covariates in a set of ANOVA's. In addition, I checked for

---

[84]   For statistical measures and estimations see for instance Hays (1994).

further influences from the students' self-assessment of accounting skills and academic performance as control variables. Interestingly, an analysis of covariance revealed that none of the covariates had significant effects when the relative amount of used cues was the dependent variable. For example, the factor score for rationality was insignificant ($F = 1.70$, $p = 0.19$), while the main effect of the amount of presented information (5, 10 or 20 cues) was still highly significant ($F = 45.87$, $p<0.001$). An analysis of covariance, with the absolute amount of information used as the dependent variable, yielded a similar result. I therefore concluded that none of the decision making styles had a significant impact, either on the relative or the absolute usage of given information. This could imply that all participants, regardless of which decision making styles they prefer, are equally affected by the usage of heuristics. The usage of heuristics seems, therefore, to be common sense.

H5: The more information cues available, the better the quality of the participant's decision.

H6: The more information cues used by a participant, the better the quality of the participant's decision.

Finally, it is essential to analyze how well the decisions were made by the participants. Given the instructions, I assume that a decision is better if it represents the solution which balances all the relevant information (following an equal weight rule). The six alternatives were ranked by this criterion and compared to the solutions calculated by the participants.

To assess the quality of the solution I determined the absolute differences between intended and reported ranks, i.e. if *Fritzbräu* should have been ranked first (according to the balanced analysis of all information given to the respondents) and a student ranked it sixth, the resulting rank difference was $|1-6| = 5$. The quality of a solution was determined by summarizing all rank differences for a participant.

Table 12: Sum of rank differences depending on absolute cues presented

Absolute cues presented	sum of rank differences		
	Mean	SD	N
5	6.4	3.6	45
10	8.0	3.5	44
20	9.2	3.7	81

Assuming that a decision will be better if it is grounded on a larger number of infor-mation cues, one can expect a lower sum of rank differences in instances in which more information has been provided. Table 12 counter-intuitively shows that the mean of the difference measure increases as the amount of information given also increases. This is supported by an ANOVA that reveals that the effect of the experi-mental variation is highly significant (F = 8.43, p< 0.001). However, keeping in mind that the heuristic usage increases relative to the amount of information given, it seems reasonable to check whether the effect diminishes when heuristic usage is controlled for. Table 13 below shows the impact of heuristic usage as the sum of rank differences

Table 13: Sum of rank differences depending on relative cues used (grouped)

Relative cues used (grouped)	sum of rank differences		
	Mean	SD	N
< = .20	10.0	3.5	69
.21 - .40	7.2	3.9	51
.41+	6.6	2.9	50

Here, I can clearly see that results are better if more information is used, which is supported by an additional ANOVA (F = 17.1, p< 0.001). If both variables - the ex-perimental variation as well as the usage of heuristics - are included in an ANOVA, only the relative usage of information remains highly significant (F = 5.32, p< 0.001). Finally, I can summarize that the amount of information presented has an influence on the relative amount of information used, which afterwards impacts the number of errors made in an investment decision. In other words: both of these two hypothesis (H5 and H6) were fully supported by the data.

Figure 21: Cue use depending on information load

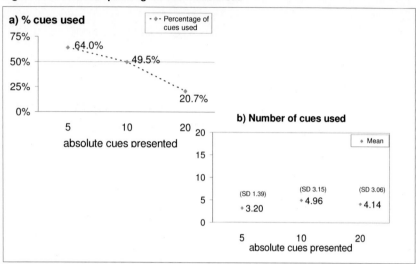

The results of the six theoretical deducted hypotheses can be summarized in the following table. I found support for H1, H3, H5 and H6; partial support for H2 and no support for H4, using various statistical measures.

Table 14: Results of the statistical analysis in Study 1

Hypo-thesis	Issue	Effect	F-value	Result
H1	Preference for heuristic so-lutions	$t = -25.95^{***}$	n.a.	✓
H2	Cue consideration	Group 1 vs. 2 d = -0.723 Group 1 vs. 3 d = -0.396 Group 2 vs. 3 d = 0.264	4.50**	✓
H3	Relative cue use	Kendall's tau-b = -0.561*** Kendall's tau-c = -0.545***	52.70***	✓
H4	Rational style vs. intuitive style	Main effect amount of informa-tion F = 45.87***	1.70 n.s	⚡
H5	Number of cues available and decision quality	n.a.	8.43***	✓
H6	Number of cues used and decision quality	n.a.	17.10***	✓

4.1.4 Discussion

Participants were placed in an environment with a prescribed "optimal decision making rule" of integrating all information in a balanced way,[85] an effectiveness dimension which was pre-tested for applicability to account for bounded rationality (Simon, 1955) and ecologic rationality (Rieskamp & Reimer, 2007). However, even under these conditions, participants still tended to use heuristics. This is in line with the findings of a broad body of relevant literature in the tradition of Herbert Simon (1955) and contrary to some research on managerial decision making (e.g. Krabuanrat & Phelps, 1998; Nutt, 1998), which claims that heuristics will not be used in well-defined decisions (such as investment decisions).

Moreover, this study demonstrates that it is the situation, rather than the participant's decision making style, which influences the use of heuristics; that it is the environment, in terms of information complexity, which affects the use of heuristics in decision making. Unsurprisingly, the average number of cues used is higher when more information is available; however, the ratio of used information relative to the total available information decreases. This implies that participants make an upfront assumption about the amount of cognitive effort necessary for completing a task.

I conclude therefore that participants decide not only in an effective but also in an efficient manner. Based on this assumption, they are more likely to engage in rational decision making in a low-information context and more likely to engage in heuristic reasoning in a high-information context (seen as an input factor, see Figure 18, p. 90). Controlling for personal decision making styles I find that, contrary to expectation (see also Furnham, 2008), these have no significant influence on the use of heuristic decision making (at least in this condition, but see the results of Study 3, p. 147ff).

Based on these results, a manager (or researcher) who wants his participants to engage in rational decision making should limit the amount of information given. However, this finding may not hold under accountability constraints, or when the par-

---

[85]   This instruction can itself be seen as a facilitating heuristic decision making, as all information is equally weighted. For the surprising and robust effectiveness of such a tallying rule, see Dawes (1979) and Hogarth and Karalaia (2005).

ticipant can make their own decision on the number of information cues provided (Lerner & Tetlock, 1999).

From a manager's perspective, the ability to influence the use of rational or heuristic decision making is not sufficient in itself. The decisions produced have to reach a high level of quality or effectiveness, as in our setting. In this study, a rational and calculable quality-criterion, the sum of rank differences, was communicated as a recommendation to the respondents. This research demonstrates that as the use of heuristics goes up, the effectiveness of the decision goes down - or, rather, that the more information used, the better the decision. This finding is an invariant of the total amount of information cues, meaning that, relative to the number of cues, a participant will perform better (in terms of effectiveness) the more cues he/she takes into account. So, from the individual perspective, the often-quoted "less-is-more" effect (Gigerenzer & Brighton, 2009) is not true. However, depending on individual cognitive efforts, a heuristic decision could still be efficient.

From a principal's perspective however, the picture is different. As the giving of less information fosters rational decision making in the agent, this results in a stunning "less-is-more" effect; the fewer cues presented, the more effective the overall decision of the agent. This effect results from the higher probability that participants will engage in cognitive decision making where they are given low numbers of cues and not from more the effectiveness of their decisions in general. Efficiency plays a minor role, as the principal is not affected by possible efforts.

A clear implication of this research for managers seeking highly effective decisions is, therefore, that they should themselves use as much information as possible but, when they are dependent on the decisions of others, managers should provide them with only a small amount of information (Milkman, et al., 2009).

Limitations and conclusion

This study is limited in a variety of ways. The most prominent, given the experimental design and sample structure, is that its validity with respect to actual investment decision making is limited. However, regarding general decision making processes, these results allow for substantial insights. The characteristics of the situation, such as the amount of information provided or the problem to be solved, account for most of the differences in the use of heuristics versus rational reasoning. Additionally no statistical manipulation check was possible within the used design. However, the analysis of verbal protocols (see Study 2, p. 129ff) of the same task revealed that participants repeated the instruction (in a think-a-loud manner), but nevertheless preferred a more frugal decision rule. Due to the qualitative nature of the interviews, no statistical measure is however possible. Future research should therefore focus on this issue and included a-priori quantifiable measures regarding a control of the experimental manipulation.

It has been demonstrated that issues of accountability also positively influence the (at least the reported) number of information cues used (H. Lee, et al., 1999). However, accountability was not included in this study (but see Study 3, p. 144ff, for the effects of accountability). As argued above, missing accountability could potentially explain differences between this study's results and those of Krabuanrat & Phelps (1998), who found that investment decisions are made according to rational decision rules. Therefore, the inclusion of accountability and different types of generic management tasks would provide fruitful ground for further studies. Related to the issue of accountability is the present study's limitation to single-person decisions. However, in in-group decision processes, explicit careful reasoning could play a role even before the actual decision is made.

Subsequent research should therefore pay attention to the use of heuristics in group-decision processes. Finally, what Libby and Lewis (1977) call self insight, that is, perceived decision quality and subjective cue usage, could be elaborated further in order to integrate this dimension into the interpretation of the results as well. This aspect is insofar of interest as it represents another promising aspect within the output dimension (as illustrated in Figure 18, p. 90). It is promising insofar, as quality is in this case is not accessed through an external (rational) yardstick (e.g. equal weight- or weighted additive rule) but through an internal evaluation.

The observed effort-reduction is in line with the suggested mechanism of heuristic reasoning by Shah and Oppenheimer (2008), however an open question concerns the nature of these heuristics, referring to the dichotomy of reasoning suggested by dual process theories (Kahneman, 2011; Stanovich & West, 2000). To what degree are these effort reduction strategies conscious (System 2) or rather unconscious (System 1)? For instance, if one subject sees a negative number in the category sales growth, does this automatically trigger a rejection (or a lower score) for this alternative? An alternative explanation could be that this (surprisingly) negative information is detected by System 1 and further elaborated by System 2. In this case System 1 works like an alarm within management accounting settings and if it rings, System 2 joins in. Future research should therefore analyze if, and to what degree decisions can be purely based on System 1 in accounting settings. The following four studies further analyze this issue from various perspectives and in particular take a closer look to what degree heuristics belong to one System or another.

4.2 Study 2: verbal protocol analysis of accounting problem solving

4.2.1 Introduction – tracking decision processes with verbal protocols

In order to better understand how heuristics are embedded in controlling decision strategies, Study 1 ("Can less-be-more in Management Accounting") was replicated, but this time using verbal protocols (cf. think-a-loud protocols (Ericsson & Simon, 1993)), with n = 17 participants, in the behavioral laboratory of a North American University.

This method is well established in behavioral accounting research (BAR), with a research history going back to the early work of Shields and colleagues (Lewis, Shields, & Young, 1983; Shields, 1980). This process tracing technique was, for example, also used by Isenberg (1986) in analyzing managerial problem solving, or more recently by Cokely and Kelly (2009) in investigating cognitive abilities and their influence on decision making under risk. That this sort of more qualitative analysis provides valuable insights with respect to accounting research, was recently stressed, for example, by Lee and Humphrey (2006), who point out that accounting "is more than a numbers game" and call for a wider mix of methods in this field.

This sort of research on process characteristics of human JDM/heuristic reasoning illustrates that the mind is not a black-box (at least not since the end of behaviorism) (Payne & Venkatraman, 2011) and there have many methods developed that allow social scientists to obtain a deeper understanding of how decisions are being made. Experiments (paper-pencil or web-based) or eye-tracking records are just two tools among many in the field of JDM research. But also more qualitative techniques such as the critical incident technique (Flanagan, 1954) have been used, defining JDM research from a rather broad perspective. One almost classic approach in this field is the analysis of verbal protocols. Its foundations can be traced back to the ideas of Watson in the 1920s (Watson, 1920), who pointed out that thinking is more than the action of language mechanisms. The psychological purpose of collecting verbal protocols as data is summarized by Ericsson and Simon (1980, p. 220)[86] as follows:

> "One of the most direct and widely used methods to gain information about subjects' internal states is to instruct them to think aloud or talk aloud. With this procedure, the heeded[87] information may be verbalized either through direct articulation or by verbal encoding of information that was originally stored in a nonverbal code. With the instruction to verbalize, a direct trace is obtained of the heeded information, and hence, an indirect one of the internal stages of the cognitive process."

Using verbal protocols for tracking decision behavior has a long tradition in JDM research (Austin & Delaney, 1998; Ericsson & Simon, 1980, 1993; Payne, 1976b). However, as Hogarth (1993, p. 410) highlights: "(…) there is enormous resistance to the use of such models. Indeed, there is a mystical belief that the mind cannot and somehow should not be modeled." Verbal protocols are, of course, not mystical mind-reading procedures; rather they are another tool with both strengths and weaknesses in analyzing the decision process. For instance according to Payne and Venkatrama (2011, p. 227) "verbal protocols are particularly valuable for studying problem representations."

JDM versus problem-solving research

In general, verbal protocols are in line with research on (complex) problem-solving or polytely (cf. complex problem solving, including many goals) (Funke, 2003). This is important, as this research differs from most JDM (or the precursor behavioral decision theory (BDT)) in some relevant aspects (Hogarth, 1993). Firstly, problem-solving research is more interested in "how" tasks are solved, compared to JDM research, in which "how well" is particularly important. In line with this basic distinction,

---

[86]   See also Konrad (2010) for a recent summary of verbal protocols as a methodology.

[87]   Ericsson and Simon (1980) use "heeded to" instead of "attended to", claiming stylistic reasons.

it is usually the case that problem-solving does not rely on normative models or other benchmarks when evaluating responses.[88]

Problem solving is thus more interested in tracing underlying processes, and not in using dependent variables as performance measures. The third key distinction addresses the general research design and the number of subjects used in studies. Problem-solving research uses within-subject design with a small number of participants, in comparison with JDM research, which usually involves large-scale between-subject design studies. So even if both fields analyze how decisions are made, there are some important distinctions to be made between the two different communities which engage in similar research questions but use different approaches. Furthermore, some issues are predominantly addressed by problem-solving research and are rarely found in JDM research. Such issues are, for example, the numerous pieces of research into "insight" or "creativity" (e.g. Sternberg, et al., 1997).

Table 15: JDM versus problem solving research

JDM research	Problem-solving research
"How well" tasks are solved using normative yardsticks such as EU theory. How judgments are made and how choices are evaluated.	"How" tasks are solved relying more on a prescriptive perspective. Research subject are mental representations which people make when making decisions.
Economics and economic theory matters (departures and enrichment from existing theories), thus more commonly found in business schools	Economics not as relevant, thus more commonly found in psychology departments
Large scale, between-subject design studies	Rather small scale, within-subject design studies

Methodological challenges for verbal protocols

Critics of verbal protocols frequently address two points. Firstly, that it is impossible for participants to have introspection with regard to their actual thoughts and to verbalize them. Secondly, they address the issue that verbalizing information could potentially affect cognitive processes, and thus verbal protocols represent no appropriate methods for analyzing JDM tasks as they have an inherent bias in their method-

---

[88]   Hogarth (1993, p. 415) even argues that "...the work of economists is irrelevant [for problem solving research]." Consequently, this scholar argues that JDM (or behavioral decision theory) research is rather found in business schools with a strong economics department, and that problem solving research is rather at home in psychology departments.

ology (for a test of validity of verbal protocols see for instance Russo, Johnson, & Stephens, 1989).

Regarding the first point (the impossibility of introspection) Ericsson and Simon (1993) argue that high level mental processes which are necessary for solving problems, progress in steps in the working memory. This temporary store for mental activities is usually accessible for conscious thoughts (see Baddeley, et al., 2009, p. for an extensive discussion of the role of working memory related processes), and thus verbal protocols can trace these processes. This theoretical point of view illustrates that verbal protocols cannot, of course, track all mental activities, and are limited to the ones currently in the working memory (cf. focal attention). This framework (which is in line with the basic distinction between automatic processes and controlled processes) can, for instance, explain the rather weak validity of retrospective protocols. Conrad et al. (2000, p. 3) also point out that "if you can not deliberately control the retrieval process [you] cannot report much about it."

With respect to the second point (the inherent bias of verbal protocols, cf. "does thinking aloud affect ones thinking" (Conrad, et al., 2000)), Simon and Ericsson (1980), analyzing a huge body of studies from the 1960s and the 1970s, already argue that "...the results of these studies consistently support our model's prediction that producing verbal reports of information directly available in propositional form does not change the course and structure of the cognitive processes." What Simon and Ericsson admit is, however, that thinking aloud could result in timelier task completion. Additionally Ericsson and Simon (1980, p. 210) highlight that this is only an effect of the instructions "if instructions require verbalization of information that would not otherwise be attended to." (but see Russo, et al., 1989 for contrary evidence).

More convincing than this early attempt to demonstrate the usefulness and validity of verbal protocols, is a recent detailed and proper meta-analysis involving 95 studies (with nearly 3,500 participants) by Fox and colleagues (2011). They picked up the criticism already faced by Ericsson and Simon ("does think aloud affect thinking") and they found that the effect size of "think-aloud" over the analyzed body of studies is only slightly above zero (r = -0.03).[89] This finding is particularly striking, and supports the claim of Ericsson and Simon, as these authors compared only studies in which verbal versus non-verbal analysis were compared, and additionally controlled for all relevant variables such as task type (non-visual versus primarily visual). Their analysis additionally supports the rather unsurprising finding that think aloud takes longer, but more surprisingly they also found that if the aloud behavior is reactive, performance is higher (distinguishing, as suggested by Ericsson and Simon (1980), between concurrent verbalization versus reactive verbalization).

Also in behavioral accounting research, verbal protocols have been used already at an early stage (see also Section 2.4, p. 46ff for the historical development of behavioral accounting research) in evaluating decisions in accounting settings (for auditing see Biggs & Mock, 1983; for management accounting see Lewis, et al., 1983). These researchers used the recommendations by Ericsson and Simon (1980) and recorded and transcribed the protocols of accounting professionals in tasks such as hypothesis development in evaluating unexpected financial developments (Bedard & Biggs, 1991). This way, these researchers departed from more static input-output models of classic experimental research and added a more process-oriented perspective to behavioral accounting research.

Verbal protocols have also been combined with experiments. For instance, Hunton and McEwen (1997) used this mixture in analyzing not only the cognitive search strategy (verbal protocols) but also controlled for forecasting accuracy (experimental design) using incentives as the independent variable. Overall, the contribution of verbal protocol analysis in behavioral accounting research is recently highlighted by Trotman et al. (2011, p. 311), reviewing 50 years of JDM research in accounting, arguing that "the findings from the protocol studies provided additional valuable descriptions of the search strategies and decision aids used by different types of decision makers."

---

[89] For a classic discussion of the importance of reporting effect sizes in behavioral sciences, see Cohen (1992). For some notes and measures of effect size calculation methods see Grissom and Kim (2005).

.

Nevertheless, analyzing the last five years (2005 onwards) of the leading accounting journals (as discussed before, see Section 2.5. p. 51ff) for the key words "verbal protocols", "verbal reports" and "protocol analysis", indicates that this method appears out of fashion, resulting in no hits when searching title, key words and abstracts. This finding is in line with a view held by Merchant (2011), who highlights that high level accounting research is more and more driven by the application of economic models and complex statistical analysis, neither of which are used in most projects using verbal protocols.

4.2.2 Method

This study (also due to the rather small sample size) can be seen to weigh more heavily on the descriptive side. The departure from prescriptive models is already shown in Study 1 in detail, so here it is of more interest to analyze and describe the underlying strategies. The only difference is that due to the design, no within-subjects design is used. In other words, my aim was to further investigate the applied decision strategies and the heuristic mechanisms that have been documented in Study 1. For instance, I was interested if they somehow resembled the heuristics described by proponents of the fast and frugal heuristics program (Gigerenzer, et al., 1999). Due to its descriptive character no hypothesis were formulated in this study.

Participants and procedure

In total, 17 students (8 male, 9 female) from an American university participated in the study. The mean age of the participants was 21.4 years (SD = 3.3). All of them had at least completed two management accounting classes in order to ensure familiarity with the basic KPIs used in the scenario. This rather small sample size is typical of problem-solving research (see the previous section). The study was conducted in the "behavioral laboratory" of a North American university. The participants were instructed in the following way: "*Think aloud as you work on the problem given. What I mean by think aloud is that I want you to tell me everything you are thinking from the time you first see the question until you give an answer.*" (Ericsson & Simon, 1993, p. 378). For a complete description of instructions of the experimental task, see Appendix p. 211ff. The protocols were digitally recorded and subsequently transcribed. The coding of the transcripts was done using *MaxQDA* software for qualitative data analysis, allowing a better handling of this sort of data as suggested by Wrona (2005).

4.2.3 Results

4.2.3.1 On the validity of the protocols

As a first step, the quantitative results (cues used) were compared to those of Study 1. This was done in order to control for any effects resulting from the changed instructions. Separate t-tests were conducted in order to check for potential differences. Additionally, effect sizes (for separate groups t-tests) were calculated using the recommendations offered by Cohen (1992). A comparison of Study 1 (in the high information load condition) (M = 4.26, SD = 3.23) with the verbal protocol analysis in the high information load condition (M = 3.40, SD = 1.52) did not result in significant differences, conditions; t(85) = 0.587, p = 0.559 n.s and only indicated a small effect size of d = 0.127.

Table 16: Comparing Study 1 and verbal protocols with high information load

	Study type	N	Mean	SD	SEM
Cues used	20 cues Study 1	82	4.26	3.23	0.36
	20 cues verbal protocols	5	3.40	1.52	0.68

Also the medium information load condition did not reveal any significant differences when comparing Study 1 (M = 4.96, SD = 3.15) and the results from the verbal protocol analysis (M = 6.00, SD = 3.74), conditions; t(47) = -0.692, p = 0.492 n.s. as well as a small effect size of d = -0.202.

Table 17: Comparing Study 1 and verbal protocols with medium information load

	Study type	N	Mean	SD	SEM
Cues used	10 cues Study 1	44	4.96	3.15	0.47
	10 cues verbal protocols	5	6.00	3.74	1.67

The condition with a low information load was in line with the other findings. There were also no significant differences between Study 1 (M = 3.22, SD = 1.38) and the verbal protocol analysis (M = 3.43, SD = 1.27), conditions; t(51) = -0.038, p = 0.705 n.s. with a marginal effect size of d = -0.01.

Table 18: Comparing Study 1 and verbal protocols with low information load

	Study type	N	Mean	SD	SEM
Cues used	5 cues Study 1	46	3.22	1.38	0.20
	5 cues verbal protocols	7	3.43	1.27	0.48

Overall, the results revealed only minimal (and insignificant, p<0.05) differences and small to marginal effect sizes, between Study 1 and Study 2, even considering the small sample size and thus the potential outliers. I thus concluded that the verbal protocols did not change the basic decision making behavior of the participants (confirming M. C. Fox, et al., 2011). As in Study 1, the GDMS had no impact on the amount of information used. For instance, the factor score for the style "rationality" was, as expected, insignificant (F = 3.21, p = 0.42).

4.2.3.2 *Code-based analysis of the protocols*

As a first step, the general use of cues was analyzed (which ones were used, and how many). As a second step, the decision rules were analyzed, coding if the search strategy matched other classic algorithms known in JDM research (see Chapter 2, p. 15ff). The simple code system for the software, based on the key concepts of JDM research as described in Chapter 2, included the labels listed in Table 19 on the next page.

Overall, these codes were used as a first approximation of what kind of information was used by the participants, what was the basic strategy in reducing the complexity, and if these strategies resembled some of the popular algorithms.

Table 19: Coding system for protocol analysis including example considerations

Protocol codes	Example considerations
KPI	When an indicator is mentioned (e.g. sales growth, ROI, employee satisfaction).
Strategy	For a general description of the decision process e.g. "*I put circles on what seems to be the best in the category and the top ones*"[VP_01]).
Cue weighting	When a comment on the cues weights was made e.g. "*based my ranking mostly on costumer satisfaction and control of supply chain*" [VP_02]).
Learning/expertise	When a decision is linked with previous experience e.g. referring to an experience during an internship [VP_17]).
Heuristics	When effort reduction is used to make a decision e.g. "*basically I just looked at the sales growth and if I see positive numbers and the negative numbers so they take a net lose every year*" [VP_11]).
Fast and Frugal	For heuristics that match those described by Gigerenzer and colleagues (1999) like TTB e.g. "*I personally like the ROI. So I guess I rank them based on that. Since there is a tie, otherwise I go here with sales growth*" [VP_08]).

This approach of using basic code schemas in analyzing verbal protocols can be seen to be in line with the distinction made by Payne (1976a)[90], who suggests four major types of statements as codes, namely goal statements, statements reflecting search, evaluation statements and comparison statements.

Using a code system for verbal protocols was also recently used by Cokely and Kelley (2009) when analyzing cognitive abilities and superior decision making.

---

[90] These codes are findings from a classic verbal protocol study by Payne (1976b), who found that with increasing complexity, the tendency to eliminate some alternatives as quickly as possible also increased. However, this verbal protocol analysis provided a richer description of which kind of heuristics are actually used, and how complexity reduction works. The verbal protocols also indicate that the process of complexity reduction that leads to heuristic solutions is rather unconscious. There was no evidence that the participants were aware of the complexity reduction in the fashion that they mentioned that they, for instance, could better calculate the ranking if it only contained a limited number of cues.

Table 20: Coding system suggested by Payne (1976a)

Protocol codes	Example considerations from Study 2
Goal statements	E.g., "Let's just see what the sale growth is in all breweries first" – this type is covered in this case by the code "**Strategy**".
Statements reflecting search	E.g., "The ROI in Fritzbräu is XX" – this type is covered in this case by the code "**KPI**".
Evaluation statements	E.g., "Well, negative sales growth is not a good thing to have" – this type is covered in this case by the codes "**weighting cues**", "**heuristics**" and 'fast and frugal".
Comparison statements	E.g., "In Sudbacher the profit growth is much better compared to Niedritzer" – this type is covered in this case by the code "**weighting cues**".

The analysis of the protocols indicated that within protocols more **KPIs** were mentioned by the participants, compared to a pure analysis of the notes[91] (as a reversed engineering mechanism). This finding is not surprising as, for instance, in some (non-compensatory) strategies, some cues are "mentioned" but instantly disregarded for later analysis or, as the protocol of one participant (VP_15) illustrates:

"I cross out business tax, though it is important as it is an expense, it is not something I would necessarily look at."

The verbal protocols indicate that the search **strategy** frequently included some kind of a deliberate elimination process with regard to cues. Thus, I conclude that the effort reduction process of excluding information is not unconscious. Rather, a strategic selection process is conducted. In order to quantify this effect, the quotient between reported cues (as found in the notes) and cues coded in the verbal protocols was calculated. For instance, if five cues were marked in the written notes and seven cues are coded in the verbal protocols, this results in a score of 0.714. This relation (with n = 17) resulted in a mean for all reports of M = 0.702 (SD = 0.271). This finding can be illustrated, for example, with one participant (VP_11). In the verbal protocol analysis, this participant mentioned seven KPIs. However, his notes clearly indicate that he only used four KPIs in his ranking strategy. This is also documented in this comment on his decision:

---

[91]   In Study 1, the inter-coder reliability indicated a satisfactory Cronbach's α of 0.936. I thus conclude that this high score allows us to conduct this estimation of KPI usage without an additional assessment of reliability measures.

> *"Sales and sales growth were the two largest factors in my deci-*
> *sions. Following these were subventions and employee satisfaction."*

This comment on his decision process illustrates that this participant reduced the complexity of the given information by focusing on a smaller amount of information than was available.

The next step in the observed pattern was typically a more compensatory way of **weighting the used cues**. A typical example for this pattern is the following protocol (VP_15):

> *"I am going to rank now the performance indicators according to*
> *those which I think are the most important. I think return on invest-*
> *ment is probably the most important one in my opinion. As the next*
> *market share is also very important. And also the control of supply*
> *chain is next. Profit growth. I am going just to use those four things*
> *to make my big decision."*

After focusing on a limited amount of information, the participants frequently ranked the remaining information, sometimes also conforming to the instructions.

This pattern of complexity reduction, which is also in line with the definition of **heuristics** as an effort reduction approach (Shah & Oppenheimer, 2008), is found in most protocols (e.g. VP_01 is prototypical, arguing: "*I just try to weigh which ones are the best or have the most important meaning*"). Participants more or less intensely reflect upon the provided cue values, but only included some of them in the final decision process. With respect to this finding, it is important to note that as in Study 1, the participants were instructed to include all available information in a balanced way in their strategy (e.g. one participant explicitly refers to the instructions (VP_09)). However, it is worth mentioning that the task in this study did not really challenge the cognitive capabilities of the participants. Even in the high information load condition, a solution using all provided information is possible (as checked in one pilot study for Study 1).

However, what the verbal protocols could not track was the reference towards **previous learning or experience.** Possibly due to the student sample, only one participant referred to his previous learning experience during an internship (VP_17), while only one participant explicitly mentioned learned facts ("Usually patents last 20 years" [VP_16]). Not all learning experience is necessarily consciously reflected in the decision process. Thus, it could still be that the participants unconsciously used, for instance, knowledge gained through accounting or finance classes. Nevertheless, if the observed complexity reduction should reflect an ecological approach of complexity reduction, some learning is absolutely necessary (Rieskamp, 2008; Rieskamp & Reimer, 2007).

Comparing the identified strategies with the **fast and frugal** mechanisms of Gigerenzer et al. (1999) some (but not all, as highlighted by Hilbig (2010)) used algorithms that resemble the TTB rule (Gigerenzer & Goldstein, 1999). For instance one participant (VP_ 3) describes his whole decision process as follows:

> "Guess I put them in order based on ROI%, so first one is Südbacher, and one starts with P (Prinzenbräu). Then after that these two have 13% almost. So I guess I go then with sales (...). So like I said in the beginning, I did it based on ROI and then for three and four they have the same ROI, so I chose the highest sales, which also had the highest brand awareness."

Like in the TTB algorithm (Gigerenzer & Goldstein, 1999) the cue with the assumed highest validity (ROI) is used to rank all alternatives. If there is a draw, the cue with the second highest validity (sales) is taken into account. Interestingly an additional cue (brand awareness) is used to underline the ranking decision. Other participants also used simple strategies but they did so, as described above, mostly after focusing on a limited number of cues.

Furthermore, a basic search pattern distinction was adopted from Shields (1980), who differentiates between two basic dimensions:

- **processing-by-parameter** (PBP; as a breadth first search pattern)
- **processing-by-unit** (PBU; as an in-depth first search pattern).

A typical PBP pattern would be, for instance, to analyze the ROI for all potential breweries (breadth). An example for PBU (depth first) would be to first analyze all KPIs for one particular company, and then switch to the next.

That a PBP pattern was attributed to the majority of participants is not particularly surprising. As expected, the participants showed no established preferences. Rather, their choice is constructed through the presented alternatives (Slovic, 1995). Within the protocols typical signs for framing effects were also identified (Tversky & Kahneman, 1986), such as with VP_07:

> "The five patents of Fritzbräu are quite impressive compared to the two of Nicebräu"

– ignoring however the fact that a large company can easily hold hundreds of patents and the five patents worked just as a frame for the decision. Within the dominant PBP strategy, two types of classic decision algorithms were also identified - elimination-by-aspects (Tversky, 1972)[92] and, as mentioned above, take-the-best (Gigerenzer & Goldstein, 1999). For example, one participant followed the single cue decision rule resembling the classic take-the best algorithm (VP_08):

> "There is a lot to choose from. I personally like the ROI. So I guess I rank them based on that. Since there is a tie, otherwise I go here with sales growth".

An example for elimination-by-aspects would be the following statement (VP_13):

> "So these are mostly random numbers of growth and one not. For sure the three with negative sales growth are borderline and I am not paying closer attention to."

4.2.4 Discussion

As illustrated in Figure 22 on the next page, the results of the experimental studies can be seen to be in line with the concept of dual process models (Evans & Frankish, 2010). It seems that a general first step in analyzing the provided KPIs, is to reduce complexity to a manageable amount. This process resembles the description of System 1 as an effortless and automatic process. As a second step, a more elaborate strategy was applied. This follows the description of System 2 as a more effortful and rule oriented mechanism (see also Section 2.7.2 on p. 70ff for a discussion of dual process theories).

---

[92] This rule begins by determining the most important attribute and then retrieves a cutoff value for that attribute. All alternatives with values below that cutoff are eliminated. The process continues with the most important remaining attribute(s), until only one alternative remains. But it is interesting to consider that, according to Tversky (1972, p. 98), elimination by aspects "[...] cannot be defended as a rational procedure of choice".

Figure 22: Experimental results as a phased strategy from a dual process perspective

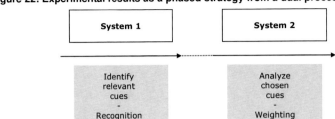

Following this argumentation, the quality of a decision does not only depend on the accurate application of certain rules (e.g. weighting some KPIs in an appropriate manner). It also depends on the set of information that is taken into account (as a potential first step in a phased strategy or as the single basis for a decision) in arriving at a more elaborate decision.

As heuristics in most dual process models would fall into the System 1 category (but see Frederick, 2002), it appears promising to further investigate if (and when) they also work as a deliberate decision strategy. What is also of interest in this manner is to what degree both System 1 and 2 have to work together in more complex tasks. Is it actually possible to solve more complicated tasks without relying completely on one System? The difficulty some authors mention in distinguishing between System 1 and 2 (e.g. Keren & Schul, 2009) also concerns this issue. Can you switch back and forth between the Systems?

One obvious limitation of verbal protocols is that they cannot naturally grasp all intuitive (System 1) thinking. However, in line with the results of this study it can also be argued that heuristics can be surprisingly conscious (System 2) effort reduction mechanisms and do not necessarily represent an automatic adaptive mechanism that rely on any sort of ecological rationality. This argumentation would also see learning/experience as well as a conscious and reflective (System 2) process.

Further research should thus replicate this study using more experienced participants (e.g. MBA students, professionals). I hypothesize that in such a sample, more references to experience/learning would be identified and ecological rationality of heuristic reasoning can be better traced.

Overall this study shows that verbal protocols, as a process tracing method (Payne & Venkatraman, 2011), can contribute some interesting insights into the decision process, particularly if combined with experimental tasks and other studies. This combination is not frequently found in *Behavioral Research in Accounting* (see Hunton & McEwen (1997) for a rare exception), and represents, in my view, many opportunities for future research in the field of JDM research in accounting. Also Bettman et al. (1991, p. 76) stress, with respect to eclectic JDM research, that: "Combinations of methods in which several complementary approaches are used in the same study seem to hold the greatest promise. Because the various methods have different strengths and weaknesses, multimethod approaches let us separate the effects of the research method from those associated with the phenomenon under study."

4.3 Study 3: on the accountability of accountants

4.3.1   Introduction – accountability in JDM research

According to Bettman, Johnson and Payne (1991), three key dimensions are identified in behavioral research, which generally determine the decision making strategy. These dimensions are: **characteristics of the person**, including cognitive abilities and prior knowledge; the **nature of the problem**, including task and context and, as the last dimension, **social context** e.g. group membership and accountability. The similarity to "Simon's scissor" (see Figure 14, p. 70), which also highlights the interaction of the individual and the environment, is no coincidence, as these authors explicitly refer to the work of this scholar.

As Studies 1 and 2 have largely focused on aspects of the first two dimensions (cf. task complexity, individual differences), this study takes a closer look at the third dimension, and introduces factor accountability as a social context variable, into the experimental design. That this small change in the settings can matter, is also highlighted by Payne (2011), who argues that: "behavior of any one individual seem to be highly contingent upon often subtle shifts in the characteristics of the problems (context) being studied (local thinking)."

As discussed in length in Section 2.7.5 (p. 83ff), accountability is a "notoriously multidimensional concept" (Lerner & Tetlock, 1999, p. 255). Dimensions include, for instance: "the mere presence of another," "identifiability", "evaluation," and "reason-giving". In this study in particular, the last two dimensions are included in the experimental design. As participants were told that their decision would be evaluated ("economic wise decision") and through the instruction that a comment on their decision (cf. the buying process of KPIs) has to be made, a high level of accountability was ensured. Additionally the presence of the experimenter can be seen as a (classic) source of accountability (Rosenthal, 1966). However, as this setting remained the same over the three studies, this effect cannot be statistically measured in this case.

The factor of accountability appears in particular to be important with regard to management accounting, as this profession cannot generally be analyzed without taking into account the social context of organizations. This importance can be illustrated through the role description of management controllers within the company, for instance by Weber et al. (1999) (see also Section 2.7.5, p. 83ff). In this approach particularly, the interaction between (top-) management and the accountant is stressed. This relationship between these two agents is thus, in addition to all contextual factors, determined by multidimensional and complex social variables such as trust or accountability.

Most scholars agree that accountability typically leads to a more effortful and self-critical search for cues when making a decision or a judgment in all kinds of settings (Larrick, 1993; H. Lee, et al., 1999; Lerner & Tetlock, 1999; Tetlock, et al., 1989). Following this argumentation, I expected participants to use more cues in a strictly experimental setting, where an economically wise investment decision was to be made in terms of the advice to spend a fixed budget. This was tested in the following hypothesis:

H1: Participants will consider a wider range of cues (compared to Study 1 in all three conditions), meaning they are buying more cues then the average number of cues used in Study 1.

Even if participants should prefer heuristic solutions in order to reduce the complexity of the available data, in line with the results of Study 1 (for a detailed review of the results see also Basel, 2010), I hypothesize that within the set or subset, an efficient use of information will take place. This assumption is in line with recent research on the use and misuse of (paid) advice (Bonaccio & Dalal, 2006; Gino, 2008). In addition, Lerner and Tetlock (1999, p. 263), with respect to cue selection in JDM, conclude: "This [cue] search leads participants to a) survey a wider range of conceivable relevant cues (tested in H1); b) pay greater attention to the cues they use (tested in H2)." Therefore, I derive the following hypothesis:

> *H2a: Participants will use the majority of the bought information (cues) based upon the notes provided to the participants and on the ranking order of the breweries.*

Additionally, as participants want to justify their decision with regard to the invested money, they will report in the comment section that they used all acquired information:

> *H2b: Participants will justify their decision by reporting the use of all acquired information in the comment section.*

However, this H2b cannot be tested statistically, as the analysis can only rely on qualitative written comments. So, in this case, a descriptive analysis of the comments will replace a statistical one.

Finally, even if Studies 1 and 2 did not indicate that decision making style (measured through the GDMS by Scott and Bruce (1995)) had an effect on the observed decision strategy, I assume that in this particular setting, decision making style will have an impact on the number of chosen cues. This hypothesis is based on the assumption that the style labeled "dependent"[93] in the GDMS, in this case leads participants to reflect more upon the evaluation of the decision and triggers a form of self-protection (Larrick, 1993). Consequently, more cues are bought.

---

[93]   According to Scott and Bruce (1997, p. 820) the dependent style is "characterized by a search for advice and direction from others."

Additionally, Scott and Bruce (1995, p. 820) point out that decision making style "…is not a personality trait, but a habit-based propensity to react in a certain way in a specific decision context." And, as this context has significantly shifted from Studies 1 and 2 to Study 3, the hypothesis is thus:

> *H3: A high score on the part of participants on the GDMS scale "dependent decision making style" will lead them to buy more cues than those scoring low on this scale.*

4.3.2   Method

Participants and procedure

In total, 31 graduate and PhD students participated in the study (13 female; 18 male). The mean age of the participants was 24.9 years (SD = 2.3). All of them had completed at least two management accounting classes, in order to ensure their familiarity with the basic KPIs used in the scenario. The study was conducted under standardized conditions within a European University. After the instructions were handed out, each participant got an envelope containing 20,000 € in toy money. Depending on the group, each KPI had a price of 1,000 € (under conditions in which up to 20 KPIs could be acquired), 2,000 € (in the 10 KPI condition) or 4,000 € (in the 5 KPI condition).

All KPIs had an equal price, and it was possible to buy all of them. Instructions only asked the participants to make "the best decision possible" and to make "an economic wise decision". As in Studies 1 and 2, the participants were instructed that they had up to 20 minutes for the task. As in the other studies, time was not intended as an independent variable, but rather as a basic frame for introducing at least some time pressure. The other instructions remained the same as in Study 1 (see Section 5.1, p. 172ff).

4.3.3 Results

I assumed that the participants would buy a larger amount of cues compared to those in Study 1 (H1), and that they would actually use them in their final decision (Gino, 2008; Larrick, 1993) (H2). This assumption was based on the fact that one important factor in JDM is self-protection and accountability (Larrick, 1993; Lerner & Tetlock, 1999). Finally, I hypothesized that in this setting the "dependent" dimension of the GDMS (Scott and Bruce, 1999) would matter, due to the concern of participants to score high on this scale in relation to the potential evaluation of others. This, for instance, can be illustrated through items 5 and 22 of the GDMS, which explicitly include: "*I use the advice of other people in making my important decisions*" (Item #5) or "*If I have the support of others, it is easier for me to make important decisions.*" (Item #22).

> H1: *Participants will consider a wider range of cues (compared to Study 1 in all three conditions), meaning they are buying more cues then the average number of cues used in Study 1.*

As a first step, the number of bought KPIs in Study 3 was compared to those used in Study 1, where all information was available for free. Separate t-tests (for independent samples) were conducted in order to check for potential differences.

Comparing Study 1 (in the high information load condition; M = 4.26, SD = 3.23) with Study 3 (accountability scenario) in the high information load condition; M = 6.58, SD = 4.62), did not result in significant differences,[94] conditions; t(92) = -1.685, p = 0.116 n.s. Interestingly the effect size in this case using t-values and df (in the separate groups t-test)[95] indicated d = -0.351, which can be interpreted as a medium effect (J. Cohen, 1992; Rosnow & Rosenthal, 1996).

---

[94] However it is important to note that the F-value gained through Levene`s test for equality of variances was F(92) = 2.538, p = 0.115 which only slightly missed a significant 0.05 value. This indicates that variances can almost be interpreted as being unequal, and under this condition t(92) = -2.199, p = 0.030** results become significant. (for a criticial discussion of significance rituals see also Sanabria & Killeen, 2007; Welkowitz, et al., 2002 for an overview of statistical measures).

[95] If not otherwise indicated in this study, effect sizes are calculated using the available t-value. This measure is usually more conservative than using means and standard deviations (Rosnow & Rosenthal, 1996). For instance, in the first condition, if M and SD had been used, the effect size would be higher with d = -0.582.

Table 21: H1 – comparison of Study 1 and 3 in 20 cue condition

	Study type	N	Mean	SD	SEM
Cues used	20 cues Study 1	82	4.26	3.23	0.36
	20 cues Study 3	12	6.58	4.62	1.33

In the medium information load study, the results comparing Study 1 (M = 4.95, SD = 3.15) with Study 3 (accountability scenario) in the medium information load condition (equal variances not assumed $F(52)$ = 9.755, p = 0.003***; M = 6.00, SD = 1.15) did not result in significant differences, conditions; $t(52)$ = -1.028, p = 0.309 n.s. But as in the high information load condition, a medium effect of d = -0.285 was computed.

Table 22: H1 – comparison of Study 1 and 3 in 10 cue condition

	Study type	N	Mean	SD	SEM
Cues used	10 cues Study 1	44	4.95	3.15	0.47
	10 cues Study 3	10	6.00	1.15	0.36

In the low information load study the results comparing Study 1 (M= 3.21, SD= 1.38) with Study 3 (accountability scenario) in the low information load condition (equal variances not assumed $F(53)$= 5.703, p= 0.021**; M= 2.89, SD= 0.93) did not result in significant differences, conditions; $t(53)$= 0.887, p= 0.388 n.s. The effect size in this case was d= 0.244, which, according to Cohen (1992), represents a medium effect.

Table 23: H1 – comparison of Study 1 and 3 in 5 cue condition

	Study type	N	Mean	SD	SEM
Cues used	5 cues Study 1	46	3.21	1.38	0.20
	5 cues Study 3	9	2.89	0.93	0.31

Obviously non-significant results do not allow a final rejection of H1 (Bortz, 2005). However, based on the results of the t-tests, I did not find any support for H1 in that participants in the accountability condition significantly bought significantly more information than was the case in Study 1. It is however likely that larger samples and a replication of Study 3 would lead to significant results, in particular in terms of the high information load condition. Nevertheless, even if participants had the chance to acquire a substantial amount of information, they refused to do so – or at least less then hypothesized.

That accountability had however some effect, can be documented through the computed effect sizes (using Cohen's d), which were all in a lower medium range between 0.351 to 0.244 (even from a conservative estimation using t-values and df instead of means and standard deviations). If H1 had been formulated in terms of effect sizes, it would have been assumed that I would find a medium to large effect (< 0.5), and thus the results of the effect sizes can be seen to be in line with the interpretation of the t-tests.

H2a: Participants will use the majority of the bought information (cues) based upon the notes provided to the participants and on the ranking order of the breweries.

Analyzing the documents of the participants revealed that, in line with H2, most of the acquired information was integrated into the ranking of the breweries (cues bought M= 5.71, SD= 3.29 versus cues used M= 5.32, SD= 3.32; t(30)= 0.654, p= 0.741 n.s; d= 0.118; in this case calculated using M and SD, due to the paired nature of the sample).

H2b: Participants will justify their decision by reporting the use of all acquired information in the comment section.

Additionally, analyzing the comments and notes made by the participants in the study (H2b), indicated that the participants checked all information in the first case (based on the notes), but that facilitating the weighting rule was than frequently applied (even simpler than the prescribed 1/N rule).

However, as tested in H1, participants still tended to follow a stunning complexity reduction mechanism. Even if you had the chance to buy up to 20 KPIs, on average only 6.58 (SD= 4.62) were bought in this condition. This does not significantly differ from the condition where up to 10 KPIs could have been bought (Mean= 6.00, SD=

1.6; t(20)= -0.386, p= 0.704 n.s.). In the condition where up to 5 KPIs could have been bought, the mean was 2.88 (SD= 0.93). As in Studies 1 and 2, all control variables and the GDMS had no effect on cue acquisition.

I also tested if any KPI out-ruled others by being purchased much more than others. My analysis revealed that the distribution of the bought cues is mostly equal, with only some minor differences. This means that the "value" of the used KPIs depends more on the subjective meaning, rather than an "innate" value (e.g. ROI is always worth more than customer satisfaction). This cannot, of course, rule out the fact that some participants might see more redundancy among the cues than others, and thus seek to acquire less information. Additionally, in a real setting, it could definitely be the case that some cues are worth more than others, but the important effect here is that this tendency was not systematic in nature.

Figure 23: Cue acquisition as a complexity reduction mechanism

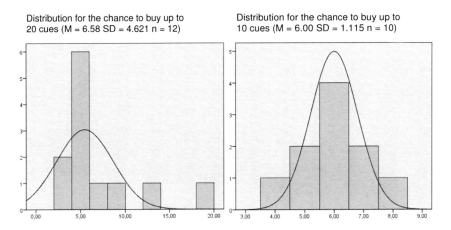

Distribution for the chance to buy up to 20 cues (M = 6.58 SD = 4.621 n = 12)

Distribution for the chance to buy up to 10 cues (M = 6.00 SD = 1.115 n = 10)

H3: A high score for participants on the GDMS scale "dependent decision making style" will lead such participants to buy more cues than those scoring low on this scale.

Finally H3 was tested to see if the "dependent" decision style dimension influences the cue acquisition behavior in the accountability setting of the experiment. The items measuring the dependent style dimension in the GDMS are #2, #5, #10, #18 and #22. As in Studies 1 and 2, a factor analysis was conducted with a median split over the factor score. Surprisingly, an effect of the GDMS "dependent" dimension was observed this time. In particular, in the high information load condition, a higher score on the factor "dependent" decision making style leads participants to buy (and thus use, see results of H2) more cues. In this condition the difference between the means was 4.50 versus 13.00, which indicates a pretty strong effect.

Table 24: H3 – Median split over factor score for "dependent" decision making style

		REGR factor score 1 for analysis 2 (binned)	
		<= .15719	.15720+
		Cues used	Cues used
		Mean	**Mean**
	5.00	3.00	2.80
Study type	10.00	5.67	6.14
	20.00	4.50	13.00

This effect was also documented in analysing the adjusted R^2 in conditions with and without this personality factor. With the factor, this measure increased from $R^2 = 0.178$ to $R^2 = 0.383$. Overall these findings indicate a pretty strong support for H3. Also the correlation coefficients for the mean factor score of the dependent dimension was significantly correlated (two tailed, Pearson) with the cues used (r= 0.421 (28), p= 0.021**. However, it has to be noted that small samples naturally tend to overestimate the Pearson correlation).

As mentioned above, this is surprising insofar as in Studies 1 and 2, no effects of any GDMS factor was observed. This can be seen as additional support for the strong effect of the context variable accountability, through the budget responsibility.

Table 25: H3 – Tests of between-subjects-effects in- and excluding the factor "dependent" decision making style

Source	Type III Sum of Squares	df	Mean Square	F	Sig.
Corrected Model	147.043(a)	3	49.014	7.005	0.001
Intercept	812.671	1	812.671	116.145	0.000
FAC1_2	64.602	1	64.602	9.233	0.005
type_aggr	91.918	2	45.959	6.568	0.005
Error	181.924	26	6.997		
Total	1.193.000	30			
Corrected Total	328.967	29			

R Squared= 0.447 (Adjusted R Squared= 0.383), DV= cues used

Source	Type III Sum of Squares	df	Mean Square	F	Sig.
Corrected Model	76.969(a)	2	38.484	4.246	0.025
Intercept	813.021	1	813.021	89.693	0.000
Study type	76.969	2	38.484	4.246	0.025
Error	253.806	28	9.064		
Total	1.209.000	31			
Corrected Total	330.774	30			

R Squared= 0.233 (Adjusted R Squared= 0.178), DV= cues used

The results of the three theoretical deducted hypotheses can be summarized in the following Table 26. I found only partial support for H1. H2 and H3 were fully supported using various statistical measures.[96]

---

[96] As suggested by APA guidelines (Wilkinson & The APA Task Force on Statistical Inference, 1999) the emphasize here is clearly in focusing on the effect sizes, as it can be assumed that large enough samples almost certainly will lead to significant (p-value based) differences (see also Vacha-Haase, Nilsson, Reetz, Lance, & Thompson, 2000).

Table 26: Results of the statistical analysis in Study 3

Dependent variable: Cue usage						
Hypo-thesis	Issue	Effect	df	t-Value	F-value	Result
H1	Cue acquisition behavior	d = -0.351 d = -0.285 d = 0.244	92 52 53	-1.685 n.s. -1.028 n.s. 0.887 n.s.	2.538 n.s. 9.755*** 5.703**	⚡
H2a	Cue usage efficiency	d = 0.118	30	0.654 n.s.	n.a.	✓
H3	Dependent decision making style	$R^2 = 0.383$	30(29)	n.a.	9.233***	✓

4.3.4 Discussion

Interpretation of the decision strategy

The strategy used by a majority of the participants can be described as a combination of decision strategies (e.g. heuristic followed by compensatory strategy) as suggested by Bettman et al. (1991) and by Payne (2011). In particular Payne (2011) highlights that the "traditional approach in decision research of assuming that people use a single compensatory decision calculus, with different parameters for different individuals, should be replaced with a more contingent multi-strategy perspective".

For instance, participants use an elimination strategy such as elimination-by-aspects (EBA - coined by Tversky (1972)) to exclude potentially irrelevant or redundant KPIs as a first step. This can explain why most participants did not consider the full extent of the available information, and focused instead on a reduced subset. As a second step, a more compensatory approach is usually chosen, such as the normative weighted additive rule (WADD). According to Bettmann et al. (1991, p. 58) the WADD rule "considers the values of each alternative on all the relative importance of the attributes". (see also section 2.5ff, p. 51 for an integration of these decision strategies into behavioral accounting research).

Instead of the WADD (which varies the cue weights), the equal weight (EQW) rule also fulfils the requirements as a compensatory strategy. In this rule, which has been promoted in particular by Dawes' improper linear models (1979) (see also section 2.3, p. 21ff of this thesis), probabilities and importance are ignored and the cue values of all cues are simply summed up. EQW is basically also applied if the prescriptive rule of the instruction in the study design ("all information should be balanced equally") is applied.

Finally, a typical compensatory strategy that fits the observed pattern with regard to the participants is the frequency of the good and bad features rule (FRQ). This heuristic, introduced by Alba and Marmorstein (1987), works by simply adding positive and negative cue values, and then picking the alternative with the largest number of positive values. For instance, one participant (VP_12) concluded:

> *"I took the decision to buy six KPIs (in my mind the most relevant). I made a matrix with the six breweries and the six KPI columns I underlined the three best performers. In the end I just ranked breweries, according to their number of top positions in each KPI"*

Additional support for this kind of decision mechanism is as well documented in the verbal protocol analysis in Study 2 (see p. 129ff) and it can be seen as a precursor to the take-the-best heuristic (Gigerenzer & Goldstein, 1999), with the difference that this rule stops after the first noticed difference and does not analyze all cues. Overall, the results are consistent with Payne et al. (1993), who argue that decision makers basically want to balance the four following goals:

- Maximizing accuracy

- Minimizing cognitive effort

- Minimizing negative decision-related emotions

- Maximizing the ease of justification of a decision to others

The use of the documented phased strategies in the accountability setting allows participants to balance the above-mentioned goals without too many tradeoffs.

Interestingly, all the documented strategies can work on a deliberate (System 2) level. This is insofar surprising as heuristics, (as already mentioned in Study 2) are described by many authors (even those who reject dual process theories for being too vague), as prototypes of System 1 behavior. For instance, the full book title of Gigerenzer´s (2007) book is: "Gut feelings: The intelligence of the unconscious" or Gilovich et al. (2002) chose the title "heuristics and biases: The psychology of intuitive judgment". Both the terms unconscious and intuitive, clearly refer to System 1 reasoning (Stanovich & West, 2000). As discussed in the conclusion of Study 1 and

Study 2 (see p. 129ff), there is future research needed regarding the interplay of the two Systems.

This issue (concerning the cooperation of the two processes) is also highlighted by Kahneman and Frederick (2005, p. 268), who argue that "System 1 and System 2 can be active concurrently, that automatic and controlled cognitive operations compete for the control of overt responses, and that deliberate judgments are likely to remain anchored on initial impressions." However, critiques of dual process models, like Kruglanski and Gigerenzer (2011, p. 98), point out that "judgments called intuitive and deliberative are both based on rules." Focusing on this rule based approach; these authors suggest a unimodel of human JDM instead of dual processes. Future research should therefore test (and compete) both approaches for a better explanation of results.

Limitations and conclusions

However, due to the small sample size, no in-depth (statistical) analysis of the applied strategies was possible. Future research should thus replicate this study using a larger sample. A potentially fruitful way of doing this could be the use of web-based quasi-experiments (Birnbaum, 2000) using *Rogator* software or *Amazon's* crowd sourcing tool *Mechanical Turk*.

The aim of this study was not to suggest a "magic number" (G. A. Miller, 1956) that represents the ideal cognitive load for the evaluation of KPIs. What the results of the study (together with Studies 1 and 2) clearly suggests however, is that participants have a preference for less complex solutions, at the price of not considering all available information (even if accountability slightly raises the number of acquired cues). This is a stunning effect in particular, as tasks like this (investment decisions) are normally associated with high information acquisitiveness.[97] This series of studies (including Studies 1 and 2), also offers multiple possibilities for future research in the area of behavioral accounting research. For instance, in this scenario, the KPIs of only comparable alternatives were used. In order to increase the validity of these kind of studies, it appears promising to also analyze non-comparable alternatives (as

---

[97]   For this tendency of management accountants to collect (potentially) useless information, see the results of Study 4 (p. 158ff).

suggested by Bettmann, et al., 1991). For example, a company can invest their profits either in an acquisition of a competitor, or it can foster its R&D activities. Both alternatives could be presented with various financial data but without allowing a direct
comparison. It appears promising to analyze what kind of decision strategies are appropriate in such a case, to see if these resemble those (for a discussion of phased
strategies see Lee et al. (1999)) found in the comparable context of Studies 1 to 3.

The results indicate that compensatory strategies were used in the second step of
the solution. This can be seen as a hint that these kinds of strategies are easier to
justify within the accountability setting. One open question in this setting is however,
why exactly this is the case. Future research should therefore address two issues:
firstly, the satisfaction with participants' made decision should be evaluated (comparing those with compensatory versus non-compensatory strategies). Secondly, it
would also be promising to evaluate the expectations that the participants have regarding their decision, for instance if they differentiate between a decision made for
themselves versus one made for others, as discussed in section 2.7.6 (p. 86ff) (for a
more detailed discussion of self-other decision-making see also Bonaccio & Dalal,
2006; Polman, 2010).

Finally the documented effect of the dependent decision making style calls for future research into decision making style factors (which should be seen separately
from personality traits according to Scott and Bruce (1995)) in management accounting (see Furnham, 2008 for a general overview of individual differences in
organizational settings). In particular, the question as to whether certain combinations of decision making style combinations lead, in accounting settings, to better
outcomes is an open issue which has not been subject to much research in the behavioral accounting research community (Gul, 1984; Hirsch & Bassler, 2010). This
approach could also represent a promising step in tracking further the (potentially)
ecological rationality of the observed complexity reduction strategies as adaptive
decision strategies.

4.4 Study 4: Choice reversal in management accounting – a quasi-experimental demonstration[98]

4.4.1 Introduction – the sure-thing principle

As mentioned in Chapter 1 (see also section 2.6, p. 63ff), some authors point out that members of the management control profession can be best thought of as chief information officers (CIO), whose function is to assure the rationality of the management (Link, 2002; J. Weber & Schäffer, 2008b). Consequently, they play a key role within organizational decision making, in requesting and evaluating incoming information (Alves, 2011; J. Weber, 2011a). The relevance of a CIO within an organizational setting can, in particular, be seen in one of the most robust findings related to psychological judgment and decision making (JDM) research:The way in which (objectively similar) information is presented (e.g. framing) hugely influences the direction of choice and decisions (e.g. Bazerman & Moore, 2009). For example, the order or reference classes in which a management controller presents information to the management can have a huge impact on the whole organization (Bonner, 2008).

The occurrence of order effects – like recency or priming effects (Hogarth & Einhorn, 1992) – in judgment and decision making indicate violation of classic normative standards of rationality, which are summarized in five axioms (Fishburn, 1981):

  i.   Order of preferences

  ii.   Choice of preferences

  iii. Transitivity of preferences

  iv.   Independence of preferences

  v.   Invariance of preferences

Order effects especially violate procedure invariance which assumes: "Normatively equivalent procedures for assessing preferences should give rise to the same preference order" (Tversky, Sattath, & Slovic, 1988, p. 371). As research has shown dif-

---

[98] An earlier draft of this study is also available online in SSRN's *Behavioral & Experimental Accounting eJournal* (see Basel, 2011). I kindly thank Rolf Brühl for fruitful comments and additional support regarding the statistical analysis of this study.

ferent elicitation procedures yield different preference orders or even more striking preference reversals (Hsee, Loewenstein, Blount, & Bazerman, 1999), I will concentrate on choice effects of information pursuit.

Despite some recent critiques, for leaving out context factors and for simply being too narrow (e.g. Gigerenzer, 1996), other concepts and approaches such as natural decision making (Lipshitz, et al., 2001) or ecological rationality (Gigerenzer & Todd, 2008) do not as yet have the same impact compared to this classic standard in JDM research (see Chapter 2 in this thesis, p. 15ff). The classic axioms (in particular the transitivity of preferences and the choice of preferences) are summarized by Stanovich (2010) as the "sure-thing-principle"[99] (Savage, 1954, p. 21) under the label "dominance". Stanovich describes this principle as follows (2010, p. 18):

> "Event X is an event that may or may not occur in the future. If you prefer prospect A to prospect B if event X happens, and you also prefer prospect A to prospect B if event X does not happen, then you definitely prefer A to B. Thus uncertainty about whether X will occur or not should have no bearing on your preference."

When a management controller is therefore portrayed as a rational agent, it can be concluded that he should fulfil the above criteria in terms of a rational decision. From this perspective, the focus of this study is to demonstrate that the daily task of management controllers with regard to acquiring and evaluating information can fundamentally depart from the above-mentioned classic axioms. In particular, it is argued that the transitivity of preferences is frequently not given in the light of newly acquired information. This assumption is based on a huge body of JDM research demonstrating that people frequently arrive at decision tasks with no clear preferences, and that the analysis of existing - and the acquisition of new information - is used to actually construct preferences (Shafir, et al., 1993; Slovic, 1995; Tversky & Shafir, 1992). For example, in evaluating the research and development (R&D) activities of a company, the sole number of patents is rarely enough to estimate if the company is performing well. Obviously the (chosen) comparison benchmark will set the stan-

---

[99] Shafir (1994, p. 404) even argues that this principle is "one of simplest and least controversial principles of rational behavior".

dard for estimating if the company is successful or not in terms of their R&D department. Consequently Bastardi and Shafir (2000, p. 216) argue:

> *"When internal attitudes are unclear, people construct or infer their attitudes partly on the basis of external cues, including their own behavior. (...) However, people can be unaware of the processes by which they reached those decisions. As a result, they are apt to misconstrue earlier decision behaviors and then form preferences consistent with such misconstrual, thus making choices they would not otherwise make."*

If your daily job as a management controller is to analyze and acquire information, it is important to distinguish different types of information (Bastardi & Shafir, 1998):

- Relevant information
- Non-instrumental information
- Instrumental information

For instance, if you want to buy a new car and it is important for you that you can plug-in your brand-new *Apple iPhone*, the information as to whether or not this is possible is relevant for you. If this information can influence whether or not you buy the car (in the event that there is no plug-in possible) this information is both relevant and influential. If you say: "Well it would have been nice to have the plug-in but, it is a great car anyway", the information is non-instrumental.

Studies in several contexts have shown that participants pursuing information are apt to weight this information higher than participants who have the information in the first place (Bastardi & Shafir, 2000; Redelmeier, Shafir, & Aujla, 2001; Young, Bauman, Chen, & Bastardi, forthcoming). However, only recently two studies in an accounting context have been conducted. Although Nelson and Tayler (2007) report that participants who created information by themselves weighted them more heavily, they did not find a choice effect.

In contrast, Smith, Tayler and Prawitt (2011) show that less experienced auditors weight in a high (litigation) risk situation more heavily and, thus, report a mitigating role of experience on choice effects. They concede that more research is necessary to clarify the role of experience under different contexts.

Another open question is which theory could address this information pursuit bias? Bastardi and Shafir propose for instance cognitive dissonance theory as one theoretical avenue to explain their findings which I will discuss in conjunction with the belief-adjustment model (Hogarth & Einhorn, 1992). This allows me to address my research questions with a social cognitive perspective. As a general framework I discuss dual-process theories and their unifying counterparts. As in detail described in Chapter 2 (p. 15ff), the overarching idea of this approaches is that of a human cognitive system which is capable of processing in different modes and constantly adapting this capability to its environment (Evans, 2008; Stanovich, 2010; Stanovich & West, 2000).

In this respect, two issues are important for this study: First, I distinguish between deliberate and intuitive processes of reasoning (as explained in section 2.7.3, p. 75ff) and judging where a deliberate process is identified with a rational, analytical, explicit and controlled process and intuitive processes are associated with a heuristic, holistic, implicit and automatic process. I will discuss the findings in the light of this dual processes. Second, I assume that intuitive processes interfere with deliberate processes. This is the social cognitive aspect: cognitive processes are influenced by social factors and hence will influence decision making (see as well the general framework of heuristic reasoning, Figure 18, p. 90)

To sum up, the contribution of this study is threefold: First, I show that participants are prone to wait for information if there is a possibility to do so. Second, participants who wait for information will give this information a higher weight and will decide in the direction of this information. Third, experienced will not differ from inexperienced management controllers in their behavior. Fourth, I frame our findings in social cognitive psychology and use a multi-processing approach to integrate our findings into behavioral accounting and into the overall framework on heuristic reasoning as laid out in Chapter 2 (p. 15ff).

4.4.2 Method

Participants and procedure

In total, 76 American and European graduate students[100] and accounting professionals participated in this between-subject design study.[101] The software *Rogator* was used as an online platform for this study. As web-based studies mostly allow no perfect control of all conditions, but as the independent variable was systematically manipulated, this study can be best classified as quasi-experimental (Birnbaum, 2000). As *Rogator* allows controlling for how long participants spend on the tasks, all participants that only took a glimpse at the task (i.e. spending only 40 seconds and less) were excluded from the study. In total, 53 participants remained in the sample. Overall, most participants belong in the age group between 26 and 30 years (range of 19 to 50 years), with 70% male and 30% female. As an incentive to participate in the study, there was a lucky draw of five Amazon vouchers involving all the participants, each worth 20 Euros.[102]

The participants received a short introduction telling them that they should imagine that they were employed in the accounting department of a large multinational company that now faces a series of problems, with regard to which important decision have to be made. In total, four different scenarios were presented to the participants. These scenarios were: an investment decision, an off-shoring decision, a fraud detection scenario and one scenario dealing with sunk costs.

The participants were separated into two groups as independent variables. Group one (A) received all the information related to the four independent accounting specific tasks right away. In group two (B), one part of the information basis was missing. These participants had the chance either to make the decision right away (without waiting for the additional information), or acquiring the additional information. This acquisition was also in some cases clearly labelled as expensive, but no "real" costs arose for the participants if they decided to wait for the extra information

---

[100] For the validity of students as surrogates for professionals in business studies, see Remus (1986). However, see also Ashton and Kramer (1980) for limitations in accounting settings.

[101] Design of the study is adopted from Bastardi and Shafir (1998).

[102] For the limited effects of financial incentives, see Camerer and Hogarth (1999).

4.4.3 Results

4.4.3.1 Scenario 1 – Investment decision

In group A (n = 22) the following scenario was presented:

Imagine you are working in the management accounting department of a large US brewing company. This company wants to enter the highly competitive German market. As a highly-skilled accountant you are asked by the CFO to evaluate various performance indicators (KPIs) of potential candidates for an acquisition. After an extensive search, you see one brewery called Prinzenbräu in Bavaria as a potential candidate. This brewery has a Return on Investment (ROI) of 13.79 % (which is really good), the sales rate is constantly rising and the brand awareness is almost 24%. However, the customer satisfaction with the main product is low, with only 13.2%. Do you:

    a) Recommend the acquisition to the CFO?   [73%]

    b) Don't recommend the acquisition to the CFO?   [27%]

In group B (n = 28) the following scenario was presented:

Imagine you are working in the management accounting department of a large US brewing company. This company wants to enter the highly competitive German market. As a highly skilled accountant you are asked by the CFO to evaluate various performance indicators of potential candidates for an acquisition. After an extensive search, you see one brewery called Prinzenbräu in Bavaria as a potential candidate. This brewery has a Return on Investment (ROI) of 13.79% (which is really good), the sales rate is constantly rising and the brand awareness is almost 24%. However, one thing you don't know at the moment is customer satisfaction. The consulting company you work with offers you the opportunity to wait one week at the end of which it will be able to deliver current numbers regarding the missing customer satisfaction. Do you:

    a) Recommend the acquisition to the CFO?   [35%]

    b) Don't recommend the acquisition to the CFO?   [0%]

    c) Wait one week (and learn about customer satisfaction) and then make your

       decision?   [65%]

If the participant chose (c) and decided to wait for the additional information the following information was then presented to him:

After one week you learn that the customer satisfaction with the main product is low, at only 13.2%. Do you.

  a) *Recommend the acquisition to the CFO?*   [46%]
  b) *Don't recommend the acquisition to the CFO?*   [54%]

Overall, the results (see Table 27 on the next page) clearly indicate that there is a high tendency for participants to acquire additional information. 65% of the participants in Group B chose to wait. However, this information might be non-instrumental if known right away. This is, in particular, relevant, as frequently information such as customer satisfaction has to be generated in a costly manner (e.g. through the help of external consultants). The external validity of this study is particularly interesting as, in real life, the amount of information that could be considered in an investment decision is almost unlimited.

As a first step of the statistical analysis, I compared the overall results of Group A and B which show that participants in Group B reversed the recommendation ($\chi 2$ (1, N = 50) = 3.4978, p < 0.06; w = 0.26).[103] This is in line with Bastardi and Shafir (1998) results, published in the *Journal of Personality and Social Psychology* (JPSP). However, I conducted further analysis. Comparing participants of Group B who did not wait for the information with Group A differ in their recommendation (p < 0.08);[104] this indicates that participants who do not wait see the omitted value of information as instrumental. Moreover, participants who waited for the information weighted this negatively labeled information and decided more often not to recommend the acquisition (p < 0.001; w = 0.56).

---

[103] I report effect size based on Cohen (1988) where w = $\sqrt{\dfrac{\chi^2}{n}}$ with small effect sizes (w = 0.1), medium effect sizes (w = 0,3) and large effect size (w = 0.5).

[104] As recommended by Hays (1994) I use Fisher exact test in case of a cell value lower than 5 and report only p-values of this test.

Table 27: Percentage of participants that recommended acquisition in condition 1 versus condition 2 in scenario 1

Condition	decision	Time of decision		Total
		Immediately	After acquisition (65)	
All Information available	recommend	73	n.a.	73
	don't recommend	27	n.a.	27
Chance for acquisition	recommend	35	11	46
	don't recommend	0	54	54

$\chi 2$ (1, N = 50) = 3.4978, p < 0.06*; w = 0.26

As expected, a t-test shows (t(48) = 2.047, p < 0.05) that participants in the uncertain situation need more response time with a medium effect size (d = 0.58).[105] Moreover, I created a slow and fast group based on above and below average response time and an experienced and an inexperienced group based on above and below average practical experience (measured with a 5-point Likert scale).

A Fisher exact test reveals that experienced participants are more often in the fast group (p_{Fet} < 0.01; w = 0.54). Overall, this indicates that experienced participants cope faster with the uncertain situation.

Further, I find evidence for a tendency to decide fast in the direction of the missing information. Participants who do not recommend the acquisition made this decision fast (p_{Fet} < 0.05; w = 0.56). I do not find significant evidence that experienced differ from inexperienced participants (p_{Fet} = 0.18; w = 0.52) in their decision after waiting. However, I do find a large effect size, which indicates that inexperienced do more often not recommend the acquisition.

---

[105] I report effect size based on Cohen (1988), where d = $\dfrac{\mu_A - \mu_B}{\sigma}$ with small effect sizes (d = 0.2), medium effect sizes (d = 0.5) and large effect size (d = 0.8).

4.4.3.2 Scenario 2 – Off-shoring decision

In group A (n = 22) the following scenario was presented:

> *Imagine your company considers launching an off-shoring project in Poland which would save a serious amount of money. You and your accounting team analyze various data from other competitors who have done the same, and come to the conclusion that one critical factor regarding the success in these projects seems that the off-shoring project is led by a local. In your company you know of one experienced top manager who is bilingual and also holds a degree from the Warsaw School of Economics and who seems perfectly suited for this job. As a backup plan you think of a young professional who has just finished his trainee programme in your company, but who is also a Polish native speaker. After consulting these two candidates, you unfortunately find out that the top manager will leave to a work for a competitor. However, the young professional would be available for this job. Do you:*
>
> *a) Recommend the launching of the off-shoring project to the CFO*   [52%]
> *b) Don't recommend the launching of the off-shoring project to the CFO*   [48%]

In group B (n = 28) the same scenario was presented. However, it differed in the end as follows:

> *(...) There are some rumours that the senior manager might not be available for this position. The younger candidate however would be definitely available. Do you:*
>
> *a) Recommend launching the project to the CFO?*   [10%]
> *b) Don't recommend launching the project to the CFO?*   [1%]
> *c) Consult the senior candidate as to whether or not he would be available for the position?*   [89%]

If the participant chose (c), and decided to wait for the additional information, the following information was then presented to him:

> *After consulting these two candidates, you unfortunately find out that the top manager will leave to work for a competitor However (as was known), the young professional would be available for this job. Do you:*
>
> *a) Recommend launching the project to the CFO?*   [45%]
> *b) Don't recommend launching the project to the CFO?*   [55%]

In this scenario more qualitative pieces of extra information could be acquired (e.g. information regarding the availability of management capacity). Again, a majority of the participants in Group B (86%) choose to wait for the extra information. Again, this information might be instrumental if known right away.

First, I compared the overall results of Group A and B which show that participants in Group B reversed the recommendation but find no significant result and a small effect size ($\chi2$ (1, N = 50) = 0.6743, p = 0.41; w = 0.11). Comparing participants of Group B who wait for the information with Group A shows no significant result ($\chi2$ (1, N = 46) = 1.3441, p = 0.27; w = 0.17).

However, as the extra information has to do with the age of the manager who will be sent to Poland, I constructed to groups based on age ("young" ranging from 18 to 30 years and "old" ranging from 31 to 50 years). I expect that the group of the younger participants will not reverse their decision and on the contrary, older partici-pants will be more impressed by the information that the experienced manager will not be available any more. As expected in the latter group 66% participants wait for the information and although due to sample size I did not find significant results (p = 0.15). I did nevertheless find a medium effect size (w = 0.4). The "bad news" regard-ing the senior manager leaving the company leads a majority of older participants to not recommend the off-shoring project. However, the young participants interestingly do not reverse their choice (p = 0.22) with a small effect (w = 0.06).

Table 28: Percentage of participants that recommended a project launch in condition 1 versus condition 2 in scenario 2

Condition	decision	Immediately	After waiting (86)	Total
		Time of decision		
All Information available	recommend	55	n.a.	55
	don't recommend	45	n.a.	45
Chance for acquisition	recommend	11	32	43
	don't recommend	3	54	57

$\chi2$ (1, N = 50) = 0.6743, p < 0.41; w = 0.11

Again a t-test shows $(t(48) = 2.047, p < 0.1)$ that participants in the uncertain situation need more response time with a medium effect size $(d = 0.51)$. Fisher's exact test reveals that experienced participants are more often in the fast group $(p_{Fet} = 0.11; w = 0.33)$. Moreover, I find evidence for a tendency to decide fast in the direction of the missing information. Participants who do not recommend the acquisition made this decision fast $(p_{Fet} = 0.11; w = 0.37)$. I do not find evidence that experienced differ from inexperienced participants $(p_{Fet} = 0.64; w = 0.14)$ in their decision after waiting.

4.4.3.3 Scenario 3 – Fraud detection

In group A $(n = 22)$ the following scenario was presented:

> *Imagine that you work in the accounting department and you are responsible for checking the sales reports of your subsidiaries. One of your subsidiaries in Hungary has performed pretty well over the last few years, with an annual sales growth of 7% (which is really outstanding for your industry). After the first monthly reports of this year arrive, you discover that approximately 150,000 € are paradoxically missing each month in the business report. Do you:*
>
> *a) Report this as an indication of fraud at the next board meeting?*   [68%]
> *b) Don't report this as an indicator of fraud at the next board meeting?*   [32%]

In group B $(n = 29)$, the same scenario was presented but which differed in the end:

> *(...) Despite the amazing growth you discover some irregularities within the reports. Do you:*
>
> *a) Report this as an indication of fraud at the next board meeting?*   [31%]
> *b) Don't report this as an indicator of fraud at the next board meeting?*   [17%]
> *c) Contact an external and expensive auditing firm to closer analyze the reports?*
>   [52%]

If the participant chose (c), and decided to wait for the additional information, the following information was then presented to him:

> *After the auditing firm closely analysed the monthly reports for this year, they discovered that approximately 150,000 € are paradoxically missing each month in the business report. Do you:*

> a) Report this as an indication of fraud at the next board meeting? [100%]
>
> b) Don't report this as an indicator of fraud at the next board meeting? [0%]

In this scenario it was explicitly mentioned that additional information comes at a cost ("external and expensive auditing firm"). This could account for the reason that in this case, less participants compare to the previous studies decided to contact the auditing firm (54%). Contrary to the first two studies I expected the participants in Group B to decide to report (recommend) even stronger than Group A. I compared the overall results of Group A and B which show that participants in Group B were almost in line with Group A ($\chi2$ (1, N = 50) = 2.2068, p = 0.14; w = 0.21). However, after waiting I find significant results (p < 0.02) with a medium effect (w = 0.4). Interestingly, the participants – after learning about the missing sum – did all report this issue to the board. They weighted the same pieces of information more heavily which enforced their tendency to report.

Table 29: Percentage of participants that recommend to report or not to report in condition 1 versus condition 2 in scenario 3

| Condition | decision | Time of decision | | Total |
		Immediately	After waiting (54)	
All Information available	report	68	n.a.	68
	don't report	32	n.a.	32
Chance for acquisition	report	32	54	86
	don't report	14	0	14

$\chi2$ (1, N = 50) = 2.2068, p < 0.14; w = 0.21

Results of the t-test get almost significant (t(48) = 1.641, p = 0.11) and show that participants with all information need less response time with a medium effect size (d = 0.47). Due to the small sample size Fisher's exact test results are not significant (p_{Fet} = 0.21; w = 0.27). In this scenario all participants who waited decided to report the fraud from which 60% decided fast.

4.4.3.4 Scenario 4 – Sunk costs

In group A (n = 22) the following scenario was presented:

> The company you work for has invested the past three years in an ambitious project in Eastern Europe. So far, over 100 billion Euros have been spent in buying a company, re-

building the infrastructure and hiring new workers. In the first year, the loss was around 40 million, in the second year the loss was 30 million, while in the third year the loss was 25 million. After these three difficult years, the CFO asks you if you think the investment is still worth the effort or if it should been sold for 80 billion Euros. Thinking about this issue you find out that there are losses of 0.5 million predicted for this year. Do you:

    a) Recommend the CFO to sell the company for 80 million €?   [23%]
    b) Don't recommend the CFO to sell the company for 80 million €?   [77%]

In group B (n = 29), the same scenario was presented. However, it differed in the end as follows:

(…) The most recent reports have not yet arrived, but you could wait a couple of weeks until the annual predictions are more accurate. Do you:

    a) Recommend the CFO to sell the company for 80 million €?   [35%]
    b) Don't recommend the CFO to sell the company for 80 million €?   [0%]
    b) Wait a couple of weeks until the predictions are more precise?   [65%]

If the participant chose (c) and decided to wait for the additional information, the following information was now presented to him:

(…) After a couple of weeks the analytic forecasts suggest that there are losses of 0.5 million € predicted for this year. Do you:

    a) Recommend the CFO to sell the company for 80 million €?   [17%]
    b) Don't recommend the CFO to sell the company for 80 million €?   [83%]

All participants (100%) who had the chance to pursuit new information waited for it. Although the tendency to recommend not selling the company increased slightly from 77% to 86%, there is no significant result ($p_{Fet} = 0.48$; w = 0.11).

This was the only scenario were no choice reversal occurred. However, the tendency to recommend not selling the company increased from 71% to 83%. From a classic sunk cost perspective (Arkes & Blumer, 1985), these costs are irreversible, and should not be relevant in a rational decision. The tendency observed here can be put in line with this seminal research that new information is valued higher than existing information. However, the amount of the new information compared to the other information was probably too small as to matter.

Table 30: Percentage of participants that recommended to sell or not to sell in condition 1 versus condition 2 in scenario 4

| Condition | decision | Time of decision | | Total |
		Immediately	After waiting (100)	
All Information available	report	23	n.a.	23
	don't report	77	n.a.	77
Chance for acquisition	report	0	14	14
	don't report	0	86	86

$p_{Fet} = 0.48; w = 0.11$

Results of the t-test are not significant ($t(48) = 1.178$, $p = 0.25$) and show that partici-pants with all information need less response time with a medium effect size ($d = 0.34$). Due to the small sample size Fisher's exact test results are not significant ($p_{Fet} = 0.41$; $w = 0.18$). Neither do I not find evidence that fast decisions, compared to slow decisions, are more likely to yield not to recommend selling the company. Nor do I find evidence that experienced differ from inexperienced participants ($p_{Fet} = 0.27$; $w = 0.28$) in their decision after waiting.

4.4.4 Discussion

In this quasi-experimental study ($n = 50$), using a between-subject design, I found evidence that the acquisition of new information, even if it is noninstrumental, fre-quently leads to choice reversals (in 2 out of 2 scenarios) or to choice enforcement (in 1 out of 2 scenarios). I further illustrate that experienced participants decide faster under uncertainty than inexperienced participants. Moreover, I did not find significant differences between experienced and inexperienced participants in their decisions after waiting.

My results have important theoretical and practical implications for research and practice in management accounting. I show that noninstrumental information may become instrumental if management controllers decide to wait for this information. This indicates that preferences are constructed during the decision process and weights of attributes are influenced by the context.

Overall, I found that participants violated procedure invariance as one of the basic assumptions of rational choice theory and they did so systematically, hence, this leads to the information pursuit bias. My findings are in line with the study of Bastardi and Shafir (1998) and of Redelmeier et al. (2001) who show that students as well as medical practitioners are affected by information pursuit bias. Due to the small sample size I report effect size, which is an indicator for practical significance and is less influenced by sample size (Grissom & Kim, 2005). Values of my effect size measures for information pursuit bias are in line with Redelmeier et al. (2001)[106]

Contrary to the findings of Smith, Tayler and Prawitt (2011), I did not find evidence that experience mitigates overweighting pursued information. There are two important caveats to this statement: First, my study did not have enough power to statistically rule out this mitigating effect of experience. Second, in one of the scenarios a medium effect size was found, which indicates that this mitigating effect may exist. However, although participants were exposed to simple and static tasks, which theoretically entailed a deliberate reasoning, overall I found they succumbed to the information pursuit bias. This raises questions about how different processes interact according to dual-process theories (see as well section 2.7.2, p. 70ff).

I suggest that according to cognitive dissonance theory (Festinger, 1962) intuitive processes may rule out deliberate processes because they are automatic and unconscious.[107] My explanation rests on the claim that participants who acquire new information and do not include it in their choice will be influenced by cognitive dissonance. Thus, in order to avoid any unpleasant feelings associated with inconsistent or non-useful choices, they may decide to rely upon these new cues (and thus regard them as instrumental). Because these processes are unconscious it is not unlikely that even experts succumb to this bias.

Additionally, I based my theoretical framework on the belief-adjusting model (Hogarth & Einhorn, 1992), which is widely used in accounting research (Bonner, 2008), but I do not use their model of equations. Instead I borrow their qualitative

---

[106]   Also Redelmeier et al. (2001) do not report effect size in their study; I calculated the missing w-values in the same fashion as I have done in this study.

[107]   In their neuroimaging study, Westen et al. (2006) find evidence that emotional processes rule out rational processes.

arguments and adopt them to my setting.[108] Insofar, I extend this model to scenarios of sequential order with a time delay. To the best of my knowledge, this has not been done before. One advantage of this model is that it represents a process model of judgment and decision making (Payne & Venkatraman, 2011) and thus is an appropriate framework to study problems on information pursuit in management accounting.

Limitations and future research directions

This study has some limitations, and some open questions could not be answered within this design. The limitations are, for example, the mixed sample of both graduate students and professionals.[109] A comparison between these two groups however did not indicate any major differences (with respect to choice reversals in scenarios 1-3). Also accounting knowledge, which was considered as an additional control variable had no effect on the choices. With respect to the external validity of the study (Loewenstein, 1999), it is important to note that here a general tendency is described, rather than having the objective of presenting a perfect picture of a real life accounting task. That this tendency is however also observed in a real life setting is, for example, documented by various studies by McKenzie (2009, p. 21), concluding that "auditors also appear to be influenced by irrelevant information when they report intervals."

Open questions address in particular the stunning effect of new information. It could be speculated that, for example, accountability ("I acquired this information so I had better use it") could play a role in this case (Lerner & Tetlock, 1999). Another, more cognitive, explanation could be that a recency effect is that new information is simply more salient then existing information (Baddeley, et al., 2009). Another explanation could also be made by arguing that participants experience cognitive dissonance (Festinger, 1962) when acquiring new information and do not include it in their choice. Thus, in order to avoid any unpleasant feelings associated with inconsistent or non-useful choices, they may decide to rely upon these new cues (and thus re-

---

[108] For those readers familiar with this model, I see sensitivity parameters α and β as a possibility to incorporate social factors in the model.

[109] It is also likely that p-values would become more significant if the whole sample was just doubled (Hays, 1994). For this reason a particular focus on effect-size was made in the results section.

gard them as instrumental). The issue of timing and request could be integrated in a follow up study. Here, additional information will be presented to the participant at a later time – even though he has not actively asked for it. Doing so allows distinguishes between the effects of accountability and recency.

Future research could address this issue by including more open questions in the design or could replicate this study using a verbal-protocol base in order to analyse how participants react to this new information. Additionally, the role of budgets and actual information costs needs to be investigated further. In this quasi-experimental setting, only the verbal information that "information is costly" was given. It would be interesting to see how participants react if they have to pay for additional information, and if this even leads to stronger effects (Gino, 2008).

Open questions would also have the chance to further analyze if there is an information asymmetry between positive versus negative newly-gathered information. For example, it could be that a negative new number has a more dramatic effect with respect to choice reversal than additional positive information. This analysis can easily be connected with classic findings in prospect theory (Kahneman & Tversky, 1979), where losses were identified as "looming larger" when compared to adequate gains. Finally, what was not collected in this study were confidence ratings. It would be interesting to ask how confident participants were in making their decision, and if the additional information significantly raises confidence.

That people have a general preference to delay decisions, even if they received no additionally information, is demonstrated by Tykocinski and Ruffle (2003).[110] These authors link this tendency with people's preference to reduce uncertainty. Indeed, they find that subjects delaying their decisions were more insecure then those making their decisions right away. In their discussion, they suggest therefore firstly to further analyze the time of delay and secondly to consider the level of confidence which is necessary for making a decision.

Another open question is the link with ecological rationality (see section 2.3, p. 21ff). Some future research should therefore identify environments where it is an

---

[110] But see the results of Schwartz and colleagues (2002), indicating that additional waiting or additional information are not necessarily associated with more satisfaction or happiness after a decision is finally made.

advantage to adapt as a result of newly acquired information. Based on these findings, it seems that the chance to gather additional information makes this piece of information relevant and instrumental. With respect to heuristic reasoning, it could also be argued from this perspective that in some environments a decision should simply rely on the latest piece of information – like a heuristic of "take-the-last" (Gigerenzer, et al., 1999).

The results of the study offer some clear advice for management accounting practitioners. When acquiring potentially costly information, it seems worth asking yourself if this new information is just relevant or if it is actually instrumental. With respect to venture-capital decisions, Price (2007) for instance, points out that: "One needs to determine what information may prove critical to the decision at hand, and, therefore is worth waiting for, and what information is unlikely to affect (and thus need not delay) the decision at hand". Or, in the words of Simon (1978, p. 13), "We cannot afford to attend to information simply because it is there."

Finally, another open question also arises naturally from these findings: Is such a shift of preferences under certain circumstances an adaptive decision mechanism? In some environments, does new information have a higher validity than the already known information (for a recent experimental study investigating this issue see Garcia-Retamero & Rieskamp, 2009)? Maybe the quote by McKenzie (2003, p. 405) hints this direction: "When a rational model fails to describe behavior, a different rational model, not different behavior, might be called for."

5 Step II: Qualitative study

5.1 Understanding the decision process – a qualitative approach

Despite the critique and challenges for finding qualitative methods, there is a strong mandate in accounting research to use more field studies in order to better understand current research issues and phenomena (for an overview of literature see Byrne & Pierce, 2007). This appears to be particularly relevant to **the case of heuristic reasoning in management accounting**; for example, a recent survey by *Accenture* (2008) among 250 executives found that 40% of all decisions are not based on analytics but on pure judgment (see also Brouthers, Andriessen, & Nicolaes, 1998; Wailgum, 2009). According to this survey, 61% of the executives answered that they relied on judgment because good or adequate data is not available and 55% highlighted that their decisions were based on qualitative and subjective factors.

What this survey leaves open, however, is the nature of the subjective decisions (also called "gut decisions" in the survey) included in this 40%. Thus, this survey provides an interesting first view on the striking impact of these kinds of decisions, but it lacks a deeper understanding of what exactly is meant by "gut decisions" and intuitive decision making (see also section 2.7.3, p. 75ff of this thesis).

Additionally, the authors of the study point out that these kind of qualitative decisions clearly represent a deficit for the companies and that companies should rely more on analytical talent and appropriate IT infrastructure and databases to support decision making. However, as documented in detail in Chapter 2 (p. 15ff), one consequence resulting from ecological rationality is precisely that more information does not necessarily lead to better predictive quality (see the discussion on "fitting versus predicting" issue on pp. 38ff and Figure 10 (p. 40) respectively). That there is demand for a "deeper understanding" (Miles & Huberman, 1994) of decision making processes is also stressed by various scholars in behavioral accounting research. For instance, Shanteau (1989, p. 174) argues that "the goal should be to understand, not just describe, judgment and decision processes (in accounting settings)".

Concerning the implementation of the ecological rationality approach by Gigerenzer et al. (2009; 2008) into a more applied setting, Neumer (2009) stresses that within this interaction model of environment and individual, the particular organizational environment has not been subject to a more detailed investigation. She additionally argues that one open issue concerns the question as to whether heuristic reasoning is actually possible within an organization. According to her, the surprising efficiency of particular heuristic solutions is no guarantee that they can also be applied in various institutions.

In order to secure this "deeper understanding" (Miles & Huberman, 1994) component, one crucial part of high-standard qualitative research is proper case selection. According to Ryan, Scapens and Theobald (2002) theoretical considerations guide the case selection (and not statistical ones). The eight cases analyzed in this study were selected using this suggestion, referring to the results of the quantitative section (see Chapter 4, p. 109ff), the theoretical framework of the decision making processes of bounded rational agents within organizations (see Chapter 2, p. 15ff) and the goals of applying a mixed methods design (Chapter 3, p. 91ff).

Throughout the theoretical sampling, the goal was to maximize the differences along the timeline (from younger to more established startups, from CEOs (managers) to controllers) and not to focus on a particular branch or industry (see Glaser & Strauss, 1967 for a discussion of maximization and minimization strategies in qualitative research).

As discussed in detail in Chapter 3 (p. 91ff), the priority of this thesis is a QUANT → qual. design, following a **deductive theoretical drive** (called model 8 by Morse, 2003), in sequential order. Thus, the central focus of the qualitative analysis is to better **explain quantitative findings** (Steckler, et al., 1992) and thus better answer open issues like the **applicability of heuristic solutions in organizational settings** and the **conceptualizations of rationality in the field** of management accounting.

Yin (2009) suggests various types of case studies.[111] Using these different suggestions, the following study is best characterized as a **descriptive case study**. This approach emphasizes the analysis of multi-dimensional phenomena in real-life contexts. With respect to the topic of this thesis, the principle research questions (see section 1.2, p. 3ff) of what triggers heuristic reasoning and what are the underlying concepts of rationality shall be investigated further. A deeper investigation of causal

---

[111] The following types are distinguished by Yin (2009): Exploratory case study, descriptive case study illustrative case study and explanatory case study.

relationships and specific configurations, which are characteristics of an explanatory study, is clearly not the goal.

5.2 Case selection and description

In order to find an organizational case study with high levels of uncertainty (which works best to represent non-routine, high-risk decisions), web-based startup companies from different fields (e.g. insurance/financial services, marketplace solutions) were chosen. A huge body of literature has documented the existence of, and some of the consequences of, this high level of uncertainty in startup companies (SuC) in various contexts (for management control systems in particular see Davila & Foster, 2007; see Katz & Green, 2011 for a general description of early-stage startup companies; E. R. Strauss, Nevries, & Weber, 2011 for another qualitative study analyzing control systems in startup companies). For instance Brouthers and colleagues (1998), analyzing 80 young firms, find that heuristics are widely in this field, used both on an individual level and in combination with more rational strategies.

The decision making processes and rationality assumptions in this field are then compared to those held by management controllers of middle to large size companies. These companies are expected to have mature management accounting systems and should thus ideally fit into the role of the CIO and rationality securer within the company (as described in detail in section 2.6, p. 63ff). The focus on startup companies (SuC, described in detail in Table 31 on the next page), besides the large and medium size companies, also has the pragmatic advantage of offering a greater chance of getting hold of top-management (CFO/CEO) members as interview partners. The downside of this focus, however, is that emerging organizations, up to a certain size, usually have no established management control system and the CEO or CFO often fulfills these functions. Davila and Foster (2005), for instance, argue that management control systems (MCS) are first introduced when the company has at least 17 or more employees. In the four analyzed cases, this applies for three out of the four cases. In order to include one young startup in the sample there was a need to make a trade-off. For this reason, the role of management controllers (Byrne & Pierce, 2007) is described from two perspectives: From the viewpoint of CEOs and from the management controllers themselves.

Table 31: Case descriptions

Name	Firm-Tag	Characteristics	Description
SuC 1	Education	Student support database (male, 27years, company founder, MSc in Business Studies)	This **emerging startup** (founded in 2008) offers online lectures, scripts and web-based tutorials for (college) students. Current priorities address the entrance into new European markets and the diversification of supply. Transfer of the web-based know-how for (public) institutions like Universities.
SuC 2	Insurance	B2B Insurance provider (male, 30 years, company founder, MSc in Business Studies)	This **emerging startup** (founded in 2008) offers risk analysis for environmental threats and insurance solution packages from partners. Their goal is to achieve higher planning security for their customers. Current priorities address the acquisition of new business partners and the development of prediction models.
SuC 3	Software	Web security solutions (male 36 years, company founder, BSc in Engineering)	**Established startup** (founded 2000) with international operations, offering web, mail and network security (coordinated multi-layer endpoint and network solutions UTM-unified threat management). Also appliances for public institutions like schools or mid-size companies.
SuC 4	Market-place	Products for young mums and babies (female, 35 years, company founder, MSc in Economics)	**Young startup** (founded 2010) offering marketplace solutions for baby clothes and the needs of young mums with up to 100.000 products. Current priorities are the design of various segments on the homepage and estimations of market volumes with respect to the collaboration with business partners in the marketplace.
MC 1	High-tech	Technical products support facility management (male, 48 years, 3 years with company, in-firm training finance and controlling)	**Medium size company** (1000 employees), founded 1927, emerging internationalization (since 2004 production and subsidiary in China), R&D and manufacturing of technical products supporting energy management, facility management. Europe wide activities and starting to penetrate Asian market.
MC 2	Recycling	Local company focusing on all areas of waste management (male, 30 years, 5 years with company, MSc in Business Studies	**Small size company** (120 employees) focusing on regional waste management), founded 1921 and family owned. Managing all aspects within the waste management supply chain (pick-up, separate, defibration, resell-sell). Overall only local to regional activities.
MC 3	Transport	Global player in railways and aircraft manufacturing (male 39 years, 8 years with company, MSc in Business Studies)	**Large company** (65.000 employees), revenue 17.71 billion $ (2011), focusing on mass transportation, aircraft and financial services. worldwide activities.
MC 4	Consumer Goods	Global Player, brand-oriented company (male 37 years, since 10 years with company, MSc in Management)	**Large company** (127.000 employees), revenue 82.56 billon $ (2011), focusing on manufacturing a wide range of consumer goods, worldwide activities

Nevertheless, a problem with validity will only arise if the suggested difference between managers and accountants (e.g. J. Weber & Schäffer, 1999) holds true. Assuming a similar cognitive architecture for both functions, the matter of heuristic reasoning in financial planning decisions (similar to those in Studies 1 to 4) should not be affected by this choice of case-study, particularly because the top management is frequently described as the key factor in setting up the management accounting system and their functions (Davila & Foster, 2005). Thus, the function/role of management controllers is reflected by the goals and concepts of the CEO/CFO and their concepts of rationality and the acceptance of heuristic solutions should also be reflected in their statements regarding these issues.

Overall, the basic procedure of the qualitative section of this thesis is based on the suggestions and guidelines by Eisenhardt (1989, p. 533) and Kvale (2007) and is specified for the particular research question of heuristic reasoning in management accounting, within a mixed methods framework.

Table 32: Qualitative research process based on Eisenhardt (1989)

Step	Activity	Reason
Getting started	Definition of research question/ a priori constructs	Provides better grounding of construct measures
Selecting cases	Theoretical, not random, sampling	Focuses efforts on theoretically useful cases – i.e. those that replicate or extend theory by filling conceptual categories (sharpens external validity)
Crafting instruments and protocols	Combination of qualitative and quantitative data	Strengthens grounding of theory by triangulation of evidence
Entering the field	Overlap data collection and analysis including field notes	Allows investigators to take advantage of emergent themes and unique case features
Analyzing data	Cross-case pattern search using divergent techniques	Forces investigators to look beyond initial impressions and see evidence through multiple lenses
Sharpening hypotheses	Search evidence for "why" behind relationships	Confirms, extends and sharpens theory
Enfolding literature	Comparison with conflicting/similar literature	Sharpens generalizability, improves construct definition, and raises theoretical level
Reaching closure	Theoretical saturation when possible	Ends process when marginal improvement becomes small

5.3 Data collection

Among the different possibilities for collecting qualitative data like document analysis or archival records (Yin, 2009), **structured interviews** (Rubin & Rubin, 2005) were selected in order to best answer the research questions and to further elaborate on the findings of the quantitative studies. All the interviews conducted, which last around 20 minutes on average each, were taped and afterwards transcribed. All the interviews were conducted in German but in order to secure a better reading flow of the thesis, all quotes were translated into English by the author. The commitment of the interview partners was secured through signing a form that stated that all information obtained during interviews will be treated as confidential and that the interviewees will be anonymous in the transcribed text.

5.3.1 Interview design and process

The interview process for (semi-) structured interviews can be separated into three basic steps: **Self-introduction**, **opening statement** and finally **detailed questions** (Kvale, 2007). In the first part, the interviewer introduces himself and the research topic (in this case a broader label, decision making in the particular company, was chosen. In the second part, issues in financial accounting[112], decision making and rationality concepts of the particular manager in each company were addressed in a generalized way. Finally, detailed questions regarding the use of heuristics in these contexts were addressed.

Overall, the interview is separated into four different sections (see Appendix p. 211ff for the full interview guide):

- **General decision making within the particular company in strategic financial accounting issues and rationality concepts:** This section analyzes the general interaction between financial planning (e.g. CFO, management controllers) and management, concerning strategic decisions and planning processes. Furthermore, in this section the interviewees are asked what they consider to be rational decision making and if they agree that management accounts can ex-

---

[112] As described above, not all young companies had established MCS. Consequently, the focus was in these cases broadened to include strategic financial decisions that would normally be fulfilled by management accountants.

hibit any form of rationality. This section concludes with asking the interviewees about the following influence factors that were identified in the quantitative section (see Chapter 4, p.109ff), namely time pressure, uncertainty factor, complexity and accountability.

- **Heuristics as a basis for making decisions:** First, the interviewees are informed what constitutes a heuristic decision (without any hint that this kind of decision mechanism can lead to good or bad outcomes). Then they are asked when they would use such a mechanism and to describe the process as accurately as possible (distinguishing between information search and information evaluation). Additional questions address issues such as learning and feedback regarding the applied strategies.

- **Integration of heuristics into organizational decisions:** In this part the influence of heuristics on broader decisions is analyzed. Interviewees are asked under which circumstances can heuristics influence larger decision processes. They are also asked if they can name any counterexamples in which another manager or accountant expressed a more intuitive view but was criticized for lack of rationality.

- **Individual decision making style:** A series of short open questions concerning the "rational" and "intuitive" dimensions from the GDMS (Scott & Bruce, 1995) are asked in this part. No quantification is intended; rather this is a control function to position the interviewee on these two dimensions.

These four sections represent both a reference towards existing literature on (heuristic) decision making (Baron, 2008) and their potential application in organizational settings. Moreover, the findings from the experimental studies (in particular studies 1 to 3) were integrated in the interview guide, allowing the eight cases to elaborate on the external validity of the results of the conducted studies, an issue frequently raised in experimental research in the social sciences (Loewenstein, 1999).

5.3.2 Transcription of the interviews

The interviews were digitally recorded and afterwards transcribed by an experienced research assistant and then additionally proofread by the author of this thesis as a double check. During the transcription process all personal information like names etc. were removed. The transcripts record literally the words spoken by the interviewees; only fill words, accents and involuntary vocalization were excluded for better reading purposes. In order to ensure a proper reading flow of the thesis, all quotes from the transcripts were translated into English. As the analysis of the transcripts was **content based** (cf. semantic analysis) and not an in-depth linguistic analysis (cf. latent analysis) this appears unproblematic. As suggested by Rubin and Rubin (2005), the interviewees had the chance to proofread the transcripts and to make additional comments on those transcripts. All of them accepted the transcripts in the form they were made. No additional comments or questions were raised in any of the eight cases.

5.3.3 Analysis of the interviews

As this study was clearly theory driven, its function is best described as an add-on of the experimental studies 1 to 4. The coding system was to a greater extent derived in a deductive, top-down way (Boyatzis, 1998). Overall, the analysis of the qualitative data can be characterized as a two-stage **thematic analysis** (B. L. Berg, 2004; Braun & Clarke, 2006; Burnard, 1991). Thematic analysis is defined by Braun and Clarke (2006, p. 80) as a method "for identifying, analyzing, and reporting pattern (themes) within data." It will be investigated, through the analysis of existing influence variables, how the themes interact (stage 1) and if new themes can emerge (stage 2). This is also done considering the overall framework of this thesis, which is summarized in Figure 18 (p. 90).

In **stage one ("coding")** the independent variables that have a demonstrable impact on heuristic reasoning were used as central reference points in analyzing the interviews. The more detailed analysis also included environmental variables. These variables included the description of the general decision making process within the company and the personal understanding of rationality in this context. As illustrated in Figure 24 on the next page, five categories and their related codes were deduced from the experimental studies and the existing body of research. These categories can be subdivided into two groups. The dark boxes refer to more **general decision making structures** on an organizational level (e.g. the openness towards advice-giving from other sources such as management controllers).

The grey boxes refer to **specific heuristic mechanisms** within the organizational context, for instance which types of strategies are used and how the success of these strategies is evaluated. Related to this issue is the question of how does the organization generate expertise and feedback. This is crucial for heuristic reasoning, when the link towards ecological rationality has to be made (see Chapter 2 p. 15ff). It is important in this context not to extend the topic towards general organizational learning. Rather, learning and expertise (as discussed in detail in Section 2.7.4, p. 79ff) are only analyzed with respect to the issue of heuristic reasoning in particular contexts. In order to get a better hold of the intensity and stages of the analyzed decision processes, some of the basic codes from Glaser's coding families (1978, described in Flick, 2005) were also included. These codes are: **Cause family** (including causes, consequences and correlations), **process family** (stages, phases and progressions) and **degree family** (amount, intensity, etc.).

Figure 24: Coding scheme based on a deductive top-down process

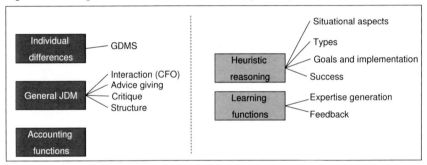

As the categories and the related codes were derived in a deductive manner, no inductive open coding (substantive coding) (Wrona, 2005) was conducted in this study, as the primary goal was not to come up with new names and identifications. Instead, the focus was on basic relationships in the first step and the development of a storyline in the second step.

In **stage two ("analyzing")**, the analysis is particularly concerned with the integration of the categories and the specification of the themes. The aim in the second stage is to develop a storyline around the four presented cases, with the goal being to reach a better understanding of heuristic reasoning in applied settings. The interplay of these two procedures and the specific goals are illustrated in Figure 25 (p.

182). In this stage, new themes can inductively emerge (Miles & Huberman, 1994) and categories can be clustered alongside identified themes.

The combination of these two stages resembles axial and selective coding, within the approach of grounded theory (A. L. Strauss & Corbin, 1998).[113] This is no coincidence, as thematic analysis can be seen as an adaptation of central grounded theory concepts (Burnard, 1991). For instance, according to Strauss and Corbin, axial coding, the second stage in the grounded theory approach, focuses on the following aspects that are also the goals of the first step of this thematic analysis:

- Causal conditions
- Contextual factors
- Actions and interactions taken in response to the phenomenon
- Consequences of actions and interactions

However, the theoretical assumptions underlying classic grounded theory are not shared in this thesis (see Braun & Clarke, 2006). For instance, the goal of this thesis is not to discover a new theory of heuristic reasoning that is somehow "grounded in the data". Furthermore, some elemental steps that are required for a proper grounded theory are not included in this study.

---

[113] These two techniques are part of the seminal concept of grounded theory (Glaser & Strauss, 1967). But for brevity's sake, only the two applied coding procedures are discussed here in short. For a detailed discussion of the application of grounded theory in accounting research in particular see Brühl et al. (2008), for a detailed grounded theory based study in Germany see Osann (2010) , or for management research in general see Douglas (2003).

Figure 25: Two stage thematic analysis procedure

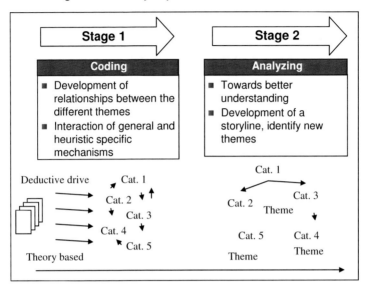

5.3.4 Some remarks on quality criteria in qualitative research

There is a long and ongoing debate (in particular in German speaking countries) regarding appropriate quality criteria in qualitative research that is often linked to the argument as to why some scholars prefer different methods over others (see Brühl & Buch, 2006; Kelle, et al., 1993; or Steinke, 2004 for an overview and critical discussion). In contrast to quantitative research, where precise measures for objectivity, reliability and validity are suggested (Bortz & Döring, 2006; Welkowitz, et al., 2002), much of this debate addresses the question as to whether the same criteria can be used for both paradigms (Altheide & Johnson, 1994).

For instance, as a prominent example, Lincoln and Guba (1985) suggest four central criteria (with only vague references towards quantitative standards) for evaluating qualitative research (the quantitative quality criteria counterpart is given in brackets): **Conformability** (objectivity), **dependability** (reliability), **credibility** (internal validity) and **transferability** (external validity).

The practicability of this approach (cf. using independent criteria for qualitative methods) is however criticized by Brühl and Buch (2006) for not being useful in a real research context. As suggested by these authors, in this thesis an approach for determining the standards of qualitative study is used that rather **resembles that used for determining quantitative standards.**[114]

Focusing on these standards is also helpful as it avoids the use of any of the conflicting criteria that are suggested for qualitative research. A more practical framework in line with this view is, for instance, suggested by Wrona (2005). This framework is particularly useful for this thesis as it is highly suitable for the qualitative content analysis (see also Mayring, 2003) of case studies (Miles & Huberman, 1994; Yin, 2009).

Thus, the following established quality criteria are used for the qualitative section of this thesis (for a detailed discussion of these criteria in an empirical mixed-methods study see also Horch, 2009):

- **Internal validity** (including construct validity). Within this criteria what is particularly important is what Yin (2009) calls "pattern matching", meaning that theoretical assumptions are challenged and further developed. Furthermore, consistency is tested with respect to a theoretical framework. In this work, internal validity is secured through the detailed theoretical foundation of what influences heuristic reasoning (see Chapter 2, p. 15ff) and the development of the interview structure throughout (see Appendix p.211ff). As requested by Yin (2009), the patterns observed in the four cases were compared with the theoretical basis of various decision making and rationality models. Additionally, the comparison with the quantitative studies (in particular 1 to 3, see Chapter 5, p.172ff) allows a solid standard of "explanation building" (Yin, 2009). Moreover, construct validity addresses the proper operationalization of the relevant variables and measures. This criteria is met, for example, through using some of the questions (namely the rational and the intuitive dimension) from the GDMS by Scott and Bruce (1995) as a basis for controlling the individual differences of the interview partner. The validity of this measure has also been recently supported by de Bruin et al. (2007).

---

[114] Other alternatives would be, as described above, to adopt independent criteria for qualitative research (Lincoln & Guba, 1985) or to skip this whole debate and reject any form of criteria, as suggested by proponents of a more constructivist view (Altheide & Johnson, 1994).

- **External validity.** Even if generalizability, in a quantitative sense, is not the goal of qualitative research (Brownell, 1995), case selection (contrasting cases, theoretical sampling) can offer the possibility of allowing some part of this criteria (Wrona, 2005; Yin, 2009) without using the large scale samples that are a prerequisite in deductive research models. This criteria is fulfilled in this work through focusing on the financial accounting aspects of web-based startup companies, where uncertainly is typically high (Davila & Foster, 2007; E. R. Strauss, et al., 2011). As the four cases can be placed on a timeline, theoretical implications that effect heuristic reasoning in the development of organizations can be drawn (Katz & Green, 2011).[115] Additionally other cases that investigate heuristic reasoning in business settings are integrated into interpreting the findings (e.g. Bedard & Wright, 1994; Krabuanrat & Phelps, 1998) and in developing the goal of a richer picture of heuristic reasoning in management accounting.

- **Reliability.** According to Flick (2006) this means that the data of the qualitative research process should be interpreted (and potentially replicated) by another scholar leading to the same findings. As replication is rather difficult in the context of this thesis, a rigid documentation of all research and interpretation steps of the qualitative study is adopted, in order to secure this standard. Transcripts, which form the basis for the interpretation process, are available for all four case-studies.[116]

- **Objectivity.** This is another criteria referring to the consistency of conclusions within the research process by two or more interpreters (Flick, 2006). The challenge with respect to this thesis, when securing this standard, is that a certain amount of theoretical JDM knowledge (e.g. concepts like ecological rationality, satisficing etc.) is absolutely essential when analyzing the interview transcripts. This is why some authors like Lisch and Kriz (Lisch & Kriz, 1978; cited in Merten,

---

[115] The reason to focus on these sorts of emerging organizations has mostly pragmatic reasons (e.g. the high impact of the individual decision maker on the organization, the possibility to get hold of top-level managers (CFOs) etc.) and thus this thesis should be seen as by no means addressing issues in the wide field of entrepreneurship, web-based startups, venture capital management etc. in detail.

[116] All quotes in this thesis are taken literally from the interviewee and interviewer. However, in order to improve the readability of the thesis, statements were translated from German into English.

1995) point out that this criteria (and respective reliability) should be excluded in qualitative research. Despite these doubts, I have tried to secure a satisfactory degree of objectivity by using established terms and theories only. These require a solid knowledge of the particular literature, which can be easily traced back through the references in this work.

Table 33: Quality criteria for qualitative research based on Wrona (2005)

Criteria	Proposition	Control in quantitative research	Possible application in qualitative research
Reliability	Degree of precision of a measurement	e.g. re-test, parallel testing etc.	Procedural reliability through explication (traceability of transcripts etc.).
Internal Validity (including construct validity)	Validness of variables within the model	Control of interfering variables	Falsification logic (search for counterevidence, use of specialized software such as *MaxQDA*).
External Validity	Generalizability	Representative sample	Theoretical sampling (maximum contrasting). Typification.
Objectivity	Results do not depend upon the researcher	Use of standardized methods and algorithms	Documentation of research process (reporting of subjective measures).

5.4 Qualitative results

The results of the qualitative study will be seen in line with the overall research design of this thesis (see Figure 26 on the next page). As described in the introduction of this thesis (see section 1.2, p. 3ff), the goal of this work is to shed some light on the phenomenon of heuristic reasoning in management accounting, considering various aspects of judgment, decision making and related issues such as the question of what constitutes rationality in business research. The qualitative study is particularly relevant for providing first insights on how the documented effects of heuristic reasoning could potentially manifest in "large worlds".

The literature on this issue is sparse, despite several calls to further analyze JDM in accounting from a more practical perspective (e.g. Shanteau, 1989), presenting an additional research gap that will be investigated in this thesis. The presentation of the results is oriented around the five deduced concepts, the related codes and the emerging themes. Overall, the qualitative data is analyzed with the focus of better understanding what can account for the existence (or non-existence) of the demonstrated causal relationships within the quantitative studies. This focus also guides that selected quotes from the transcripts.

Figure 26: Research design

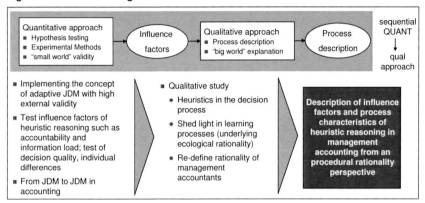

5.4.1 General decision making procedures and rationality conceptualizations

The first two themes that emerged out of the analysis of the interviews is the distinction between **ideal decision making and rationality** assumptions of the interviewees and the **applied decision strategies and mechanisms**. The interviewees, of the established and the emerging startups in particular, acknowledged that their decision making is strategic; financial decisions are frequently not guided by rationality standards. Rationality to them is typically defined through quantitative data and their precise compensatory analysis. However, the actual quality of this data is not mentioned. This view on rationality is very similar to one of classic economic rationality, as described in Chapter 2 of this thesis (p. 15ff). For example, the interviewee of SuC_02 points out that:

> "Rationality is for sure based on numbers." (Interview SuC_02)

In addition:

> "Without any sort of financial data I cannot make decisions" (Interview SuC_02)

Alternatively, the importance of the inclusion of numbers in making rational decisions is highlighted:

> *"Rationality is based on numbers and if decisions are number-based they are more likely to be rational than decisions that are based on gut feelings."* (Interview SuC_03)

As assumed through the case selection and the literature on decision making in startups (Katz & Green, 2011), the actual decision making did not match greatly with these rationality conceptualizations:

> *"Making rational decisions that are purely based on knowledge is, in the stage where we are right now, almost impossible."* (Interview SuC_02)

Or:

> *"There are some web-based startup companies where you have comparison data, but this is not the case for us. That is why our planning process is rather made-up out of thin air. Now a little less, but in the beginning it was extreme."* (Interview SuC_01)

These are typical statements that reflect the departure from self-set rationality standards in the daily tasks. The interviewees recognize that this standard is, in most cases, impossible to fulfill, but the statements lack a redefinition of rationality for their particular circumstances. For instance, in the case of the insurance company (HR_02), the interviewee stresses the novel circumstances in his area that make certain quantitative estimations impossible:

> *"There is a lack of historical data and no financial information or numbers to base your decision upon."* (Interview SuC_02)

Nevertheless, quantitative, number-based information and its optimal evaluation represents the gold standard for rational decision making and the fact that this is, in many cases, impossible for startup companies does not change this perspective. As uncertainty is particularly high for the young startup company (SuC_04), a slight difference in the rationality conceptualization is observed. Here the interviewee points out that in his particular business environment "trial and error" decision making are actually considered as rational and the importance is to be "honest to yourself and make improvements or leave the decision behind."

A departure from the number-based (ideal) strategy is, however, reported in different stages of the decision making process. The interviewees argue that they, both in information search and in information evaluation, use shortcuts in order to facilitate this process. That these sorts of patterns are documented elsewhere in this study (see results of Study 2, section 4.2.3.2, p. 132ff), supports the **existence of phased strategies** (H. Lee, et al., 1999) in high-stakes decision making (in terms of money and risk). However, the interview data could not reveal if there is a particular preference for compensatory followed by non-compensatory strategies or vice versa. In the case of the established startup SuC_03, a search mechanism is described using a compensatory-non-compensatory order, in novel circumstances:

> *"The process works that we systematically analyze the market. This is a very precise process, and then you look at certain aspects and make an instant decision."* (Interview SuC_03)

Interestingly one of the controllers included the need to rely on intuition in his definition of rationality, arguing:

> *"There is no such thing as 100% reliable data for predicting the future. So it's about estimating, balancing reasons and trying to make with your experience the right decision."* (Interview MC_01)

As in the startup companies, rationality typically included hard (financial) facts and numbers. However, the controllers seem to know that even numbers and bean counting does not reduce uncertainty to zero. In addition, one of the controllers points our that there are different ways of approaching a rational decision:

> *"For the management rationality is for sure more than this [financial data], because they want to consider or influence different factors. In our company brands play a very important role. Thus, you should also keep an eye on the customer in making the strategically right decisions. For example, from a mar-*

keting perspective. However, these factors are harder to quantify then the fi-
nancial impact of a decision." (Interview MC_04)

5.4.2 Accounting functions

As only the mature startup company has an established accounting system, the
other cases with the startup group address the issue of financial planning and cost
calculation. These kinds of tasks are usually fulfilled at a later stage (as in SuC_03)
by the accounting department. Thus, the interviews in SuC_01 to SuC_04 can be
seen as descriptions of what kind of roles an accounting system should have and
what roles the management controller should play within the company.

The interviewees from the startup companies see the role of the accountant as
that of a person providing a certain service, rather than that of an actual decision
maker. This service orientation of the accounting function is in line with the overall
framework of this thesis, that sees the function of management accounting as being
to assure the rationality (of the management) (J. Weber & Schäffer, 1999). This is
important insofar as, in this function, the operationalization of rationality for the management controller represents an important issue.

> *"The management accounting, in our case a single person, does not make de-*
> *cisions so that the management can decide, rather he provides numbers and*
> *maybe interprets them in his own view."* (Interview SuC_01)

Or:

> *"The management controller prepares options so that the management can de-*
> *cide (...). You basically deliberate how a project or an investment should look*
> *then the management controller provides different scenarios upon which the fi-*
> *nal decision is based."* (Interview SuC_03)

For instance, the results of study 4 (p. 158ff) on choice reversal and the tendency to
collect all available information becomes more relevant in the light of this conceptualization of management controllers. If their job is to prepare and interpret numbers
then it is a matter of fact that both potential biases and potential adaptive decision
mechanisms influence the company's overall decision making to a large degree.

The controlling professionals see themselves as well as advisors to the management and agree that they should assure the rationality of the management. However, they do not see controllers as decision makers. Rather they present different alternatives and challenge the decisions made by others. At the most, they are seen as "pre-decision makers" (MC_04). The rationality principle, as suggested by Weber (see section 2.6., p. 63ff) is seen as a accurate description of their role:

> "The quote of assuring the rationality is from Jürgen Weber, the rationality principle. This sounds a little bit academic, understood as: the controller should approve or disapprove the intuition of the management, I would agree with this statement." (Interview SuC_01)

5.4.3 Heuristic types and implementation

The interviews clearly indicate that heuristics and their popular connotation as "gut feelings" influence the strategic planning function to a large degree. This is the case both in startups (in line with finding from Brouthers, et al., 1998) and (more surprisingly) also from the controller perspective. However, the analysis of the qualitative data implies that a specification of these heuristics, in rather neutral terms, appears difficult for the interviewees.

For instance, no interviewee describes heuristic reasoning in the way of a "single cue decision rule" (Gigerenzer, et al., 1999). It is likely that the individual steps of a decision process are not usually identifiable, resembling the basic elements of the working memory (Baddeley, et al., 2009). It seems that the interviewees are not fully aware of where their gut feeling is actually coming from. Interestingly, in the mature startup (SuC_03) the interviewee points out that the influence of decisions arrived at by heuristics is so strong that it can later influence the information search and its evaluation:

> "You catch yourself with a decision that is made based on your gut feeling that is additionally verified and you make an analysis that is not really outcome oriented. But in many cases this is a speed advantage founder lead startups have." (Interview SuC_03)

The interviewees from both seem aware that there is a trade-off between high accuracy and the use of faster decision processes. In the mature startup (SuC_03), the

company policy is, according to the interviewee, that it is better to make five decisions fast and take the risk that one to two prove to be wrong than to wait too long
before making a decision.

The reported applications of heuristics are typically investment decisions and
forecasting scenarios, resembling the scenario used in studies 1 to 3. Interestingly,
even in high-stake decisions. For instance, one interviewee (MC_01) reports that a
large multi-million acquisition was based on a gut feeling of the management. Another controller (MC_03) point out that heuristics guide the forecasting process regarding the efficient distribution of resources and they are in particular used for discovering irregularities in different departments.

Using heuristics in making predictions is also a basic requirement for using them
in an adaptive way (see Chapter 2, on the distinction between fitting and predicting,
p. 38ff). In the emerging startup (SuC_01) in the education industry, the interviewee
gives the example that the development of new content areas is guided by a heuristic decision process and, in particular, the first step is to invest a certain amount of
time and to contact relevant business partners.

Furthermore, the success of particular advertisements is estimated using a heuristic rule ("just pick out a few channels and see if it works" [Interview SuC_01]).[117] The
interview partner of the insurance startup (SuC_02), points out that the high level of
uncertainty makes it absolutely essential to rely on gut feeling, however they try to
match their gut feelings with quantitative data. The gut feeling is in this way
"adapted". In the established startup (SuC_03), the further development of the product portfolio is directed by heuristic decisions:

> *"Products we like or that appear intuitively right to us will be developed or*
> *bought. The involvement of customers or partners is rather low in these cases."*
> (Interview SuC_03)

In the young startup (SuC_04), a very detailed description of an investment decision
in a new business branch is documented. The implementation of such a new busi-

---

[117]   The success of heuristics and analyzing customer activities has also recently demonstrated in a
series of empirical studies (Wübben & Wangenheim, 2008).

ness idea and the related financial investment is based on a heuristic decision made in the evaluation of certain information:

> *"Of course we will make a small test before implementing the decision to a larger degree. But the first decision to make this test is pure gut feeling to us. We believe that customers want such a product and a survey costs a lot of money and we don't know if people answer it honestly – so we can try it right away on our own."* (Interview SuC_04)

Here it becomes clear that in particular the very first step in the decision process can be triggered by heuristics (cf. gut feelings). This finding is in line with a large body of psychological research showing that simple action plans (or implementation intentions) can influence motivation and decisions over a longer period of time (Geen, 1995; Gollwitzer & Bargh, 1996; Mook, 1996).

5.4.4 Learning functions

In the case of the established startup, the interviewee stresses the importance of pattern matching. The described process resembles the concept of an adaptive decision mechanism in various contexts, where a certain form of recognition is positively related to the cue validity (Goldstein & Gigerenzer, 2002; Payne, et al., 1993). This learning function and pattern recognition is only mentioned by the established startup, which could be seen as a form of more mature and adaptive heuristic processes (Baylor, 2001).

> *"(...) you try to recognize particular patterns and I am sure that the matching works, meaning that you have already seen a similar one, even if it is not identical."* (Interview SuC_03)

In all analyzed cases from the startup group extended networks are used to gain additional expertise. Frequently personal information or advice is preferred over web-based sources. Thus, as discussed in Chapter 2 (see p. 15ff), small samples are preferred over larger samples (as long as the web-based source is an accumulation of data). The interviewees from the startup companies typically assume that this kind of source has a higher validity for investment related decisions.

"(…) if I am stocked up at a certain point, I contact my network or the associates, where we have a lot of experienced people. If it is a very precise issue im also browsing the web, but if decision have to be made and perspectives to be modified I prefer the personal level." (Interview SuC_02)

Interestingly, at a later stage of the interview in SuC_01, the interviewee points out that intuition and experience are closely related. This case indicates that there is some knowledge about potential mechanisms that allow adaptive decision making like in SuC_03 where the importance of "pattern matching" is stressed. Despite these relationships the meaning of rationality is not further modified e.g. if I see a well-known pattern I do not have to collect additional numbers etc.

The controllers of the startups are mostly older than the interviewees are and they report that they gather feedback from the management in a double-loop fashion. Interestingly, one interviewee (MC_01) highlights that learning occurs in particular then, when he leaves his desk and participates in meeting and exchanges with the management. He explicitly mentions that he searches for the decision algorithms that are used by the management in order to adapt his own decision making behavior. That trail-and-error learning is also commonplace in large companies as in startups is documented in interview with MC_03:

"We are typically learning through our mistakes. Concerning the forecast for instance, we used to take all information we received for granted and we had massive deviations. Based on that we calculated our own forecast system." (MC_03)

5.4.5 Individual differences

The items from the GDMS (Scott & Bruce, 1995) were used to get an impression of potential individual differences between the four cases. The responses, weighted either in favor of the statement (+; e.g. "quite often; basically all the time if it makes sense"), against it (-) or neutral (+/–) can be compared with the statements regarding the use of heuristics and the conceptualizations of rationality. What this inventory of course cannot measure is if there are differences between an ideal decision and how decisions are made on a daily basis. For instance one interviewee (SuC_03) acknowledges, with respect to item #4 (I make decisions in a logical and systematic way): "I wish I would to so, but this is for sure not the case all the time".

As mentioned above, the cases indicate that there are some discrepancies be-tween the way what is seen as a rational decision and the use of intuitive strategies and/or heuristics. For instance in all cases I found support for the statement of item #7 (*When making decisions, I consider various options in terms of a special goal*) within the rational dimension. At the same time the majority of the interviewees high-lights that they (at least partially) "trust their inner feelings" (Item #6), they rely upon their instincts (item #8) and their intuition (item #1). This tension between a norma-tive form of rationality and intuition is not only particularly strong within the analyzed field of startup companies, it is also found in the analysis of the interviews with the controllers.

Comparing the answers from both groups, with respect to individual differences, indicated that here we have the impression that the differences between these two groups can be seen as rather marginal. Only item #1 ("When I make decisions, I tend to rely on my intuition") points towards some differences. An explanation for this may be that the controllers overall agree with their role of assuring the rationality and thus are more reluctant to rely more on their intuition.

Table 34: GDMS responses of the eight cases[118]

		SuC 01	SuC 02	SuC 03	SuC 04	MC 01	MC 02	MC 03	MC 04
1.	When I make decisions, I tend to rely on my intuition (I)	+	+	+	−	+ / −	+	+ / −	+ / −
2.	When I make a decision, it is important to me to feel the decision is right than to have a rational reason for it (I)	−	−	−	−	−	−	−	+ / −
3.	I double-check my information sources to be sure I have the right facts before making decisions (R)	+ / −	+	+	+	+	+	+	+
4.	I make decisions in a logical and systematic way (R)	+	+	−	+	+	+	+	+
5.	My decision making requires careful thought (R)	+ / −	+	+	+	+	+	+	+
6.	When making decisions, I trust my inner feelings and reactions (I)	+ / −	+ / −	+	−	+ / −	+ / −	+ / −	+ / −
7.	When making decisions, I consider various options in terms of a special goal (R)	+	+	+ / −	+	+	+	+	+
8.	When making decisions, I rely upon my instincts (I)	+ / −	+ / −	+	+	+ / −	+	+	+ / −
9.	I generally make decisions that feel right to me (I)	−	−	−	+ / −	−	−	−	+
10.	I usually have a rational basis for making decisions (R)	+	−	+	+	+	+	+	+

5.4.6 Conclusion

The starting point for this qualitative study was that startup entrepreneurs often use intuition in making important decisions (Mitchell, Friga, & Mitchell, 2005). The high levels of uncertainty they face, the high financial risk and low organizational hierar-

---

[118] R = rational scale; I = intuitive scale within GDMS

chies makes this field a suitable area to study as well the role of heuristic reasoning and the need for assuring the rationality of the decision making process. This field can also ideally be contrasted with the decisions (and heuristics) made by controllers in larger companies. Overall, the results of the qualitative study indicate that the results of the experimental studies (in particular 1 to 3) also match those in "large worlds". Heuristics and intuitive strategies play an important role, also in large-scale financial investment decisions and in forecasting estimations within the analyzed cases. The described role of management controllers within the four companies (in the MC sample) is in line with Weber's et al. (1999; 1999) "assuring the rationality of the management" concept.

Following this framework (and following the results of the experimental studies within this thesis), heuristics can actually effect the organizational decision process at various stages. Firstly, when the accountant prepares the numbers and offers potential solutions to the management. Secondly, when the management picks one of these options. Consequently, the importance of analyzing adaptive decision mechanisms lay in particular in the interaction process between management and accounting department. Thus, considering both perspectives (manager and accountant) is considered as the most fruitful approach in investigating this dyad.

The content analysis revealed three main themes. On the one hand, the **conceptualization of rationality**, which is classical number based and includes an optimal evaluation of all (available) information. On the other hand, the second theme is the **actual decision process** (and the related use of heuristics). Despite the normative yardstick proposed by most the interviewees, they depart from it for various, well known, reasons (high uncertainty, information too expensive, competitive advantage of making fast decisions). All the influence variables, analyzed in the quantitative studies are seen as key factors in their decision making process. The third theme is the description of **decision processes as phased strategies**, where compensatory strategies are combined with non-compensatory ones.

Figure 27: Identified themes

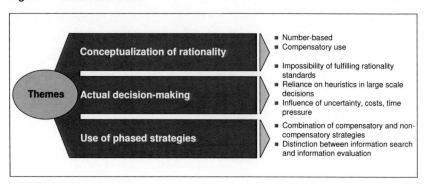

As mentioned above, the limitations of this study include the difficulty to reason from the analyzed sample upon the more complex decisions made in large accounting departments (even if some controllers were included in the sample). Young startups have no established accounting standards and only the more mature company (SuC_03) had a real management accounting system. However, the decision making of the CEOs highly determines of what kind of system is later adopted (Davila & Foster, 2005) and what kind of risks the company is later willing to take (and in particular based on what kind of data basis).

Future research should in particular address the issue to deeper understand adaptive decision mechanisms in this kind of setting. Some of the cases clearly point out the importance of pattern recognition and experience when relying on intuitive strategies etc., but no substantial redefinition of rationality (or the function of management controllers respectively) occurred. The second issue that future research should take into account is the interaction of management and accounting department at the later stage of the company and if rationality is actual defined in different ways by both parties; or how far the original conceptualization of rationality of the founder determines the role of the management controller.

Emerging psychological concepts like dual process theories (see 2.7.2, p. 72ff) and recent emerging research topics like self-other decision making (see 2.7.6, p. 88ff) provide a valuable (theoretical) starting point for analyzing these kind of issue and to further deepen the understanding of heuristic reasoning in accounting related settings.

6   Final summary and conclusion

6.1 Contributions and added value of the overall work

Within this thesis, the (empirically demonstrated) research gap (the lack of process models within behavioral accounting research, using current JDM models and concepts) is approached by the analysis of heuristic reasoning in management accounting. This was done through the combination of quantitative (mostly experimental) and qualitative methods (structured interviews) in a so-called mixed methods design. The five empirical studies were guided by five overall research questions (see section 1.2, p. 3ff), which addressed aspects such as: when are heuristics used, and if there is evidence for their adaptive character in accounting settings. Furthermore, the role of individual differences was addressed and a description of the search strategies from a process perspective was provided.

Contributions from the conceptual part (Chapters 2 and 3)

The analysis of research on heuristics and heuristic reasoning published in leading accounting journals (see Table 6, p. 61) revealed that there is a constant (slightly increasing) stream of research on this issue. However, to a large degree, these publications are duplications of classic findings in the heuristics and biases tradition, and have merely been transferred into accounting settings (this critique is already stressed by Hogarth, 1991). Scholars in this field rarely point out potential benefits from departures of economic rationality and economic models (for an empirical exception see Bedard & Wright, 1994; Lingnau, 2006; Lingnau & Walter, 2011 for an exception regarding the theoretical perspective).

However, there are at least some scholars that recognize that there is a mismatch between the requirements of unbounded rationality and the uncertainty and increasing complexity of the modern business world. For instance Luft and Shields (2009, p. 275), on the one hand, in their recent review of psychology models of management accounting, highlight: "Decisions that use non-compensatory models are not based on all of the available information are therefore likely to result in poorer decisions." On the other hand, the same authors Luft and Shields stress (p. 210) (even in the same review): "We often do not know whether the solutions provided by simplified economic models in fact perform better in complex natural settings than decision makers' cognitively simplified decision models do."

The buzzword of adaptive decision making (Payne, et al., 1993) is nevertheless rarely mentioned in behavioral accounting research and if it is mentioned, it is within the context of second best decisions (e.g. Bonner, 2008; Luft & Shields, 2009; Shanteau, 1989; Trotman, et al., 2011). This is surprising, as management accounting deals, by definition, with the optimal and efficient distribution of (limited) resources (see for example Brühl, 2009) and heuristics represent exactly this (defining cognitive effort, time and money as potential resources) (Conslisk, 1996).

Thus, the contribution of the theoretical part of this work is to introduce and integrate emerging concepts like ecological rationality (for a definition see Rieskamp & Reimer, 2007) and adaptive decision strategies (e.g. Gigerenzer, 2002) and linking them with pressing issues in behavioral accounting research. This sort of rationality conceptualization can outline under what circumstances departures from economic rationality can lead to efficient decisions.

Additionally, this more open framework, as laid out in this thesis, integrates findings and conceptualizations of current cognitive research that are seen as key concepts in investigating and interpreting JDM processes. These concepts are for instance the dual process model approaches (for an extensive review see Evans & Frankish, 2010) and emerging areas of research such as self-other decision making (for a recent review on this issue, see Bonaccio & Dalal, 2006). Together with traditional fields within a behavioral accounting research focus like expertise (e.g. Snowball, 1980), this theoretical framework (see Chapter 2, p. 15ff, of this thesis for a detailed description) allows behavioral accounting researchers to better classify their own research into the various existing streams and traditions in behavioral accounting research and to add recent tendencies and findings from cognitive and social psychology.

For instance concepts such as intuition or intuitive decision strategies are frequently vaguely defined in many business studies (including behavioral accounting research), whereas current psychological research provides a detailed definition and measures for this phenomena. In a review of psychology models of management accounting by Luft and Shields (2009), the case of deliberative versus intuitive decision making is also identified as an emerging theme in this field highlighting the importance for more detailed theoretical frameworks such as those proposed in this thesis.[119]

Generally speaking, concepts such as ecological rationality and adaptive decision making represent important new directions for JDM research and the relevance for behavioral accounting research is documented in this thesis. That behavioral accounting researchers should integrate this kind of progression is also highlighted by Bonner (1999, p. 395), who argues: "Studying JDM issues in accounting requires an understanding of the logical progression of JDM research in general and the peculiarities that an applied field adds to this logical progression." With respect to the German accounting community, Hirsch (2007) even laments that behavioral accounting research in general is totally underdeveloped in this national community. Consequently, introducing more crisp psychological concepts as described here represents a chance for increasing research activity in behavioral accounting research.

The contribution with respect to the methodology of the chosen mixed methods approach (Tashakkori & Teddlie, 2003) is the linking of the "small worlds" of the experimental tasks in Study 1 to 4 with the "large worlds" of the analyzed qualitative cases from Study 5. This kind of combination is rarely documented in general JDM research, despite the repeating call to analyze JDM processes in accounting also in more applied settings (Bonner, 2008) and the documented prevalence of non-compensatory strategies in top-management decision making (Accenture, 2008; Wailgum, 2009) or in high stake trading decisions (Haug & Taleb, 2011). The challenge of transferring JDM findings into a broader (organizational) context is as well recently picked up by Staw (2010, p. 411), who argues that:

> *"Many of the limiting factors [of transferring JDM findings into organizational/business settings] stem from well-known problems of ex-*

---

[119] Luft and Shields (2009) also mention main themes in existing behavioral accounting research. These are: framing and reference points (subjective valuations of management accounting related monetary payoffs); social influence on management accounting (subjective valuations of non-monetary payoffs); limitations on learning (acquiring and subjectively estimating parameters and variables in management accounting related decision models) and predictably simplified subjective decision models for management accounting related tasks.

ternal validity. Others result from the paradigm of laboratory based JDM studies, where a phenomenon is distilled to its narrowest form and contextual variables are systematically removed. In its search for parsimonious cause-effect relationships, JDM research often misses (or willfully avoids) many of the most crucial elements of work behavior, making judgment and decision research less interesting and relevant to organizational researchers."

In order to increase the relevance of JDM findings for more macro settings, Staw (2010) suggests that scholars in JDM should consider integrating qualitative methods in their research designs. Providing a theoretical basis for this sort of research design is another major contribution of this work. The justification for this kind of method combination from a philosophy of science point of view, is described in Chapter 3 (p. 91ff), referring not only to a pragmatist angle (for a summary of this standpoint see Hookway, 2008) but also on the necessity of the research context (Brühl, 2010) and classifying research on heuristic reasoning within the larger context of evolutionary (psychological) based approaches (Buss, 1995).

Consequently the notion of bounded rationality as proposed by Simon (e.g. 1990) is in its evolutionary connotation not subject to falsification, rather, the argument that this sort of cognitive (hard-wired) limitation leads to a series of unavoidable systematic lapses in human judgment, is questioned. This course of action relies of the framework of Imre Lakatos "proofs and refutations" (Lakatos & Musgrave, 1970), in which the core theory (here, evolutionary theory) is not subject to direct criticism. Rather the protective belt of assumptions (here, the consequences resulting from bounded rationality) that are based on this theory is subject to critique. This allows the integration of diverse concepts such as ecological rationality and heuristics and biases.

Contributions of the empirical studies (Chapters 4 and 5)

Various scholars point out that the (in particular German) management accounting community lacks empirical studies that build on emerging trends within the field of psychology and cognitive sciences (e.g. Hirsch, 2007; Hogarth, 1991; Lingnau & Walter, 2011). The four quantitative studies (described in Chapter 4, p. 109ff) and the qualitative study (described in Chapter 5, p. 172ff) build on the theoretical foundation laid out in Chapter 2 (p. 15ff) and can thus be seen as a response to this call.

The particular contribution of the empirical studies is that they integrate various relevant variables within management accounting JDM research, combining classic lab experiments (for a discussion of psychological methodology see also Kempf, 2006) with other methods such as verbal protocols (Ericsson & Simon, 1993) and web based quasi-experimental investigations (Birnbaum, 2000). This eclectic multi-method approach (and adding a qualitative cross validation with Study 5, p. 176ff) reduces the risk of little external validity (Loewenstein, 1999) and allows a description of a more complete picture of heuristic reasoning in management accounting.

In line with classic studies in JDM and information processing in management accounting (e.g. Lewis, et al., 1983; Payne, 1976b; Shields, 1980) the studies support the finding of general preferences for heuristic solutions in accounting settings. However, the interpretation and analysis of the findings goes beyond these classics. For instance, the introduction of less-is-more effects (Basel, 2010; Gigerenzer, 2006), adaptive decision making (and also the information pursuit bias in Study 4, p. 158ff) has so far not been documented in behavioral accounting literature to the best of my knowledge. Additionally, the findings of the empirical studies (in particular Study 2, p. 129ff) allow integration of the application of (potentially adaptive) heuristics within the model of phased strategies (H. Lee, et al., 1999) in decision making. This transfer is novel to behavioral accounting research and represents another contribution of this work. Additionally, this study represents an approach to provide a more process oriented description of JDM in accounting settings (as requested for instance by Payne & Venkatraman, 2011). To my knowledge the process description has mostly been ignored in existing accounting JDM research (Trotman, et al., 2011).

Many scholars in behavioral accounting research (e.g. Shields, 2002) assume that the task is the most relevant factor in analyzing the decision making processes of management accountants. However, the results of Study 3 (p. 144ff) clearly indicate that a dependent decision making style (using the GDMS by Scott & Bruce, 1995) matters in contexts were accountability is high. Whereas this finding is not surprising from a psychological perspective (see Lerner & Tetlock, 1999), this stunning effect has been mostly excluded within current behavioral accounting research. Combining behavioral accounting topics with appropriate and validated instruments, such as the GDMS (for a validity analysis see Bruine de Bruin, et al., 2007; Scott & Bruce, 1995), represents a fruitful approach for accounting research.

The major contribution of the qualitative study and the conducted thematic analysis (Braun & Clarke, 2006) is the finding of the mismatch between ideal rational decisions and their application in applied contexts. It seems there is some sort of naturalistic rationality, which is the "applied" version of rationality in business settings and economic rationality that is based on the classic axioms described in Chapter 2 (p. 15ff).[120] Despite the impossibility of fulfilling the standards for a perfect rational decision, the interviewees surprisingly saw this form of economic rationality as their benchmark for a rational decision. So even if a concept like ecological rationality exists in the models of some psychologists or organizational behavior scholars, the results of this study represent reasonable doubts that practitioners will depart from this economic gold standard.

6.2 Limitations of the research design

Most of the limitations of this thesis relate to a particular study. For this reason, they were previously discussed in the appropriate sections of Studies 1 through 5. This section, therefore, only includes a brief summary of the general limitations of the overall research design. In general, these limitations inform future research directions as well.

First, only some variables that influence heuristic reasoning were analyzed in this thesis (see Figure 18. p. 90). Achievement of the overall goal to describe heuristic reasoning in management accounting was limited to the analyzed variables that were selected in light of current JDM research as key variables (Baron, 2008). Consequently, the investigated aspects of JDM and heuristic reasoning, respectively, in this thesis represented a tradeoff between a detailed analysis of certain factors that focused on subtle manipulation shifts, rather than practical relevance, and a complete description of heuristic reasoning in management accounting that was an inch deep, but an ocean wide.

---

[120] This mismatch between an economic and a naturalistic approach is also documented in other areas. For instance Fox and Tannenbaum (2011, p. 1) point out that on the one hand, in economics and finance risk is defined in terms of "variance in the probability distribution over possible outcomes". On the other hand experienced managers define risks in terms of "exposure to possible negative outcomes, rather than variance over outcomes or some other quantifiable construct." Examples like these question the external validity of some economic models and the underlying picture of human information processing.

As stressed in all studies, most participants in the empirical investigations were students. The number of experienced participants, such as in Study 4, was relatively small. This was a limitation of Study 4, as experienced managers were affected by novel information differently than younger professionals and students (see p. 166ff). Therefore, future researchers in this area should recruit a more balanced sample of professionals and students (but see Remus, 1986). The findings of this research could also further clarify the role of experience in accounting settings and the reliance upon heuristics, even in settings in which accountability is high (see the results of Study 3, p. 147ff).

One general limitation of the overall research design was the comparison of relatively large samples in empirical studies with a relatively small sample of eight individuals. A small sample is not uncommon in qualitative research. Even single-case studies can frequently provide valuable insights (Yin, 2009). However, a fair comment could address this issue, given that one goal of this thesis was to approach heuristic reasoning using a mixed-method design. Therefore, a wider range of interviews with a more detailed analysis would have promoted understanding of the decision process. However, conducting additional studies and collecting more data would have gone beyond the scope of this thesis.

6.3 Future research directions

Within each of the five studies, several points regarding future research directions were proposed. In sum, several issues were present in almost every study that represent promising and fruitful areas for future behavioral accounting research. The five issues ranged from specific issues, such as information asymmetries, to more general issues, such as the further integration of current cognitive and social psychological models into behavioral accounting research. One example of a potentially fruitful area involves the concept of fluency, which is briefly introduced here. Each of them is a large field within behavioral research. In addition, adoption into behavioral accounting research is guided by successful examples from other disciplines.

(1) The yardstick issue

One frequently mentioned issue that arises in testing the efficiency of decision strategies is the yardstick problem. This means if you want to test if one decision mechanism, like a simple heuristic is superior, you need an external criterion in order to compare it to other benchmarks like more compensatory strategies. In the development of the fast and frugal program, mostly simple (win/loss) outcomes such as Wimbledon tennis matches were used in order to demonstrate the efficiency of heuristic solutions (Gigerenzer, et al., 1999), however in business settings (cf. accounting settings) simple win/loss situations are scarce, as one usually faces multiple degrees of freedom in these sort of tasks. In order to overcome this difficulty, well-defined forecasting scenarios in production scheduling could potentially represent promising future research directions in analyzing the efficiency of heuristic reasoning in accounting settings. The advantage of this field is that there are right answers and some plans do provide better output than others.

Another solution to this issue would be that of leaving the yardstick in accounting tasks as an np-hard problem behind and thus focus more on the descriptive models of accounting JDM and focus more on what Simon (1976) calls procedural rationality. A simple yet promising approach in this tradition would be to start a more inductive based research approach, using qualitative research techniques in estimating what kind of yardsticks are actually used by professionals (besides market responses and cash flow calculations) and then continue with more quantitative models.

(2) Extending the process perspective of heuristic reasoning

Focusing on procedural rationality means that future research in behavioral accounting should concentrate on a richer description of JDM process models. Besides the verbal protocols, also used in this thesis (see Study 2, p. 129ff), there is a wide range of possibilities to further track the decision process.

Mouselab or eye-tracking methods just represent two well-established ones (for an overview of process-tracing methods see Schulte-Mecklenbeck, Kühberger, & Ranyard, 2011). In particular further innovative combinations of different process tracing methods represent promising approaches towards a further maturation of behavioral accounting research.

(3) Information cost and information asymmetries

In describing mechanisms of bounded rationality, frequently the tradeoff between costs and time is mentioned (e.g. Conlisk, 1996). In accounting settings, these costs can frequently be attributed to real values stemming from the costs of benchmarks or expensive databases. Whereas Study 3 (p. 144ff) introduced some form of budget responsibility, there are many open issues than can be addressed in future research analyzing the effects of information acquisition behavior in particular related to its costs.

The issue of information asymmetries concerns the fact that information with a positive content is differently evaluated compared to information with a negative content (see also the discussion of Study 4, p. 171ff). This finding is related to the value function within prospect theory (Kahneman & Tversky, 1983) (see also section 2.3.4, p. 28ff and Figure 7, p. 30), which states that for instance the subjective value from a 100.- € gain is completely different compared to that of a 100.- € loss.

Transferring this robust finding into behavioral accounting research offers various aspects for future research. In particular, with respect to heuristic reasoning from a dual process theory perspective (see section 2.7.2, p. 70) it can be speculated that different values also influence the operating System 1 or 2 and the interaction mode between those two processes. For instance, a positive value is less likely to activate System 2 reasoning compared to a negative value, which might work as a alarm clock, activating the self-aware modus operandi of System 2.

(4) Self-other decision making

One of the most promising fields for future JDM research in management accounting is the field of self-other decision making (Bonaccio & Dalal, 2006), as many of the emerging research issues, highlighted for instance by Bonner (2008) or Shields and Luft (2009), can be approached from this perspective. The dyad of manager and (management) accountant is also a typical research subject (and starting point) within the various attempts in defining the role of management accountants within the organization (Brühl, 2009; J. Weber & Schäffer, 2008b). The analysis of this dyad offers multiple open research questions ranging from information distortion in this relationship (Polman, 2010) to the integration of dual process (Evans & Frankish, 2010) models within this dyad.

(5) Further integration of cognitive models – the case of fluency

Another promising future research direction for behavioral accounting research is in the further integration of state of the art cognitive models. One promising concept is fluency, which is of particular interest for management control research, as it deals with the underlying qualities of information that influences its processing speed (assuming that controllers daily task is to analyze and interpret large information sets)

Oppenheimer (2008, p. 237) defines fluency as "the participative experience of ease or difficulty associated with completing a mental task." This increasingly popular concept helps researchers to better understand the cognitive mechanisms of heuristic reasoning. It is especially attractive in the field of JDM (Judgment and Decision Making), where heuristics (of all kinds) might be preferred over more complex decision making strategies using free parameters. Fluency can also be seen in line with the classic work of Brunswick (1957), who stresses that proximal cues are crucial for making inferences about distal properties.

The influence and robustness of fluency has been shown in various areas, such as strategy selection (Bröder & Gaissmaier, 2007), and choice (Alter & Oppenheimer, 2006). Alter and Oppenheimer (2006) illustrate in their study why this concept is so relevant to business studies as well. The authors provide an interesting insight into the role of fluency in the stock market. They show that in the initial weeks following their first appearance on the stock market, companies with easier to pronounce names (as a proxy for fluency) significantly outperform the stocks of companies with more complex, or difficult to pronounce names. This shows that brand names function as a proxy for a company's value. One explanation for this finding could be that brokers rely on heuristic one-cue decision making when selecting a portfolio of emerging new companies. Using this theory I might assume that the fictitious company "Broody" would outperform the (equally hypothetical) company "Broodpzcinskij", as the former is easier to pronounce, and thus has a higher level of fluency. A similar finding has also been found for consumer products in a study conducted by Novemsky and colleagues (2007). In examples of successful decision making, the affect of fluency is more difficult to ascertain. How adaptive is "adaptive enough" to rely on this shortcut and make it a "tool" for successful decision making? Some of the fast and frugal heuristics suggested by Gigerenzer and colleagues (Gigerenzer, et al., 1999) would require more subtle adaptive mechanisms.

Alter and colleagues (2007) also suggest that fluency could be a trigger for heuristic reasoning. In their study, participants used heuristics when they experienced fluency, and otherwise used systematic processing. These results corroborate with the aforementioned dual process model approach, because they describe a mechanism that can "switch a gear" between Systems 1 and 2.

I can draw an example of fluency and ecological rationality that can be applied in a business context from Kruglanski and Gigerenzer's discussion of the fluency heuristic: they suggest that "when a person requesting advice for a choice between A and B is impressed by how quickly the responder answered "A" and takes this speed as clear evidence for A" (2011, p. 100). For instance if a manager asks a financial accountant which of the two production sites has a lower profitability, and he answers "B" without a glimpse, the manager might conclude that this fast response was based on the accountants' solid knowledge of the data and of the significant difference between the two sites. Thus, the reaction time can be used as a proxy for the validity of the inference, and as a cue for its ecological rationality.

6.4 Overall conclusion

More than 30 years ago, behavioral accounting research pioneer John Dickhaut asked (management) accountants how they coped with the tremendous uncertainty that they faced in their jobs. One individual stated, "Son, there's no uncertainty in this accounting department" (quoted in Dickhaut, 1976, p. 181). Thirty years later, findings from a growing body of behavioral accounting research have revealed that this optimistic view stems from relatively wishful thinking. It is even possible that it is an example of an existing, profession-rooted overconfidence bias and that the same errors and lapses of human decision making are found within (management) accounting as in all other studied fields (Bazerman & Moore, 2009; Kahneman, 2011; Kotchetova & Salterio, 2004).

Whereas some scholars in behavioral accounting research continue to replicate studies in the fashion of these heuristics and biases tradition, which was ironically dubbed as the quest for "the error of the day" by Goldstein (2010), this thesis is an attempt to move beyond a pure summary of irrationalities that management controllers commit. The introduction or integration of concepts, such as adaptive decision making and procedural and ecological rationality and also dual process theories, helps to explain why these errors occur and calls into question whether they are errors at all.

This work is an initial attempt to provide a more accurate description of the JDM processes of management controllers in light of these new ideas. The subject of heuristics and heuristic reasoning served as a showcase for analyzing this issue. As complexity of worldwide databases and the amount of available data grows every day, this descriptive approach to examining how heuristics are used by individuals who should reduce this complexity or assure the rationality of others, such as management controllers, appears to be even more relevant today than it was 30 years ago. However, I state that this complexity is not solved by more complex descriptions of decision making behavior (including extending the number of free parameters) but rather by focusing on simple and robust (see Coughlan et al., 2010) models from a process perspective.

Appendix

1. Assessment of general decision making style (GDMS) by Scott and Bruce (1995)

(R = rational; I = intuitive; D = dependent; S = spontaneous; A = avoidant; C = control question)

		Strongly agree	agree	neutral	disagree	Strongly disagree
1	When I make decisions, I tend to rely on my intuition (I)	+ +	+	o	–	– –
2	I rarely make important decisions without consulting other people (D)	+ +	+	o	–	– –
3	When I make a decision, it is important for me to feel the decision is right than to have a rational reason for it (I)	+ +	+	o	–	– –
4	I double-check my information sources to be sure I have the right facts before making decisions (R)	+ +	+	o	–	– –
5	I use the advice of other people in making my important decisions (D)	+ +	+	o	–	– –
6	I put off making decisions because thinking about them makes me uneasy (A)	+ +	+	o	–	– –
7	I make decisions in a logical and systematic way (R)	+ +	+	o	–	– –
8	When making decisions I do what feels natural at the moment (S)	+ +	+	o	–	– –
9	I generally make snap decisions (S)	+ +	+	o	–	– –
10	I like to have someone steer me in the right direction when I am faced with important decisions (D)	+ +	+	o	–	– –
11	My decision making requires careful thought (R)	+ +	+	o	–	– –
12	When making decisions, I trust my inner feelings and reactions (I)	+ +	+	o	–	– –
13	When making decisions, I consider various options in terms of a special goal (R)	+ +	+	o	–	– –
14	I avoid making important decisions until the pressure is on (A)	+ +	+	o	–	– –
15	I often make impulsive decisions (S)	+ +	+	o	–	– –
16	When making decisions, I rely upon my instincts (I)	+ +	+	o	–	– –
17	I generally make decisions that feel right to me (I)	+ +	+	o	–	– –

18	I often need assistance of other people when making important decisions (D)	+ +	+	o	–	– –
19	I postpone decision making whenever possible (A)	+ +	+	o	–	– –
20	I often make decisions on the spur of the moment (S)	+ +	+	o	–	– –
21	I often put off making important decisions (A)	+ +	+	o	–	– –
22	If I have the support of others, it is easier form e to make important decisions (D)	+ +	+	o	–	– –
23	I generally make important decisions at the last minute (A)	+ +	+	o	–	– –
24	I make quick decisions (S)	+ +	+	o	–	– –
25	I usually have a rational basis for making decisions (R)	+ +	+	o	–	– –
26	I consider myself as an above-average student (C)	+ +	+	o	–	– –
27	I consider my skills in management control (accounting) as above average (C)	+ +	+	o	–	– –

2. Interview Guide

A: General decision making in strategic financial/accounting decisions

1. How do you describe the general interaction between management and financial planning (CFO/accounting department) concerning strategic decisions? For instance is the goal rather to check already made decisions, chose   between alternatives or come up with own suggestions?

    a) How do management accountants/CFOs participate in the decision making process in your company?

    b) Is their a way to come up with own suggestions or critique or is rather a controlling function of the management's decisions the goal of these positions?

    c) Do you consider the management accountants as the advice giver of the management?

2. To which degree do you agree with the following statements?

    a) "Management accountants shall assure the rationality of the management"?

    b) "Management accountants make decisions so that the management can decide"?

    c) Do you see any major differences between information acquisition and evaluation between management and accounting/financial department?

3. How would you define rationality regarding decision making?

4. How does information search work in your company for important non-routine decisions?

    a) Do you see any major differences between information acquisition and evaluation between management and accounting/financial department?

5. How do the following variables effect these processes (information search and evaluation)

    a) time pressure

    b) degree of uncertainty

    c) complexity

    d) accountability of the decision

B: When are heuristics used as a decision basis?

1. Which individual heuristics do you use in your (daily) tasks? Can you remember a particular situation in which you relied on a heuristic?

    a) In which situations you generally rely on heuristics?

    b) Please describe these heuristic(s) as accurate as possible

    c)   Was this heuristic rather used in information acquisition or information evaluation?

    d)   Did you use the heuristic(s) rather in routine decisions or in novel circumstances?

    e)   How do you evaluate the success of the applied heuristic?

    f)   Which role is played of experience and expertise in applying heuristics?

2.   How and from whom do you receive feedback regarding your decisions?

3.   How does your organization support learning processes and how do you reach expertise in your tasks??

C: How are heuristics implemented into organizational decisions?

1.   How can individual heuristics be implemented into organizational decision processes?

    a)   Are there any differences if these heuristics come from the same or from a different hierarchy level?

    b)   Do you remember any specific situations in your team, where someone referred to a heuristic he used?

2.   Can you also remember a counterexample where someone relied on his intuition, but you questioned the rationality basis for this decision?

3.   How far do you see your organization as open minded to integrate intuition based decisions of single members?

D: Individual characteristics concerning decision making behavior

1.   When I make decisions, I tend to rely on my intuition.

2.   When I make a decision, it is important to me to feel the decision is right than to have a rational reason for it.

3.   I double-check my information sources to be sure I have the right facts before making decisions.

4.   I make decisions in a logical and systematic way.

5.   My decision making requires careful thought.

6.   When making decisions, I trust my inner feelings and reactions.

7.   When making decisions, I consider various options in terms of a special goal.

8.   When making decisions, I rely upon my instincts.

9.   I generally make decisions that feel right to me.

10. I usually have a rational basis for making decisions.

3. Standard Think-Aloud Instructions

based on Ericsson and Simon (1993, p. 378) and Austin and Delaney (1998, p. 56):

In this experiment, I am interested in what you think about when you find answers to some questions that I am going to ask you to answer. In order to do this I am going to ask you to THINK ALOUD as you work on the problem given. What I mean by think aloud is that I want you to tell me EVERYTHING you are thinking from the time you first see the question until you give an answer. I would like you to talk CONSTANTLY from the time I present each problem until you have given your final answer to the question. I do not want you to try to plan out what you are saying or try to explain to me what you are saying. Just act as if you are alone in the room speaking to yourself. It is most important that you keep talking if you are silent for any long period of time I will ask you to talk. Do you understand what I want you to do?

[...]

References

Accenture. (2008). Most U.S. companies say business analytics still future goal, not present reality. Retrieved from http://newsroom.accenture.com/article_display.cfm?article_id=4777

Agor, W. H. (1990). *Intuition in organizations : leading and managing productively.* Newbury Park: Sage

Ahrens, T. (1999). *Contrasting involvements : A study of management accounting practices in Britain and Germany.* Amsterdam: Harwood Academic.

Ahrens, T., & Chapman, C. S. (2007). Doing qualitative field research in management accounting: Positioning data to contribute to theory. In C. S. Chapman, A. Hopwood & M. D. Shields (Eds.), *Handbook of management accounting research* (pp. 299-318). Oxford: Elsevier.

Alba, J. W., & Marmorstein, H. (1987). The effects of frequency knowledge on consumer decision making. *Journal of Consumer Research, 14*(1), 14-25.

Alter, A. L., & Oppenheimer, D., M. (2006). Predicting short-term stock fluctuations by using processing fluency. *Proceedings of the National Academy of Sciences of the United States of America, 103*, 9369-9372.

Alter, A. L., Oppenheimer, D. M., Epley, N., & Eyre, R. N. (2007). Overcoming Intuition: Metacognitive Difficulty Activates Analytic Reasoning. *Journal of Experimental Psychology: General, 136*(4), 569-576.

Altheide, D. L., & Johnson, J. M. (1994). Criteria for assessing interpretive validity in qualitative research. In N. K. Denzin & Y. S. Lincoln (Eds.), *Handbook of qualitative research* (pp. 485-499). Thousand Oaks: Sage

Alves, M. (2011). *Accounting data for managerial decision-making purposes.* Paper presented at the 34th annual congress of the European Accounting Association (EAA) 2011, Rome, Italy.

American Psychological Association. (1974). *Standards for educational and psychological tests.* Washington, D.C.: American Psychological Association.

Ansari, S., & Euske, K. J. (1987). Rational, rationalizing, and reifying uses of accounting data in organizations. *Accounting, Organizations and Society, 12*(6), 549-570.

Anthony, R. N., & Govindarajan, V. (2001). *Management control systems* (10 ed.). New York: Mc Graw-Hill.

Argyris, C. (1953). Human problems with budgets. *Harvard Business Review, 31*(1), 97-110.

Ariely, D. (2008). *Predictably irrational: The hidden forces that shape our decisions.* New York: Harper

Ariely, D. (2010). *The upside of irrationality : the unexpected benefits of defying logic at work and at home.* New York: Harper.

Arkes, H. R., & Blumer, C. (1985). The psychology of sunk cost. *Organizational Behavior and Human Decision Processes, 35*(1), 124-140.

Arrow, K. J. (2004). Is bounded rationality unboundedly rational? Some ruminations. In M. Augier & J. G. March (Eds.), *Models of a man essays in memory of Herbert A. Simon* (pp. 47-55). Cambridge: MIT Press.

Ashton, R. H. (1974a). Behavioral implications of information overload in managerial accounting reports. *Cost and Management, July-August.*

Ashton, R. H. (1974b). An experimental study of internal control judgments. *Journal of Accounting Research, 12*(1), 143-157.

Ashton, R. H. (2010). Quality, timing, and luck: looking back at Ashton (1974). *Auditing: A Journal of Practice & Theory, 29*(1), 3-13.

Ashton, R. H., & Ashton, A. H. (1995). *Judgment and decision-making research in accounting and auditing.* Cambridge: Cambridge University Press.

Ashton, R. H., & Kramer, S. S. (1980). Students As surrogates in behavioral accounting research: some evidence. *Journal of Accounting Research, 18*(1), 1-15.

Astebro, T., & Elhedhli, S. (2006). The effectiveness of simple decision heuristics: forecasting commercial success for early-stage ventures. *Management Science, 52*(3), 395-409.

Atkinson, J. W. (1957). Motivational determinants of risk-taking behavior. *Psychological Review, 64*(6), 359-372.

Atkinson, J. W., & Raynor, J. O. (1976). *Personality, motivation, and achievement.* Washington, D.C.: Hemisphere.

Austin, J., & Delaney, P. F. (1998). Protocol analysis as a tool for behavioral analysis. *The Analysis of Verbal Behavior, 15*, 41-56.

Axelrod, R. (1984). *The evolution of cooperation.* New York: Basic Books, Inc. Publishers.

Ayton, P., & Fischer, I. (2004). The hot hand fallacy and the gambler's fallacy: Two faces of subjective randomness? *Memory & Cognition, 32*(8), 1369-1378.

Baddeley, A. D., Eysenck, M. W., & Anderson, M. (2009). *Memory.* Hove: Psychology Press.

Balakrishnan, R., & Sivaramakrishnan, K. (2002). A critical overview of the use of full cost data for planning and pricing. *Journal of Management Accounting Research, 14*(1), 3-31.

Bamber, M. E. (1993). Opportunities in behavioral accounting research. *Behavioral Research in Accounting, 5*, 1-29.

Barnard, C., I. (1938). *The functions of the executive.* Cambridge: Harvard University Press.

Baron, J. (2008). *Thinking and deciding* (4 ed.). New York: Cambridge University Press.

Baron, J., & Hershey, J. C. (1988). Outcome bias in decision evaluation. *Journal of Personality and Social Psychology, 54*(4), 569-579.

Basel, J. S. (2010). *Can less-be-more in Management Accounting?* Paper presented at the Behavioral Decision Research in Management (BDRM) Conference, Carnegie Mellon University, Pittsburgh, PA.

Basel, J. S. (2011). Choice reversal in management accounting: a quasi-experimental demonstration. *SSRN eLibrary.* from http://ssrn.com/paper=1955874

Basel, J. S., & Brühl, R. (2011). Concepts of rationality in management research. From unbounded rationality to ecological rationality. Berlin: ESCP Europe Wirtschaftshochschule Berlin.

Bastardi, A., & Shafir, E. (1998). On the pursuit and misuse of useless information. *Journal of Personality and Social Psychology, 75*(1), 19-32.

Bastardi, A., & Shafir, E. (2000). Nonconsequential reasoning and Its consequences. *Current Directions in Psychological Science, 9*(6), 216-219.

Baylor, A. L. (2001). A u-shaped model for the development of intuition by level of expertise. *New Ideas in Psychology, 19*(3), 237-244.

Bazerman, M. H., & Moore, D. A. (2009). *Judgment in managerial decision making* (7 ed.). New York: Wiley.

Becker, G. (1976). *The economic approach to human behavior.* Chicago: University of Chicago Press.

Beckmann, D., & Huch, B. (2002). Controllingverständnis – dogmatisch oder pragmatisch? Zum paradigmatischen Kern des Controlling. In J. Weber & B. Hirsch (Eds.), *Controlling als akademische Disziplin* (pp. 145-160). Wiesbaden: Deutscher Universitäts-Verlag.

Bedard, J. C., & Biggs, S. F. (1991). Pattern recognition, hypotheses generation, and auditor performance in an analytical task. *The Accounting Review, 66*(3), 622-642.

Bedard, J. C., & Wright, A. M. (1994). The functionality of decision heuristics: reliance on prior audit adjustments in evidential planning. *Behavioral Research in Accounting, 6*, 62-89.

Bell, J. F. (1967). *A history of economic thought.* New York: Ronald Press.

Bendor, J. (2001). Bounded rationality. In N. J. Smelser & P. B. Baltes (Eds.), *International Encyclopedia of the Social & Behavioral Sciences* (pp. 1303-1307). Amsterdam: Elsevier.

Benston, G. J. (1963). The role of the firm's accounting system for motivation. *The Accounting Review, 38*(2), 347-354.

Berg, B. L. (2004). *Qualitative research methods for the social sciences.* Boston: Allyn and Bacon.

Berg, N. (2010). Behavioral Economics. In R. C. Free (Ed.), *21st Century Economics:A Referencee Handbook.* Thousand Oaks: Sage

Berg, N., & Gigerenzer, G. (2010). As-if behavioral economics: neoclassical economics in disguise? *History of Economic Ideas, 18*(1), 133-165.

Bernoulli, D. (1738/1954). Exposition of a new theory on the measurement of risk. *Econometrica, 22*(1), 22-36.

Betsch, C. (2008). Chronic preferences for intuition and deliberation in decision making: Lessons learned about intuition from an individual diferences approach. In H. Plessner, C. Betsch & T. Betsch (Eds.), *Intuition in judgment and decision making* (pp. 231-248). Mahwah: Lawrence Erlbaum.

Bettman, J. R., & Park, C. W. (1980). Eeffects of prior knowledge and experience and ohase of the choice process on consumer decision processes: A protocol analysis. *Journal of Consumer Research, 7*, 234-249.

Bettmann, J. R., Johnson, E. J., & Payne, J. W. (1991). Consumer decision making. In T. S. Robertson & H. H. Kassarjian (Eds.), *Handbook of consumer behavior* (pp. 50-84). Englewood Cliffs: Prentice-Hall.

Biggs, S. F., & Mock, T. J. (1983). An investigation of auditor decsion processes in the evaluation of internal controls and audit scope decisions. *Journal of Accounting Research, 21*(1), 234-255.

Binmore, K. G. (2007). *Game theory : a very short introduction.* New York: Oxford University Press.

Birnbaum, M. H. (1999). How to Show That 9 < 221: Collect Judgments in a Between-Subjects Design. *Psychological Methods, 4*(3), 243-249.

Birnbaum, M. H. (2000). *Psychological experiments on the internet.* San Diego: Academic Press.

Birnberg, J. G. (2009). A proposed framework for behavioral research in accounting. Pittsburgh University.

Birnberg, J. G., Luft, J., & Shields, M. D. (2007). Psychology theory in management accounting research. In C. S. Chapman, A. G. Hopwood & M. D. Shields (Eds.), *Handbook of Management Accounting Research* (Vol. 1, pp. 113-135). Amsterdam: Elsevier.

Birnberg, J. G., & Shields, J. F. (1989). Three decades of behavioral accounting research: a search for order. *Behavioral Research in Accounting, 1*, 23-74.

Bonaccio, S., & Dalal, R. S. (2006). Advice taking and decision-making: An integrative literature review, and implications for the organizational sciences. *Organizational Behavior and Human Decision Processes, 101*(2), 127-151.

Bonner, S. E. (1999). Judgment and decision-making research in accounting. *Accounting Horizons, 13*(4), 385-398.

Bonner, S. E. (2008). *Judgment and decision making in accounting.* Upper Saddle River: Pearson Prentice Hall.

Booth, P., & Schulz, A. K. D. (2004). The impact of an ethical environment on managers' project evaluation judgments under agency problem conditions. *Accounting, Organizations and Society, 29*(5-6), 473-488.

Bortz, J. (2005). *Statistik für Human- und Sozialwissenschaftler* (6 ed.). Heidelberg: Springer.

Bortz, J., & Döring, N. (2006). *Forschungsmethoden und Evaluation für Human- und Sozialwissenschaftler* (4 ed.). Heidelberg: Springer.

Bowler, P. J. (2009). Darwin's Originality. *Science., 323*(5911), 223.

Boyatzis, R. E. (1998). *Transforming qualitative information : thematic analysis and code development*. Thousand Oaks: Sage

Boyd, R., & Richardson, P. J. (2005). *The origin and evolution of cultures*. New York: Oxford University Press.

Brändle, M. (2007). *Strategisches Controlling auf Märkten im Wandel: Führungsunterstützung durch Inhalte, Prozesse und Verhalten*. Frankfurt am Main: Lang.

Braun, V., & Clarke, V. (2006). Using thematic analysis in psychology. *Qualitative Research in Psychology, 3*(2), 77-101.

Brehm, S. S., Kassin, S. M., & Fein, S. (2002). *Social Psychology* (5 ed.). Boston: Houghton Mifflin

Bröder, A., & Gaissmaier, W. (2007). Sequential processing of cues in memory-based multiattribute decisions. *Psychological Bulletin Review, 14*, 895-900.

Brouthers, K., Andriessen, F., & Nicolaes, I. (1998). Driving blind: Strategic decisionmaking in small companies. *Long Range Planning Long Range Planning, 31*(1), 130-138.

Brown, H. I. (1978). On being rational. *American Philosophical Quarterly, 15*(4), 241-248.

Brown, L. D., & Huefner, R. J. (1994). The familiarity with and perceived quality of accounting journals: views of senior accounting faculty in leading U.S. MBA programs. *Contemporary Accounting Research, 11*(1), 223-250.

Brownell, P. (1995). *Research methods in management accounting*. Melbourne: Coopers & Lybrand

Brühl, R. (2009). *Controlling: Grundlagen des Erfolgscontrollings* (2 ed.). München: Oldenbourg.

Brühl, R. (2010). Handlungserklärungen in einer erkenntnispluralistischen Methodologie. Betriebswirtschaftliche Handlungstheorien und Methodenkombinationen. In T. Wrona & G. Fandel (Eds.), *Zeitschrift für Betriebswirtschaft* (Vol. 80, pp. 44-76).

Brühl, R., & Buch, S. (2006). Einheitliche Gütekriterien in der empirischen Forschung? Objektivität, Reliabilität und Validität in der Diskussion: ESCP-EAP Europäische Wirtschaftshochschule Berlin.

Brühl, R., Horch, N., & Orth, M. (2008). Grounded Theory und ihre bisherige Anwendung in der empirischen Controlling- und Rechnungswesenforschung. *Zeitschrift fur Planung und Unternehmenssteuerung, 19*(3), 299-323.

Bruine de Bruin, W., Fischhoff, B., & Parker, A. M. (2007). Individual differences in adult decision-making competence. *Journal of Personality and Social Psychology, 92*(5), 938-956.

Bruns, W. J., & DeCoster, D. T. (1969). *Accounting and its behavioral implications*. New York: McGraw-Hill.

Bruns, W. J., & DeCoster, D. T. (1970). Review of Accounting and Its Behavioral Implications. *Accounting Review, 45*(2), 387-389.

Brunswick, E. (1957). Scope and aspects of the cognitive problem. In H. Gruber, K. R. Hammond & R. Jessor (Eds.), *Contemporary approaches to cognition* (pp. 5-31). Cambridge: Harvard University Press.

Buller, D. J. (2005). Evolutionary psychology: the emperors new paradigm. *Trends in Cognitive Sciences, 9*(6), 277-283.

Burgstahler, D., & Sundem, G. L. (1989). The evolution of behavioral accounting research in the United States, 1968-1987. *Behavioral Research in Accounting, 1*(1), 75-108.

Burnard, P. (1991). A method of analysing interview transcripts in qualitative research. *Nurse Education Today, 11*, 461-466.

Buss, D. M. (1995). Evolutionary Psychology: A New Paradigm for Psychological Science. *Psychological Inquiry, 6*(1), 1-30.

Byrne, S., & Pierce, B. (2007). Towards a more comprehensive understanding of the roles of management accountants. *European Accounting Review, 16*(3), 469-498.

Camerer, C. (1992). Recent test of generalizations of expected utility theory. In W. Edwards (Ed.), *Studies in risk and uncertainty: No. 2. Utility theories: Measurement and applications* (pp. 207-251). Norwell: Kluwer Academic Pub.

Camerer, C. (1998). Bounded rationality in individual decision making. *Experimental Economics, 1*(2), 163-183.

Camerer, C., & Hogarth, R. M. (1999). The effect of financial incentives on performance in experiments. *Journal of Risk and Uncertainty, 19*(1), 7-42.

Camerer, C., Loewenstein, G., & Rabin, M. (2003). *Advances in behavioral economics. The roundtable series in behavioral economics.* Princeton: Princeton University Press.

Carlile, P. R., & Christensen, C. M. (2004). The cycles of theory building in management research. *Harvard Business School Workingpaper, 05-057.*

Carnap, R. (1960). Theoretische Begriffe der Wissenschaft. Eine logische und methodologische Untersuchung. *Zeitschrift für philosophische Forschung, 14,* 209-233, 571-598.

Casey, C. J., Jr. (1980). Variation in accounting information load: The effect on loan officers' predictions of bankruptcy. *The Accounting Review, 55*(1), 36-49.

Casey, C. J., Jr. (1982). Coping with information overload: The need for empirical research. *Cost and Management, 4,* 31-38.

Chase, V. M., Hertwig, R., & Gigerenzer, G. (1998). Visions of rationality. *Trends in Cognitive Sciences, 2*(6), 206-214.

Christensen, C. M., & Sundahl, D. M. (2001). The process of building theory. *Harvard Business School Workingpaper, 02-016.*

Cloyd, C. B., & Spilker, B. (2000). Confirmation bias in tax information search: A comparison of law students and accounting students. *Journal of American Taxation Association, 22*(2), 60-71.

Cohen, J. (1988). *Statistical analysis for the behavioral sciences* (2 ed.). Hillsdale: Lawrence Earlbaum.

Cohen, J. (1992). A power primer. *Quantitative Methods in Psychology, 112*(1), 155-159.

Cohen, L. J. (1981). Can human irrationality be experimentally demonstrated? *Behavioral and Brain Sciences, 4*, 317-370.

Cokely, E. T., & Kelley, C. M. (2009). Cognitive abilities and superior decision making under risk: a protocol analysis and process model evaluation. *Judgment and Decision Making, 4*(1), 20-33.

Conlisk, J. (1996). Why bounded rationality? *Journal of Economic Literature, 34*(2), 669-700.

Connolly, T., Arkes, H. R., & Hammond, K. R. (2000). *Judgment and decision making: An interdisciplinary reader.* Cambridge: Cambridge University Press.

Conrad, F., Blair, J., & Tracy, E. (2000). Verbal reports are data! A theoretical approach to cognitive interviews. *Proceedings of the National Academy of Sciences of the United States of America.*

Conslisk, J. (1996). Why bounded rationality? *Journal of Economic Literature, 34*, 669-700.

Cosmides, L., & Tooby, J. (1994). Better than rational: evolutionary psychology and the invisible hand. *American Economic Review, 84*(2), 327-332.

Cosmides, L., & Tooby, J. (2005). Neurocognitive adaptions designed for social exchange. In D. M. Buss (Ed.), *The handbook of evolutionary psychology* (pp. 584-627). Hoboken: Wiley.

Coughlan, A. T., Choi, S. C., Chu, W., Ingene, C. A., Moorthy, S., Padmanabhan, V., et al. (2010). Marketing modeling reality and the realities of marketing modeling. *Marketing Letters, 21*(3), 317-333.

Creswell, J. W. (Ed.). (2003). *Research design. Qualitative, quantitative, and mixed methods approaches* (2 ed.). Thousand Oaks: Sage

Creswell, J. W., & Plano Clark, V. L. (2007). *Mixed methods research.* Thousand Oaks: Sage.

Creswell, J. W., Plano Clark, V. L., Gutmann, M. L., & Hanson, W. E. (2003). Advanced mixed methods research designs. In A. Tashakkori & C. Teddlie (Eds.), *Handbook of mixed methods in social & behavioral research* (pp. 209-240). Thousand Oaks: Sage.

Cronshaw, S. F., & Alexander, R. A. (1985). One answer to the demand for accountability: Selection utility as an investment decision. *Organizational Behavior and Human Decision Processes, 35*(1), 102-118.

Dane, E., & Pratt, M. G. (2007). Exploring Intuition and Its Role in Managerial Decision Making. *The Academy of Management review., 32*(1), 33.

Darwin, C. (1872). *The origin of species by means of natural selection ; or, The preservation of favored races in the struggle for life.* Chicago: Rand, McNally.

Davidson, H. J., & Trueblood, R. M. (1961). Accounting for decision-making. *The Accounting Review, 36*(4), 577-582.

Davila, A., & Foster, G. (2005). Management accounting systems adoption decisions: evidence and performance implications from early-stage/startup companies. *The Accounting Review., 80*(4), 1039-1068.

Davila, A., & Foster, G. (2007). Management control systems in early-stage startup companies. *The Accounting Review, 82*(4), 907-937.

Dawes, R. M. (1979). The robust beauty of improper linear models in decision making. *American Psychologist, 34*, 571-582.

DellaVigna, S. (2009). Psychology and economics: evidence from the field. *Journal of Economic Literature, 47*(2), 315-372.

DeMiguel, V., Garlappi, L., & Uppal, R. (2009). Optimal versus naive diversification: How inefficient is the 1/N portfolio strategy? *Review of Financial Studies, 22*(5), 1915-1953.

Deutsch, M., & Krauss, R. (1965). *Theories of social psychology.* New York: Basic Books.

Devine, T. C. (1960). Research Methodology and Accounting Theory Formation. *Accounting Review, 35*(3), 387-399.

Dewey, J. (1938). *Logic. The theory of inquiry.* New York: Henry Holt.

Dickhaut, J. W. (1973). Alternative information structures and probability revisions. *The Accounting Review, 48*(1), 61-79.

Dickhaut, J. W. (1976). Discussion of experiments in the heuristics of human information processing. *Journal of Accounting Research, 14*, 188-195.

Diijksterhuis, A., Bos, M. W., Nordgren, L. F., & van Baaren, R. B. (2006). On making the right choice: The deliberation-without-attention effect. *Science, 311*, 1005-1007.

Dijksterhuis, A., & Aarts, H. (2010). Goals, attention, and (un)consciousness. *Annual Review of Psychology, 61*, 467-490.

Dijksterhuis, A., Bos, M. W., Nordgren, L. F., & van Baaren, R. B. (2006). On Making the Right Choice: The Deliberation-Without-Attention Effect. *Science., 311*(5763), 1005.

Dijksterhuis, A., & Nordgren, L. (2006). A Theory of Unconscious Thought. *Perspectives on Psychological Science, 1*(2), 95-109.

Dilthey, W. (1977). *Descriptive psychology and historical understanding.* The Hague: Nijhoff.

Douglas, D. (2003). Grounded theories of management: a methodological review. *Management Research News, 26*(5), 44-52.

Driver, M. J., & Mock, T. J. (1975). Human information processing, decision style theory, and accounting information systems. *The Accounting Review, 50*(3), 490-508.

Drury, C. (1997). *Management accounting for business decisions.* London: International Thomson Business Press.

Dyckhoff, H., & Ahn, H. (2001). Sicherstellung der Effektivität und Effizienz der Führung als Kernfunktion des Controlling. *Kostenrechnungspraxis, 45*, 111-121.

Dyckman, T. R. (1964). The Effects of alternative accounting techniques on certain management decisions. *Journal of Accounting Research, 2*(1), 91-107.

Einhorn, H. J., & Hogarth, R. M. (1981). Behavioral decision theory: Processes of judgment and choice. *Journal of Accounting Research, 19*(1), 1-31.

Eisenführ, F., & Weber, M. (2003). *Rationales Entscheiden*. Heidelberg: Springer.

Eisenhardt, K. M. (1989). Building theories from case study research. *Academy of Management Review, 14*(4), 532-550.

Elio, R. (2002). Issues in common sense reasoning and rationality. In R. Elio (Ed.), *Common sense, reasoning and rationality* (pp. 3-36). New York: Oxford University Press.

Eppler, M. J., & Mengis, J. (2004). The concept of information overload: A review of literature from organizational science, accounting, marketing, MIS, and related disciplines. *The Information Society, 20*, 325-344.

Epstein, S., Lipson, A., Holstein, C., & Huh, E. (1992). Irrational reactions to negative outcomes: evidence for two conceptual systems. *Journal of Personality and Social Psychology, 62*(2), 328-339.

Ericsson, K. A. (2006). Protocol analysis and expert thought. Concurrent verbalizations of thinking during experts' performance on representative tasks. In K. A. Ericsson, N. Charness, P. J. Feltovich & R. R. Hoffmann (Eds.), *The cambridge handbook of expertice and expert performance* (pp. 223-241). Cambridge: Cambridge University Press.

Ericsson, K. A., Andersson, P., & Cokely, E. T. (2006). *The enigma of financial expertise: Superior and reproducible investment performance in efficient markets*. Paper presented at the Proceedings of the 28th Annual Meeting of the Cognitive Science Society, Mahwah, New Jersey.

Ericsson, K. A., Prietula, M., J., & Cokely, E. T. (2007). The making of an expert. *Harvard Business Review, 85*, 114-121.

Ericsson, K. A., & Simon, H. A. (1980). Verbal reports as data. *Psychological Review, 87*(3), 215-250.

Ericsson, K. A., & Simon, H. A. (1993). *Protocol analysis: verbal reports as data* (6 ed.). Cambridge: MIT Press.

Ettenson, R., Shanteau, J., & Krogstad, J. (1987). Expert judgment: Is more information better? *Psychological Reports*, 227-238.

Evans, J. S. B. T. (2008). Dual-Processing accounts of reasoning, judgment, and social cognition. *Annual Review of Psychology, 59*, 255-278.

Evans, J. S. B. T. (2010). *Thinking twice. Two minds in one brain*. Oxford: Oxford University Press.

Evans, J. S. B. T., & Frankish, K. (2010). *In two minds: dual process and beyond*. Oxford: Oxford University Press.

Fasolo, B., McClelland, G., & Todd, P. M. (2007). Escaping the tyranny of choice: when fewer attributes make choice easier. *Marketing Theory, 7*(1), 13-26.

Feigenbaum, E. A., & Feldman, J. (1963). *Computers and thought*. New York: McGraw-Hill.

Feilzer, M. Y. (2010). Doing mixed methods research pragmatically. Implications for the rediscovery of pragmatism as a research paradigm. *Journal of Mixed Methods Research, 4*(1), 6-16.

Fertakis, J. P. (1969). On communication, understanding, and relevance in accounting reporting. *The Accounting Review, 44*(4), 680-691.

Festinger, L. (1962). *A theory of cognitive dissonance*. Stanford: Stanford University Press.

Fiedler, K. (1988). The dependence of the conjunction fallacy on subtle linguistic factors. *Psychological Research, 50*, 123-129.

Fishburn, P. C. (1981). Subjective expected utility: A review of normative theories. *Theory and Decision, 13*, 139-199.

Fisher, J. G., Frederickson, J. R., & Peffer, S. A. (2006). Budget negotiations in multi-period settings. *Accounting, Organizations and Society, 31*(6), 511-528.

Flanagan, J. C. (1954). The critical incident technique. *Psychological Bulletin, 51*(4), 327-358.

Flick, U. (2005). *Qualitative Sozialforschung. Eine Einführung* (3 ed.). Reinbek bei Hamburg: Rowohlt.

Flick, U. (2006). *An introduction to qualitative research* (3 ed.). Thousand Oaks: Sage.

Foran, M. F., & Don, T. D. (1974). An experimental study of the effects of participation, authoritarianism, and feedback on cognitive dissonance in a standard setting situation. *The Accounting Review, 49*(4), 751-763.

Fox, C., R., & Tannenbaum, D. (2011). The elusive search for stable risk preferences. *Frontiers in Psychology, 2*(1), 1-4.

Fox, M. C., Ericsson, K. A., & Best, R. (2011). Do procedures for verbal reporting of thinking have to be reactive? A meta-analysis and recommendations for best reporting methods. *Psychological Bulletin, 137*(2), 316-344.

Frankish, K. (2010). Dual-process and dual-system theories of reasoning. *Philosophy Compass, 5*(10), 914-926.

Frederick, S. (2002). Automated choice heuristics. In T. Gilovich, D. Griffin & D. Kahneman (Eds.), *Heuristics and biases: The psychology of intuitive judgment* (pp. 548-558). Cambridge: Cambridge University Press.

Frey, B. S., & Benz, M. (2004). From imperialism to inspiration: A survey of economics and psychology. In A. Marciano, J. B. Davis & J. Runde (Eds.), *Elgar companion to economics and philosophy* (pp. 61-83). Cheltenham: Edward Elgar.

Friedman, M., & Savage, L. (1948). The utility analysis of choice involving risk. *Journal of Political Economy, 4*, 463-474.

Funder, D. C. (1987). Errors and mistakes: Evaluating the accuracy of social judgment. *Psychological Bulletin, 101*(1), 75-90.

Funke, J. (2003). *Problemlösendes Denken.* Stuttgart: Verlag W. Kohlhammer.

Furnham, A. (2008). *Personality and intelligence at work : exploring and explaining individual differences at work.* London: Routledge.

Garcia-Retamero, R., & Rieskamp, J. (2009). Do people treat missing information adaptively when making inferences? *The Quarterly Journal of Experimental Psychology, 62*(10), 1991-2013.

Geen, R. G. (1995). *Human motivation: A social psychological approach.* Pacific Grove: Brooks/Cole Pub.

Gibbons, M., Salterio, S., & Webb, A. (2001). Evidence about auditor – client management negotiation concerning client's financial reporting. *Journal of Accounting Research, 39*(3), 535-563.

Gigerenzer, G. (1991). How to make cognitive illusions disappear: Beyond "heuristics and biases.". *European Review of Social Psychology, 2*, 83-115.

Gigerenzer, G. (1996). On narrow norms and vague heuristics: A reply to Kahneman and Tversky (1996). *Psychological Review, 103*(3).

Gigerenzer, G. (1997). Bounded rationality: Models of fast and frugal inference. *Swiss Journal of Economics and Statistics, 133*(2/2), 201-218.

Gigerenzer, G. (1998). Surrogates for theory. *Theory & Psychology, 8*(2), 195-204.

Gigerenzer, G. (2002). The adaptive toolbox. In G. Gigerenzer & R. Selten (Eds.), *Bounded rationality: the adaptive toolbox* (pp. 38-50). Cambridge: The MIT Press.

Gigerenzer, G. (2006). Bounded and rational. In R. J. Stainton (Ed.), *Contemporary debates in cognitive science* (pp. 115-133). Oxford: Blackwell.

Gigerenzer, G. (2007). *Gut feelings : The intelligence of the unconscious.* New York: Viking.

Gigerenzer, G., & Brighton, H. (2009). Homo heuristicus: Why biased minds make better inferences. *Topics in Cognitive Science 1*(1), 107-143.

Gigerenzer, G., & Gaissmaier, W. (2011). Heuristic decision making. *Annual Review of Psychology, 62*, 451-482.

Gigerenzer, G., & Goldstein, D. G. (1996). Reasoning the fast and frugal way: Models of bounded rationality. *Psychological Review, 23*(4), 650-669.

Gigerenzer, G., & Goldstein, D. G. (1999). Betting on one good reason: the take the best heuristic. In G. Gigerenzer, P. M. Todd & The ABC Research Group (Eds.), *Simple heuristics that make us smart* (pp. 75-95). New York: Oxford University Press.

Gigerenzer, G., Hertwig, R., Hoffrage, U., & Sedlmeier, P. (2008). Cognitive illusions reconsidered. In C. R. Plott & V. L. Smith (Eds.), *Handbook of experimental economics results. [Volume 1]* (pp. 976-986). Amsterdam: North Holland.

Gigerenzer, G., & Regier, T. (1996). How do we tell an association from a rule? Comment on Sloman (1996). *Psychological Bulletin, 1*, 23-26.

Gigerenzer, G., & Selten, R. (2002). Rethinking rationality. In G. Gigerenzer & R. Selten (Eds.), *Bounded rationality: the adaptive toolbox* (pp. 1-12). Cambridge: The MIT Press.

Gigerenzer, G., & Todd, P. M. (1999). Fast and frugal heuristics: the adaptive toolbox. In G. Gigerenzer, P. M. Todd & The ABC Research Group (Eds.), *Simple heuristics that make us smart* (pp. 3-34). New York: Oxford University Press.

Gigerenzer, G., & Todd, P. M. (2008). Rationality the fast and frugal way: introduction. In C. R. Plott & V. L. Smith (Eds.), *Handbook of experimental economics results. [Volume 1]* (pp. 976-986). Amsterdam: North Holland.

Gigerenzer, G., Todd, P. M., & the ABC Research Group. (1999). *Simple heuristics that make us smart.* New York: Oxford University Press.

Gilovich, T. (1991). *How we know what isn't so : the fallibility of human reason in everyday life.* New York: Free Press.

Gilovich, T., & Griffin, D. (2002). Heuristics and biases: Then and now. In T. Gilovich, D. Griffin & D. Kahneman (Eds.), *Heuristics and biases: The psychology of intuitive judgment* (pp. 1-18). Cambridge: Cambridge University Press.

Gilovich, T., Griffin, D., & Kahneman, D. (2002). *Heuristics and biases: The psychology of intuitive judgment.* Cambridge: Cambridge University Press.

Gino, F. (2008). Do we listen to advice just because we paid for it? The impact of advice cost on its use. *Organisational Behavior and Human Decision Processes, 107*, 234-245.

Gladwell, M. (2005). *Blink : The power of thinking without thinking.* New York: Little Brown and Co.

Glaser, B. G., & Strauss, A. L. (1967). *The discovery of grounded theory; strategies for qualitative research.* Chicago: Aldine.

Goldstein, D. G. (2010). What is the field of judgment and decision making (JDM)? Retrieved from http://www.decisionsciencenews.com/2010/10/11/what-is-jdm/

Goldstein, D. G., & Gigerenzer, G. (2002). Models of ecological rationality: The recognition heuristic. *Psychological Review, 109*(1), 75-90.

Gollwitzer, P. M., & Bargh, J. A. (1996). *The psychology of action : linking cognition and motivation to behavior.* New York: Guilford Press.

Greene, J. C., & Caracelli, V. J. (2003). Making paradigmatic sense of mixed methods practice. In A. Tashakkori & C. Teddlie (Eds.), *Handbook of mixed methods in social & behavioral research* (pp. 91-110). Thousand Oaks: Sage.

Greene, J. C., Caracelli, V. J., & Graham, W. J. (1989). Toward a conceptual framework for mixed-method evaluation designs. *Educational Evaluation and Policy Analysis, 11*(3), 255-274.

Grissom, R. J., & Kim, J. J. (2005). *Effect sizes for research : a broad practical approach.* Mahwah: Lawrence Erlbaum Associates.

Gul, F. A. (1984). The joint and moderating role of personality and cognitive style on decision making. *The Accounting Review, 59*(2), 264-277.

Harless, D. W., & Camerer, C. (1994). The predictive utility of generalized expected utility theories. *Econometrica, 62*(16), 1251-1289.

Hastie, R., & Dawes, R. M. (2010). *Rational choice in an uncertain world. The psychology of judgment and decision making* (2 ed.). Los Angeles: Sage.

Haug, E. G., & Taleb, N. N. (2011). Option traders use (very) sophisticated heuristics, never the black scholes merton formula. *Journal of Economic Behavior and Organization, 77*(2), 97-106. Retrieved from http://ssrn.com/paper=1012075

Hayes, S. C. (1986). The case of the silent dog - verbal reports and the analysis of rules: A review of Ericsson and Simon´s protocol analysis: Verbal reports as data. *Journal of the experimental analysis of behavior, 45*, 351-363.

Hays, W. L. (1994). *Statistics* (5 ed.). Belmont: Wadsworth.

Heath, L. (2001). Triangulation: Methodology. In N. J. Smelser & P. B. Baltes (Eds.), *International Encyclopedia of the Social and Behavioral Sciences* (pp. 15901-15906). Amsterdam: Elsevier.

Helliar, C. V., Lonie, A. A., Power, D. M., & Sinclair, C. D. (2002). Managerial attitudes to risk: a comparison of Scottish chartered accountants and U.K. managers. *Journal of International Accounting, Auditing & Taxation, 11*(2), 165.

Hempel, C. G. (1965). Aspects of scientific explanation *Aspects of scientific explanation. And other essays in the philosophy of science* (pp. 331-504). New York: The Free Press.

Hertwig, R., & Herzog, S. M. (2009). Fast and frugal heuristics: Tools of social rationality. *Social Cognition, 27*(5), 661-698.

Hertwig, R., Hoffrage, U., & the ABC Research Group. (in press). *Simple heuristics in a social world.* New York: Oxford University Press.

Heukelom, F. (2005). The origin of prospect theory, or testing the intuitive statistician. *Tinbergen Institute Discussion Paper, 2005-11/2.*

Heukelom, F. (2007a). What Simon says. *Tinbergen Institute Discussion Paper, 2007-005/1.*

Heukelom, F. (2007b). Who are the behavioral economists and what do they say? *Tinbergen Institute Discussion Paper, 2007-020/1.*

Hilbig, B. E. (2010). Reconsidering "evidence" for fast-and-frugal heuristics. *Psychonomic Bulletin & Review, 17*(6), 923-930.

Hilbig, B. E., & Richter, T. (2010). Homo heuristicus outnumbered: comment on Gigerenzer and Brighton (2009). *Topics in Cognitive Science, 3*(1), 187-196.

Hilbig, B. E., Scholl, S. G., & Pohl, R. F. (2010). Think or blink - is the recognition heuristic an "intuitive" strategy? *Judgment and Decision Making, 5*(4), 300-309.

Hirsch, B. (2007). *Controlling und Entscheidungen : Zur verhaltenswissenschaftlichen Fundierung des Controllings.* Tübingen: Mohr Siebeck.

Hirsch, B., & Bassler, A. (2010). The impact of managers personality on visualization of management accounting data. *SSRN eLibrary.* Retrieved from http://ssrn.com/paper=1609728

Hodgkinson, G. P., & Healey, M. P. (2008). Cognition in organizations. *Annual Review of Psychology, 59*, 387-417.

Hoetker, G. (2005). How much you know versus how well I know you: selecting a supplier for a technically innovative component. *Strategic Management Journal, 26*(1), 75-96.

Hoffrage, U., & Reimer, T. (2004). Models of Bounded Rationality: The Approach of Fast and Frugal Heuristics. *management revue, 15*(4), 437-459.

Hofstedt, T. R., & Kinard, J. C. (1970). A strategy for behavioral accounting research. *The Accounting Review*, 38-54.

Hogarth, R. M. (1978). A note on aggregating opinions. *Organizational Behavior and Human Performance, 21*(1), 40-46.

Hogarth, R. M. (1987). *Judgment and choice. The psychology of decision* (2 ed.). Chichester: Wiley.

Hogarth, R. M. (1991). A perspective on cognitive research in accounting. *Accounting Review, 66*(2), 277-290.

Hogarth, R. M. (1993). Accounting for decisions and decisions for accounting. *Accounting, Organizations and Society, 18*(5), 407-424.

Hogarth, R. M. (2002). Deciding analytically or trusting your intuition? The advantages and disadvantages of analytic and intuitive thought. Universitat Pompeu Fabra. Departament d'Economia y Empresa.

Hogarth, R. M., & Einhorn, H. J. (1992). Order effects in belief updating: The belief-adjustment model. *Cognitive Psychology, 24*(1), 1-55.

Hogarth, R. M., & Karelaia, N. (2005). Simple models for multiattribute choice with many alternatives: When it does and does not pay to face trade-offs with binary attributes. *Management Science, 51*(12), 1860-1872.

Holland, P. (1986). Statistics and causal inference. *Journal of the American Statistical Association, 81*(396), 945-960.

Hookway, C. (2008). Pragmatism. In E. N. Zalta (Ed.), *The Stanford Encyclopedia of Philosophy (Fall 2008 Edition)*.

Horch, N. (2009). *Management control of global supply chains*. Köln: Eul.

Horgan, J. (1995). The New Social Darwinists. *Scientific American., 273*(4), 150-157.

Horváth, P. (2009). *Controlling* (11 ed.). München: Vahlen.

Hsee, C. K., Loewenstein, G. F., Blount, S., & Bazerman, M. H. (1999). Preference reversals between joint and separate evaluations of options: A review and theoretical analysis. *Psychological Bulletin 125*(5), 576-590.

Hsee, C. K., & Zhang, J. (2004). Distinction bias: Misprediction and mischoice due to joint evaluation. *Journal of Personality and Social Psychology, 86*, 680-695.

Hunton, J. E., & McEwen, R. A. (1997). An Assessment of the relation between analysts' earnings forecast accuracy, motivational incentives and cognitive information search strategy. *The Accounting Review, 72*(4), 497-515.

Iselin, E. R. (1988). The effects of information load and information diversity on decision quality in a structured decision task. *Accounting, Organizations and Society, 13*(2), 147-164.

Iselin, E. R. (1993). The effects of the information and data properties of financial ratios and statements on managerial decision quality. *Journal of Business Finance & Accounting, 20*, 249-267.

Isenberg, D. J. (1984). How senior managers think. *Harvard Business Review, 62*(6), 81-90.

Isenberg, D. J. (1986). Thinking and managing: A verbal protocol analysis of managerial problem solving. *Academy of Management Journal, 29*(4), 775-788.

Jackson, N., & Carter, P. (1993). 'Paradigm Wars': A response to Hugh Willmott. *Organization Studies, 14*(5), 721-725.

Johnson-Laird, P. N. (1983). *Mental Models. Towards a cognitive science of language, inferences, and consciousness.* Cambridge: Cambridge University Press.

Johnson, B. R., Onwuegbuzie, A. J., & Turner, L. A. (2007). Toward a definition of mixed methods research. *Journal of Mixed Methods Research, 1*(2), 112-133.

Johnson, J. G., & Raab, M. (2003). Take The First: Option-generation and resulting choices. *Organizational behavior and human decision processes., 91*(2), 215.

Johnson, W. B. (1983). "Representativeness" in judgmental predictions of corporate bankruptcy. *The Accounting Review, 58*(1), 78.

Jonas, E., Schulz-Hardt, S., & Frey, D. (2005). Giving advice or making decisions in someone else's place: the influence of impression, defense, and accuracy motivation on the search for new information. *Personality and Social Psychology Bulletin, 31*(7), 977-990.

Jones, B. D. (1999). Bounded rationality. *Annual Review of Political Science, 2*, 297-321.

Kahn, B. E., & Baron, J. (1995). An exploratory study of choice rules favored for high-stakes decisions. *Journal of Consumer Psychology, 4*, 305-328.

Kahneman, D. (2011). *Thinking, fast and slow.* New York: Farrar, Straus and Giroux.

Kahneman, D., & Frederick, S. (2002). Representativeness revisited: Attribute substitution in intuitive judgment In T. Gilovich, D. Griffin & D. Kahneman (Eds.), *Heuristics and biases: The psychology of intuitive judgment* (pp. 49-81). Cambridge: Cambridge University Press.

Kahneman, D., & Frederick, S. (2005). A model of heuristic judgment. In K. J. Holyoak & R. G. Morrison (Eds.), *The Cambridge handbook of thinking and reasoning* (pp. 267-293). New York: Cambridge University Press.

Kahneman, D., & Klein, G. (2009). Conditions for intuitive expertise. *American Psychologist, 64*(6), 515-526.

Kahneman, D., & Lovallo, D. (1993). Timid choices and bold forecasts: A cognitive perspective on risk taking. *Management Science, 39*(1), 17-31.

Kahneman, D., & Tversky, A. (1972). Subjective probability: A judgment of representativeness. *Cognitive Psychology, 3*, 430-454.

Kahneman, D., & Tversky, A. (1979). Prospect theory: An analysis of decision under risk. *Econometrica, 47*(2), 263-291.

Kahneman, D., & Tversky, A. (1981). The framing of decisions and the psychology of choice. *Science, 211*, 453-458.

Kahneman, D., & Tversky, A. (1983). Choices, values, and frames. *American Psychologist, 39*(4), 341-350.

Kahneman, D., & Tversky, A. (1996). On the reality of cognitive illusions. *Psychological Review, 103*(3), 582-591.

Kahneman, D., & Tversky, A. (2000). *Choices, values, and frames*. New York: Russel Sage Foundation.

Kaplan, R. S., & Norton, D. P. (1992). The Balanced Scorecard: measures that drive performance. *Harvard Business Review, 74*(January/February), 71-79.

Kappler, E. (2002). Controlling enthält keinen Kern – aber eine Theorie In J. Weber & B. Hirsch (Eds.), *Controlling als akademische Disziplin* (pp. 161-190). Wiesbaden: Deutscher Universitäts-Verlag.

Katz, J. A., & Green, R. P. (2011). *Entrepreneurial small business*. New York: McGraw-Hill

Kelle, U. (2007). *Die Integration qualitativer und quantitativer Methoden in der empirischen Sozialforschung. Theoretische Grundlagen und methodologische Konzepte*. Wiesbaden: VS Verlag für Sozialwissenschaften.

Kelle, U., Kluge, S., & Prein, G. (1993). Strategien der Geltungssicherung in der qualitativen Sozialforschung zur Validitätsproblematik im interpretativen Paradigma. Bremen: Sonderforschungsbereich 186; Arbeitspapier Nr. 24

Kempf, W. (2006). *Forschungsmethoden der Psychologie. Zwischen naturwissenschaftlichem Experiment und sozialwissenschaftlicher Hermeneutik. Band I: Theorie und Empirie* (2 ed.). Berlin: Irena Regener.

Keren, G., & Schul, Y. (2009). Two is not always better than one. *Perspectives on Psychological Science, 4*(6), 533-550.

Keren, G., & Teigen, K., H. (2004). Yet another look at the heuristics and biases approach. In D. J. Koehler & N. Harvey (Eds.), *Blackwell Handbook of Judgment and Decision Making* (pp. 89-109). Malden: Blackwell Publishers Ltd.

Ketelaar, T., & Ellis, B. J. (2000). Are Evolutionary Explanations Unfalsifiable? Evolutionary Psychology and the Lakatosian Philosophy of Science. *Psychological Inquiry, 11*(1), 1-21.

Khatri, N., & Ng, H. A. (2000). The role of intuition in strategic decision making. *Human Relations, 53*(1), 57-86.

Klaes, M., & Sent, E.-M. (2005). A conceptual history of the emergence of bounded rationality. *History of Political Economy, 37*(1), 27-59.

Klein, G. (1993). *Sources of power: How people make decisions*. Cambridge: MIT Press.

Koch, C. (2004). Behavioral Economics und das Entscheidungsverhalten des Wirtschaftsprüfers - Ein Forschungsüberblick. Mannheim: Universität Mannheim.

Konrad, K. (2010). Lautes Denken. In G. Mey & K. Mruck (Eds.), *Handbuch Qualitative Forschung in der Psychologie* (pp. 476-490). Wiesbaden: VS Verlag für Sozialwissenschaften.

Kotchetova, N., & Salterio, S. (2004). Judgment and decision-making accounting research. A quest to improve the production, certivication, and use of accounting information. In D. J. Koehler & N. Harvey (Eds.), *Blackwell Handbook of Judgment and Decision Making* (pp. 547-565). Malden: Blackwell Publishing Ltd.

Krabuanrat, K., & Phelps, R. (1998). Heuristics and rationality in strategic decision making: An exploratory study. *Journal of Business Research, 41*(1), 83-93.

Kray, L. J. (2000). Contingent Weighting in Self-Other Decision Making. *Organizational Behavior and Human Decision Processes, 83*(1), 82-106.

Kruglanski, A. W., & Gigerenzer, G. (2011). Intuitive and deliberate judgments are based on common principles. *Psychological Review, 118*(1), 97-109.

Kuhn, T. S. (1972). *The structure of scientific revolutions* (2 ed.). Chicago: The University of Chicago Press.

Kvale, S. (2007). *Doing interviews*. London: Sage.

Laibson, D., & Zeckhauser, R. (1998). Amos Tversky and the ascent of behavioral economics. *Journal of Risk and Uncertainty, 16*, 7-47.

Lakatos, I., & Musgrave, A. (1970). *Criticism and the growth of knowledge : proceedings of the International Colloquium in the Philosophy of Science.* London: Cambridge University Press.

Lakatos, I., Worrall, J., & Currie, G. (1978). *Philosophical papers of Imre Lakatos. Vol.1, The methodology of scientific research programmes.* Cambridge: Cambridge University Press.

Larrick, R. P. (1993). Motivational factors in decision theories: The role of self-protection. *Psychological Bulletin, 113*(3), 440-450.

Lee, B., & Humphrey, C. (2006). More than a numbers game: qualitative research in accounting. *Management Decision, 44*(2), 180-197.

Lee, H., Herr, P. M., Kardes, F. R., & Kim, C. (1999). Motivated Search: Effects of Choice Accountability, Issue Involvement, and Prior Knowledge on Information Acquisition and Use. *Journal of Business Research, 45*(1), 75-88.

Lehrer, J. (2010). *How we decide*. New York: Houghton Mifflin Harcourt.

Lenat, D. B. (1982). The nature of heuristics. *Artificial Intelligence, 19*(2), 189-245.

Lerner, J. S., & Tetlock, P. E. (1999). Accounting for the effects of accountability. *Psychological Bulletin, 125*(2), 255-275.

Lewis, B., Shields, M. D., & Young, S. M. (1983). Evaluating human judgments and decision aids. *Journal of Accounting Research, 21*(1), 271-285.

Libby, R. (1975). Accounting ratios and the prediction of failure: some behavioral evidence. *Journal of Accounting Research, 13*(1), 150-161.

Libby, R. (1981). *Accounting and human information processing : Theory and applications.* Englewood Cliffs: Prentice-Hall.

Libby, R. (1985). Availability and the generation of hypotheses in analytical review. *Journal of Accounting Research, 23*(2), 648-667.

Libby, R., & Lewis, B. L. (1977). Human information processing research in accounting: The state of the art. *Accounting, Organizations and Society, 2*(3), 245-268.

Libby, R., & Luft, J. (1993). Determinants of judgment performance in accounting seetings: Ability, knowledge, motivation, and environment. *Accounting, Organizations and Society, 18*(5), 425-451.

Lincoln, Y. S., & Guba, E. G. (1985). *Naturalistic inquiry.* Beverly Hills: Sage.

Lindenberg, S. (1992). The method of decreasing abstraction. In J. S. Coleman & T. J. Fararo (Eds.), *Rational choice theory. Advocacy and critique* (pp. 3-20). Newbury Park: Sage.

Lingnau, V. (2006). Controlling – ein kognitionsorientierter Ansatz, *Beiträge zur Controlling-Forschung* (2 ed., Vol. 4). Technical University Kaiserslautern, Germany.

Lingnau, V., & Walter, K. (2011). Psychologische Paradigmen für die Controllingforschung, *Beiträge zur Controlling-Forschung* (Vol. 17). Technical University Kaiserslautern, Germany.

Link, J. (2002). Controlling in der Defensive? Die Zuständigkeiten für Informationssyteme im Widerstreit. In J. Weber & B. Hirsch (Eds.), *Controlling als akademische Disziplin* (Vol. 1, pp. 39-48). Wiesbaden: Deutscher Studien Verlag.

Lipsey, R. G., & Lancaster, K. (1956). The General Theory of Second Best. *The Review of Economic Studies, 24*(1), 11-32.

Lipshitz, R., Klein, G., Orasnu, J., & Salas, E. (2001). Taking stock of naturalistic decision making. *Journal of Behavioral Decision Making, 14*, 331-352.

Lisch, R., & Kriz, J. (1978). *Grundlagen und Modelle der Inhaltsanalyse : Bestandsaufnahme und Kritik.* Reinbek: Rowohlt

Locke, J. (1689). *An essay concerning human understanding, and a treatise on the conduct of the understanding.* London: Goerge Routledge & Sons.

Loewenstein, G. (1999). Experimental economics from the vantage point of behavioral economics. *The Economic Journal, 109*(2), 25-33.

Loewenstein, G., & Lerner, J. S. (2003). The role of affect in decision making. In R. J. Davidson, K. R. Scherer & H. H. Goldsmith (Eds.), *Handbook of affective sciences* (pp. 619-642). Oxford: Oxford University Press.

Lopes, L. L. (1987). Between hope and fear: The psychology of risk. *Advances in Experimental Psychology, 20*, 255-295.

Lopes, L. L. (1992). Three misleading assumptions in the customary rhetoric of the bias literature. *Theory and Psychology, 2*, 231-236.

Lord, A. T. (1989). The development of behavioral thought in accounting, 1952-1981. *Behavioral Research in Accounting, 1*, 124-149.

Lord, A. T. (1992). Pressure: A methodological consideration for behavioral research in auditing. *Auditing: A Journal of Practice & Theory, Fall*, 90-108.

Luce, R. D. (2000). *Utility of gains and losses measurement –theoretical and experimental approaches.* Hove: Lawrence Erlbaum.

Luckett, P. F., & Eggleton, I. R. (1991). Feedback and management accounting: A review of research into behavioural consequences. *Accounting, Organizations and Society, 16*(4), 371-394.

Luft, J. (1997). Fairness, ethics and the effect of management accounting on transaction costs. *Journal of Management Accounting Research, 9*, 199-216.

Luft, J. (2011). *Psychology models in empirical research in management accounting and control.* Paper presented at the ERMAC, Vienna, Austria.

Luft, J., & Shields, M. D. (2003). Mapping management accounting: graphics and guidelines for theory-consistent empirical research. *Accounting, Organizations and Society, 28*(2/3), 169-249.

Luft, J., & Shields, M. D. (2009). Psychological models of management accounting. *Foundations and Trends in Accounting, 4*(3-4), 199-345.

Lukka, K., & Kasanen, E. (1995). The problem of generalizability: Anecdotes and evidence in accounting research. *Accounting, Auditing & Accountability Journal, 8*(4), 71-90.

March, J. G., & Shapira, Z. (1987). Managerial Perspectives on Risk and Risk Taking. *Management Science, 33*(11), 1404-1418.

Martignon, L., & Hoffrage, U. (1999). Why does one-reason work? A case study in ecological rationaliy. In G. Gigerenzer, P. M. Todd & The ABC Research Group (Eds.), *Simple heuristics that make us smart* (pp. 119-140). Oxford: Oxford University Press.

Matsumoto, Y. (2007). Seeking a realistic way of individual decision making. *Global Business and Economics Review, 9*(2/3), 126-150.

Maxcy, S. J. (2003). Pragmatic threads in mixed methods research in the social sciences: the search for multiple modes of inquiry and the end of the philosophy of formalism. In A. Tashakkori & C. Teddlie (Eds.), *Handbook of mixed methods in social & behavioral research* (pp. 51-89). Thousand Oaks: Sage.

Mayring, P. (2003). *Qualitative Inhaltsanalyse. Grundlagen und Techniken* (8 ed.). Weinheim, Basel: Beltz.

McAllister, D. W., Mitchell, T. R., & Beach, L. R. (1979). The contingency model for the selection of decision strategies: An empirical test of the effects of significance, accountability, and reversibility. *Organisational Behavior and Human Decision Processes, 24*, 228-244.

McClelland, D. C. (1951). *Personality.* New York: William Sloane.

McClelland, D. C. (1964). *The roots of consciousness.* Princeton: Van Nostrand.

McKenzie, C. R. M. (2003). Rational models as theories - not standards - of behavior. *Trends in cognitive sciences, 7*(9), 403-406.

McKenzie, C. R. M. (2009). Business & Psychology: The growing trend of judgment and decision making. *Rady Business Journal, Summer 2009*, 17-22.

Merchant, K. (2011). *Trends in management control research.* Paper presented at the ERMAC, Vienna, Austria.

Merten, K. (1995). *Inhaltsanalyse : Einführung in Theorie, Methode und Praxis.* Opladen: Westdeutscher Verlag.

Meyer, M. (2005). Akteursmodell und ökonomischer Ansatz – Eine Verhältnisbestimmung. *WHU Working Paper, 106*(Mai 2005).

Miles, M. B., & Huberman, M. A. (1994). *Qualitative data analysis: An expanded sourcebook* (2 ed.). Thousand Oaks: Sage.

Milkman, K., Chugh, D., & Bazerman, M. (2009). How Can Decision Making Be Improved? *Perspectives on Psychological Science, 4*(4), 379-383.

Miller, C. C., & Ireland, R. D. (2005). Intuition in strategic decision making: Friend or foe in the fast-paced 21st century? *Academy of Management Executive, 19*(1), 19-30.

Miller, G. A. (1956). The magical number seven plus minus two: Some limits on our capacity for processing information. *Psychological Review, 63*, 81-97.

Miller, H. (1972). Environmental complexity and financial reports. *The Accounting Review, 47*(1), 31-37.

Mirowski, P. (2002). *Machine Dreams, Economics becomes a Cyborg Science.* Cambridge: Cambridge University Press.

Mischel, W. (1968). *Personality and assessment.* New York: Wiley.

Mischel, W., Shoda, Y., & Smith, R. E. (2007). *Introduction to personality : toward an integration* (8 ed.). Hoboken: Wiley.

Mises, L. v. (1966). *Human action. A treatise on economics* (3 ed.). Chicago: Henry Regnery.

Mitchell, J. R., Friga, P. N., & Mitchell, R. K. (2005). Untangling the Intuition Mess: Intuition as a Construct in Entrepreneurship Research. *Entrepreneurship Theory and Practice, 29*(6), 653-679.

Molina-Azoín, J. F. (2011). The use and added value of mixed methods in management research. *Journal of Mixed Methods Research, 5*(1), 7-24.

Mook, D. G. (1996). *Motivation. The organization of action.* New York: W.W. Norton.

Morgan, D. L. (2007). Paradigms lost and paradigms regained: methodological implications of combining qualitative and quantitative methods. *Journal of Mixed Methods Research, 1*(1), 48-76.

Morgan, M. S. (2006). Economic man as a model man: ideal types, idealization and caricatures. *Journal of the History of Economic Thought, 28*(1), 1-27.

Morse, J. M. (2003). Principles of mixed methods and multimethod research design. In A. Tashakkori & C. Teddlie (Eds.), *Handbook of mixed methods in social & behavioral research* (pp. 180-208). Thousand Oaks: Sage.

Mullainathan, S., & Thaler, R. H. (2000). Behavioral Economics. *Massachusetts Institute of Technology. Department of Economics Working Paper Series, 00-27.*

Nelson, M. W., & Tayler, W. B. (2007). Information pursuit in financial statement analysis: Effects of choice, effort, and reconciliation. *The Accounting Review* *82*(3), 731-758.

Neumer, J. (2009). Gemeinsame Entscheidungsfindung: Perspektiven, Ansatzpunkte und blinde Flecken. *Institut für Sozialwissenschaftliche Forschung e.V. (ISF) München, Working Paper.*

Newell, A. (1990). *Unified theories of cognition.* Cambridge: Harvard University Press.

Newell, B. R., Weston, N. J., & Shanks, D. R. (2003). Empirical tests of a fast-and-frugal heuristic: Not everyone "takes-the-best". *Organizational behavior and human decision processes., 91*(1), 82-96.

Newman, I., & Benz, C. R. (1998). *Qualitative-quantitative research methodology: exploring the interactive continuum.* Carbondale, Illinois: Souther Illinois University Press.

Nisbett, R. E., & Wilson, T. D. (1977). Telling more then we can know: Verbal reports on mental processes. *Psychological Review, 84*, 231-259.

Novemsky, N., Dhar, R., Schwarz, N., & Simonson, I. (2007). Preference Fluency in Choice. *JMR, Journal of marketing research., 44*(3), 347.

Nutt, P. C. (1998). Evaluating alternatives to make strategic choices. *Omega 26*(3), 333-354.

Oppenheimer, D., M. (2003). Not so fast! (and not so frugal!): rethinking the recognition heuristic. *Cognition, 90*, B1-B9.

Oppenheimer, D., M. (2008). The secret life of fluency. *Trends in Cognitive Sciences, 12*(6), 237-240.

Ortmann, A., Gigerenzer, G., Borges, B., & Goldstein, D. G. (2008). The recognition heuristic: A fast and frugal way to investment choice? In C. Plott, R. & V. Smith, L. (Eds.), *Handbook of Experimental Economics Results* (Vol. 1, pp. 993-1003). Amsterdam: Elsevier.

Osann, M. (2010). *Freiwillige Berichterstattung über immaterielle Ressourcen : ein deskriptiv-explikatives Mehrebenenmodell.* Lohmar: Eul.

Oswick, C., & Barber, P. (1998). Personality type and performance in an introductory level accounting course: a research note. *Accounting Education, 7*(3), 249-254.

Owhoso, V. E., Messier, W. F., Jr., & Lynch, J. G., Jr. (2002). Error detection by industry-specialized teams during sequential audit review. *Journal of Accounting Research, 40*(3), 883-900.

Parikh, J., Neubauer, F.-F., & Lank, A. G. (1994). *Intuition : the new frontier of management.* Cambridge: Blackwell.

Patton. (1990). *Qualitative evaluation and research methods* (2 ed.). Newbury Park, CA: Sage.

Payne, J. W. (1976a). Heuristic search processes in decision making. *Advances in Consumer Research, 3*(1), 321-327.

Payne, J. W. (1976b). Task complexity and contingent processing in decision making: An information search and protocol analysis. *Organizational Behavior and Human Performance, 16*(2), 366-387.

Payne, J. W. (2011). *Complexity and decision making under risk.* Paper presented at the International Conference on Behavioral Decision Making (ICBDM), Interdisciplinary Center (IDC) Herzliya, Tel Aviv, Israel.

Payne, J. W., Bettman, J. R., & Johnson, E. J. (1993). *The adaptive decision maker.* Cambridge: Cambridge University Press.

Payne, J. W., & Venkatraman, V. (2011). Opening the black box: Conclusions to a handbook of process tracing methods for decision research. In M. Schulte-Mecklenbeck, A. Kühberger & R. Ranyard (Eds.), *A handbook of process tracing methods for decision research. A critical review and user's guide* (pp. 223-249). New York: Psychology Press.

Peirce, C. S. (1960). *Pragmatism and pragmaticism, Band V, Scientific metaphysics, Band VI.* Cambridge, Massachusetts: Harvard University Press.

Persky, J. (1995). Retrospectives: The ethology of homo economicus. *The Journal of Economic Perspectives, 9*(2), 221-231.

Pinker, S. (1997). *How the mind works.* New York: Norton.

Pinker, S. (2002). *The blank slate: The modern denial of human nature.* New York, N.Y.: Viking.

Plaschke, F., Roghé, F., & Günther, F. (2011). The art of planning. *Boston Consulting Group White Paper.*

Plott, C. R., & Smith, V. L. (2008). *Handbook of experimental economics results.* (Vol. 1). Amsterdam; Oxford: North Holland.

Polman, E. (2010). Information distortion in self-other decision making. *Journal of Experimental Social Psychology, 46*, 432-435.

Popper, K. (1959). *The logic of scientific discovery.* New York: Basic Books, Inc. Publishers.

Popper, K. (1967). Das Rationalitätsprinzip. In K. Popper & D. Miller (Eds.), *Ausgewählte Texte zu Erkenntnistheorie, Philosophie der Naturwissenschaften, Metaphysik, Sozialphilosophie* (pp. 350-359). Tübingen: Mohr Siebeck.

Powalla, C. (2010). Heuristiken im Rahmen der strategischen Analyse. Ein Vergleich der Prognosekraft von VRIO-Framework und Rekognitionsheuristik. Unpublished Dissertation. Freie Universität Berlin.

Price, W. (2007). Decision making and the venture capital process. Retrieved from http://willprice.blogspot.com/2007/05/decision-making-and-venture-capital.html

Psillos, S. (2007). Contemporary perspectives on explanation. In T. A. F. Kuipers (Ed.), *Handbook of philosophy of science: general philosophy of science - focal issues* (pp. 97-173). Amsterdam: Elsevier.

Putnam, H. (1974). The "corroboration" of theories. In P. A. Schilpp (Ed.), *The Philosophy of Karl Popper* (pp. 221-240). La Salle: Open Court.

Redelmeier, D. A., Shafir, E., & Aujla, P. S. (2001). The beguiling pursuit of more information. *Medical Decision Making, 21*(5), 374-379.

Reichenbach, H. (1938). *Experience and prediction. An analysis of the foundations and the structure of knowlegde*. Chicago: University of Chicago Press.

Reimer, T., Hoffrage, U., & Katsikopoulos, K. (2007). Entscheidungsheuristiken in Gruppen. *NeuroPsychoEconomics, 2*(1), 7-29.

Remus, W. (1986). Graduate students as surrogates for managers in experiments on business decision making. *Journal of Business Research, 14*(1), 19-25.

Rieskamp, J. (2008). The importance of learning when making inferences. *Judgment and Decision Making, 3*(3), 261-277.

Rieskamp, J., & Otto, P., E. (2006). SSL: A theory of how people learn to select strategies. *Journal of Experimental Psychology: General, 135*(2), 207-236.

Rieskamp, J., & Reimer, T. (2007). Ecological rationality. In R. F. Baumeister & K. D. Vohs (Eds.), *Encyclopedia of Social Psychology* (Vol. 1, pp. 273-274). Thousand Oaks: Sage.

Robbins, P., & Aydede, M. (2009). *The Cambridge handbook of situated cognition*. Cambridge: Cambridge University Press.

Roberts, S., & Pashler, H. (2000). How persuasive is a good fit? A comment on theory testing. *Psychological Review, 107*(2), 358-367.

Rorty, R. (1986). Pragmatism, Davidson and truth. In E. LePore (Ed.), *Truth and interpretation* (pp. 333-355). Oxford: Basil Blackwell.

Rosenberg, A. (2008). *Philosophy of social science* (3 ed.). Boulder: Westview Press.

Rosenthal, R. (1966). *Experimenter effects in behavioral research*. New York: Appleton-Century-Crofts.

Rosnow, R. L., & Rosenthal, R. (1996). Computing contrasts, effect sizes, and counternulls on other people's published data: general procedures for research consumers. *Psychological Methods 1*(4), 331-340.

Ross, L., Greene, D., & House, P. (1977). The false consensus effect: An egocentric bias in social perception and attribution processes. *Journal of Experimental Social Psychology, 13*(3), 279-301.

Rowan, R. (1990). Listen for those warning bells. In W. H. Agor (Ed.), *Intuition in organizations* (pp. 195-204). Thousand Oaks: Sage

Rubin, H. J., & Rubin, I. S. (2005). *Qualitative interviewing. The art of hearing data* (2 ed.). Thousand Oaks: Sage.

Rugg, M. D., & Yonelinas, A. P. (2003). Human recognition memory: a cognitive neuroscience perspective. *Trends in Cognitive Sciences, 7*(7), 313-319.

Russo, J., Johnson, E., & Stephens, D. (1989). The validity of verbal protocols. *Memory & Cognition, 17*(6), 759-769.

Ryan, B., Scapens, R. W., & Theobald, M. (2002). *Research method and methodology in finance and accounting* (2 ed.). London: Thomson.

Salas, E., Rosen, M. A., & DiazGranados, D. (2010). Expertise-Based intuition and decision making in organizations. *Journal of Management 36*(4), 941-973.

Sale, J. E. M. (2002). Revisiting the quantitative-qualitative debate: implications for mixed-methods research. *Quality and Quantity, 36*(1), 43-53.

Salmon, W. C. (1989). Four decades of scientific explanation. In P. Kitcher & W. C. Salmon (Eds.), *Scientific explanation* (Vol. XIII, pp. 3-219). Minneapolis: University of Minnesota Press.

Samuels, R., & Stich, S. P. (2004). Rationality & psychology. In A. R. Mele & P. Rawling (Eds.), *The Oxford handbook of rationality* (pp. 297-300). Oxford: Oxford University Press.

Samuels, R., Stich, S. P., & Bishop, M. (2002). Ending the rationality wars: how to make dispute about human rationality disappear. In R. Elio (Ed.), *Common sense, reasoning and rationality* (pp. 236-268). New York: Oxford University Press.

San Miguel, J. G. (1976). Human information processing and its relevance to accounting: A laboratory study. *Accounting, Organizations and Society, 1*(4), 357-373.

Sanabria, F., & Killeen, P. R. (2007). Better statistics for better decisions: Rejecting null hypotheses statistical tests in favor of replication statistics. *Psychology in the Schools, 44*(5), 471-481.

Savage, L. J. (1954). *The Foundation of Statistics*. New York: John Wiley and Sons, Inc.

Schäffer, U. (2002). Rationalitätssicherung der Führung und Controlleraufgaben. In J. Weber & B. Hirsch (Eds.), *Controlling als akademische Disziplin* (Vol. 1, pp. 99-111). Wiesbaden: Deutscher Studien Verlag.

Schäffer, U., & Weber, J. (2001). *Rationalitätssicherung der Führung : Beiträge zu einer Theorie des Controlling*. Wiesbaden: Deutscher Universitäts-Verlag.

Schick, A. G., Gordon, L. A., & Haka, S. (1990). Information overload: A temporal approach. *Accounting, Organizations and Society, 15*(3), 199-220.

Schmidt, A. (2011). *The professionalization of controllers in Germany*. Paper presented at the 27th doctoral colloquium in accounting (EAA) 2011, Siena, Italy.

Schulte-Mecklenbeck, M., Kühberger, A., & Ranyard, R. (2011). *Opening the black box: Conclusions to a handbook of process tracing methods for decision research*. New York: Psychology Press.

Schwartz, B. N., Ward, A., Monterosso, J., Lyubomirsky, S., White, K., & Lehman, D. R. (2002). Maximizing versus satisficing: Happiness is a matter of choice. *Journal of Personality and Social Psychology, 83*(5), 1178-1197.

Schwarz, N. (2004). *The paradox of choice: Why more is less*. New York: Ecco.

Scott, S. G., & Bruce, R., A. (1995). Decision-making style: The development and assessment of a new measure. *Educational and Psychological Measurement, 55*(5), 818-831.

Secchi, D., & Bardone, E. (2010). *Does bounded rationality need an update?* Paper presented at the Behavioral Decision Making in Management (BDRM), Pittsburgh, PA.

Sedlmeier, P. (2009). Beyond the significance test ritual. What is there? *Zeitschrift für Psychologie, 217*(1), 1-5.

Seligman, M., & Kahana, M. (2009). Unpacking Intuition: A Conjecture. *Perspectives on Psychological Science, 4*(4), 399-402.

Selten, R. (2002). What is bounded rationality? In G. Gigerenzer & R. Selten (Eds.), *Bounded rationality: The adaptive toolbox* (pp. 13-36). Cambridge: The MIT Press.

Sen, A. (2002). *Rationality and freedom.* Cambridge: Harvard University Press.

Sent, E.-M. (2004). Behavioral economics: how psychology made its (limited) way back into economics. *History of Political Economy, 36*(4), 735-760.

Shadish, W. R., Cook, T. D., & Campbell, D. T. (2002). *Experimental and quasi-experimental designs for generalized causal inferences.* Boston: Houghton Mifflin.

Shafir, E. (1994). Uncertainty and the difficulty of thinking through disjunctions. *Cognition, 50*, 403-430.

Shafir, E., & LeBoeuf, R. A. (2002). Rationality. *Annual Review of Psychology, 53*(1), 491-517.

Shafir, E., Simonson, I., & Tversky, A. (1993). Reason-based choice. *Cognition, 49*, 11-36.

Shah, A., K., & Oppenheimer, D., M. (2008). Heuristics made easy: An effort-reduction framework. *Psychological Bulletin, 134*(2), 207-222.

Shanteau, J. (1989). Cognitive heuristics and biases in behavioral auditing: review, comments and observations. *Accounting, Organizations and Society, 14*(2), 165-177.

Shanteau, J. (1992). How much information does an expert use? Is it relevant? *Acta Psychologica, 81*, 75-86.

Shaw, M., & Constanzo, P. (1982). *Theories of social psychology* (2nd ed.). New York: Mc Graw-Hill.

Shields, M. D. (1980). Some effects on information load on search patterns used to analyze performance reports. *Accounting, Organizations and Society, 5*(4), 429-442.

Shields, M. D. (1983). Effects of inormation supply and demand on judgment accuracy: Evidence from corporate managers. *The Accounting Review, 58*(2), 284-303.

Shields, M. D. (2002). *Psychology and Accounting* (4 ed.). Stuttgart: Schäffer-Poeschel.

Shields, M. D. (2009). "What a long, Interesting trip it's been" through the behavioral accounting literature: A personal perspective. *Behavioral Research in Accounting, 21*(2), 113-116.

Sieber, S. D. (1973). The integration of fieldwork and survey methods. *American Journal of Sociology, 73*, 1335-1359.

Siegel, G., & Ramanauskas-Marconi, H. (1989). *Behavioral Accounting.* Cincinnati: South-Western Pub.

Simnet, R. (1996). The effects of information selection, information processing and task complexity on predictive accuracy of auditors. *Accounting, Organizations and Society, 21*(7-8), 699-719.

Simon, H. A. (1945). *Administrative behavior. A study of decision-making processes in administrative organization* (1 ed.). New York: The Free Press.

Simon, H. A. (1955). A behavioral model of rational choice. *Quarterly Journal of Economics, 69*(1), 99-118.

Simon, H. A. (1972). How big is a chunk? *Science, 183*(4142), 482-488.

Simon, H. A. (1976). From substantive to procedural rationality. In S. J. Latsis (Ed.), *Methods and appraisal in economics* (pp. 129-148). Cambridge: Cambridge University Press.

Simon, H. A. (1978). Rationality as process an as product of thought. *American Economic Review, 68*(2), 1-16.

Simon, H. A. (1979). Rational decision making in business organizations. *American Economic Review, 69*(4), 493-513.

Simon, H. A. (1986). Rationality in psychology and economics. *The Journal of Business, 59*(4), 209-224.

Simon, H. A. (1990). Invariants of human behavior. *Annual Review of Psychology, 41*(1), 1-19.

Simon, H. A. (1993). A behavioral model of rational choice. In S. Maital & S. L. Maital (Eds.), *Economics and Psychology* (pp. 229-248). Hants: Edward Elgar.

Simon, H. A. (1997). *Models of Bounded Rationality. Volume 3, Empirically Grounded Economic Reason.* Cambridge, Mass.: MIT Press.

Simon, H. A. (2000). Bounded rationality in social science: Today and tomorrow. *Mind & Society, 1*, 25-39.

Simonson, I. (1989). Choice based on reasons: The case of attraction and compromise effects. *Journal of Consumer Research, 16*, 158-174.

Simonson, I., & Nowlis, S. (1998). Constructive decision making in a social context: Unconventional choices based on reasons. unpublished manuscript: Stanford University

Simonson, I., & Nye, P. (1992). The effect of accountability on susceptibility to decision errors. *Organizational Behavior and Human Decision Processes, 51*(3), 416-446.

Sloman, S., A. (1996). The empirical case for two systems of reasoning. *Psychological Bulletin, 119*(1), 3-22.

Slovic, P. (1969). Analyzing the expert judge: A descriptive study of a stockbroker's decision process. *Journal of Applied Psychology, 53*, 255-263.

Slovic, P. (1995). The construction of preference. *American Psychologist, 50*(5), 364-371.

Smith, J. F., & Kida, T. (1991). Heuristics and biases: Expertise and task realism in auditing. *Psychological Bulletin, 109*(3), 472-489.

Smith, M. L. (1994). Qualitative plus/versus quantitative: The last word. In C. S. Reichardt & S. F. Rallis (Eds.), *The qualitative-quantitative debate: new perspectives* (Vol. 61, pp. 37-44). San Francisco: Jossey-Bass.

Smith, S. D., Tayler, W. B., & Prawitt, D. F. (2011). The effect of information pursuit on auditors judgments and confidence. *SSRN eLibrary.* Retrieved from http://ssrn.com/paper=1872387

Smith, V. L. (1994). Economics in the laboratory. *Journal of Economic Perspectives, 8*(1), 113-131.

Smith, V. L. (2003). Constructivist and Ecological Rationality in Economics. *American Economic Review, 93*(3), 465-508.

Snowball, D. (1980). Some effects of accounting expertise and information load: An empirical study. *Accounting, Organizations and Society, 5*(3), 323-338.

Snowball, D. (1986). Accounting laboratory experiments on human judgment: Some characteristics and influences. *Accounting, Organizations and Society, 11*(1), 47-69.

Sprinkle, G. B. (2003). Perspectives on experimental research in managerial accounting. *Accounting, Organizations and Society, 28*, 287-318.

Stanovich, K. E. (1999). *Who is rational? Studies of individual differences in reasoning.* Mahwah: Lawrence Erlbaum Associates.

Stanovich, K. E. (2004). *The robot's rebellion : finding meaning in the age of Darwin.* Chicago: University of Chicago Press.

Stanovich, K. E. (2010). *Decision making and rationality in the modern world.* New York: Oxford University Press.

Stanovich, K. E., & West, R. (2000). Individual differences in reasoning: Implications for the rationality debate. *Behavioral and Brain Sciences, 23*, 645-726.

Staw, B. M. (2010). The trouble with JDM: some limitations to the influence of JDM on organizational research. *Industrial and Organizational Psychology, 3*(4), 411-416.

Steckler, A., McLeroy, K. R., Goodman, R. M., Bird, S. T., & McCormick, L. (1992). Toward integrating qualitative and quantitative methods: an introduction. *Health Education Quarterly, 19*(1), 1-8.

Stedry, A. C. (1960). *Budget control and cost behavior.* Englewood Cliffs, New Jersey: Prentice-Hall.

Steinke, I. (2004). Quality criteria in qualitative research. In U. Flick, E. v. Kardorff & I. Steinke (Eds.), *A companion to qualitative research* (pp. 184-190). Thousand Oaks: Sage.

Sternberg, R. J. (2003). *Cognitive Psychology* (3 ed.). Toronto: Thomson Wadsworth.

Sternberg, R. J., O'Hara, L. A., & Lubart, T. I. (1997). Creativity as investment. *California Management Review, 40*(1), 8-21.

Stevens, J. R. (2010). Rational decision making in primates: the bounded and the ecological. In M. L. Platt & A. A. Ghazanfar (Eds.), *Primate neuroethology* (pp. 98-116). New York: Oxford University Press.

Stigler, G. J. (1961). The economics of information. *American Economic Review, 69*, 213-225.

Stone, E. R., Yates, A. J., & Caruthers, A. S. (2002). Risk taking in decision making for others versus the self. *Journal of Applied Social Psychology, 32*(9), 1797-1824.

Strauss, A. L., & Corbin, J. M. (1998). *Basics of qualitative research : techniques and procedures for developing grounded theory*. Thousand Oaks: Sage

Strauss, E. R., Nevries, P., & Weber, J. (2011). The emergence of management control Systems: a resource dependency perspective. *SSRN eLibrary*. Retrieved from http://ssrn.com/paper=1881464

Streim, H. (1975). Heuristische Lösungsverfahren Versuch einer Begriffsklärung. *Mathematical Methods of Operations Research, 19*(5), 143-162.

Swain, M. R., & Haka, S., F. (2000). Effects of information load on capital budgeting decisions. *Behavioral Research in Accounting, 12*, 171-199.

Tashakkori, A., & Teddlie, C. (1998). *Mixed methodology. Combining qualitative and quantitative approaches*. Thousand Oaks: Sage.

Tashakkori, A., & Teddlie, C. (Eds.). (2003). *Handbook of mixed methods in social & behavioral research*. Thousand Oaks: Sage.

Tayler, W. B., Smith, S. D., & Prawitt, D. F. (2011). The effect of information pursuit on auditors' judgments and confidence. from http://ssrn.com/abstract=1872387

Tetlock, P. E. (2002). Social functionalist frameworks for judgment and choice: Intuitive politicians, theologians, and prosecutors. *Psychological Review, 109*(3), 451-471.

Tetlock, P. E., & Boettger, R. (1994). Accountability amplifies the status quo effect when change creates victims. *Journal of Behavioral Decision Making, 7*(1), 1-23.

Tetlock, P. E., Lerner, J. S., & Boettger, R. (1996). The dilution effect: judgmental bias, conversational convention, or a bit of both? *European Journal of Social Psychology, 26*(6), 915-934.

Tetlock, P. E., Skitka, L., & Boettger, R. (1989). Social and cognitive strategies for coping with accountability: conformity, complexity, and bolstering. *Journal of Personality and Social Psychology, 57*(4), 632-640.

Thaler, R. H. (1993). *Advances in behavioral finance. The roundtable series in behavioral economics*. New York: Russel Sage Foundation.

Thaler, R. H., & Sunstein, C. R. (2003). Libertarian Paternalism. *American Economic Review, 93*(2), 175-179.

Thaler, R. H., & Sunstein, C. R. (2008). *Nudge - improving decisions about health, wealth, and happiness*. New Haven: Yale University Press.

Thayer, H. S. (1967). Pragmatism. In P. Edwards (Ed.), *The Encyclopedia of Philosophy* (Vol. 5, pp. 430-436). New York: Macmillan.

Thompson, J. (1967). *Organizations in action*. New York: Mc Graw-Hill.

Thorngate, W. (1980). Efficient decision heuristics. *Behavioral Science, 25*(3), 219-225.

Todd, P. M. (2007). Coevolved cognitive mechanisms in mate search. In J. Forgas, M. G. Haselton & W. v. Hippel (Eds.), *Evolution and the social mind: Evolutionary psychology and social cognition* (pp. 145-159). New York: Psychology Press: Taylor & Francis Group.

Todd, P. M., & Gigerenzer, G. (2003). Bounding rationality to the world. *Journal of Economic Psychology, 24*(1), 143-165.

Todd, P. M., Neil, J. S., & Paul, B. B. (2001). Heuristics for Decision and Choice *International Encyclopedia of the Social & Behavioral Sciences* (pp. 6676-6679). Oxford: Pergamon.

Tooby, J., & Cosmides, L. (2005). Conceptual foundations of evolutionary psychology. In D. M. Buss (Ed.), *The handbook of evolutionary psychology* (pp. 5-67). Hoboken: Wiley.

Tost, L. P., Gino, F., & Larrick, R. P. (2010). *Power, competiveness, and advice taking: Why the powerful don´t listen*. Paper presented at the Behavioral Decision Research in Management (BDRM) Conference, Pittsburgh, PA.

Tribe, L. H. (1973). Technology assessment and the fourth discontinuity: The limits of instrumental rationality. *Southern California Review of Law, 46*(3), 617-660.

Trotman, K. T., Tan, H. C., & Ang, N. (2011). Fifty-year overview of judgment and decision-making research in accounting. *Accounting & Finance, 51*(1), 278-360.

Tuttle, B., & Burton, F. G. (1999). The effects of a modest incentive on information overload in an investment analysis task. *Accounting, Organizations and Society, 24*(8), 673-687.

Tversky, A. (1972). Elimination by aspects: A theory of choice. *Psychological Review, 79*(4), 281-299.

Tversky, A., & Kahneman, D. (1973). Availability: A heuristic for judging frequency and probability. *Cognitive Psychology, 5*, 207-232.

Tversky, A., & Kahneman, D. (1974). Judgment under uncertainty: Heuristics and biases. *Science, 185*, 1124-1131.

Tversky, A., & Kahneman, D. (1986). Rational Choice and the Framing of Decisions. *Journal of Business, 59*(4), S251-S278.

Tversky, A., & Koehler, D. J. (1994). Support Theory: A nonextensional representation of subjective probability. *Psychological Review, 101*(4), 547-567.

Tversky, A., Sattath, S., & Slovic, P. (1988). Contingent weighting in judgment and choice. *Psychological Review 95*(3), 371-384.

Tykocinski, O. E., & Ruffle, B. J. (2003). Reasonanble reasons for waiting. *Journal of Behavioral Decision Making, 16*(2), 147-157.

Vacha-Haase, T., Nilsson, J. E., Reetz, D. R., Lance, T. S., & Thompson, B. (2000). Reporting practices and APA editorial policies regarding statistical significance and effect size. *Theory & Psychology, 10*(3), 413-425.

Vaivio, J. (2008). Qualitative management accounting research: rationale, pitfalls and potential. *Qualitative Research in Accounting & Management, 5*(1), 64-86.

Van der Rijt, J.-W. (2006). The ruin of homo oeconomicus. *London School of Economics Working Paper Series.*

Vera-Muñoz, S. C., Shackell, M., & Buehner, M. (2007). Accountants' usage of causal business models in the presence of benchmark data. *Contemporary Accounting Research, 24*(3), 1015-1038.

Volnhals, M., & Hirsch, B. (2009). Information Overload bei Managern. Implikationen der Informationsüberlastung für das Controlling. *CFO aktuell, 3*(2), 72-75.

von Hayek, F. A. (1937). Economics and knowledge. In F. A. von Hayek (Ed.), *Individualism amd economic order* (pp. 33-56). Chicago: University of Chicago Press.

von Hayek, F. A. (1979). *The counter-revolution of science: studies on the abuse of reason* (2 ed.). Indianapolis: Liberty Fund.

von Neumann, J., & Morgenstern, O. (1944). *Theory of games and economic behavior.* Princeton: Princeton University Press.

Wailgum, T. (2009). To hell with business intelligence: 40 percent of execs trust gut. Retrieved from http://blogs.cio.com/thomas_wailgum/to_hell_with_business_intelligence_40_percent_of_execs_trust_gut?page=0

Watson, J. B. (1920). Is thinking merely the action of language mechanisms? *British Journal of Psychology, 11*, 87-104.

Weber, E. U., & Hsee, C. K. (2000). Culture and individual judgment and decision making. *Applied Psychology: An International Review, 49*(1), 32-61.

Weber, E. U., & Johnson, E. J. (2009). Mindful judgment and decision making. *Annual Review Psychology, 60*(1), 53-85.

Weber, J. (2011a). The development of controller tasks: Explaining the nature of controllership and its changes. *Journal of Management Control, 22*(1), 25-46.

Weber, J. (2011b). Genese des Akteursmodells. In M. Meyer & J. Weber (Eds.), *Controlling und begrenzte kognitive Fähigkeiten. Grundlagen und Anwendungen eines verhaltensorientierten Ansatzes* (pp. 15-26). Wiesbaden: Gabler.

Weber, J., & Schäffer, U. (1999). Sicherstellung der Rationalität von Führung als Aufgabe des Controlling? *Die Betriebswirtschaft, 59*, 731-747.

Weber, J., & Schäffer, U. (2008a). *Einführung in das Controlling* (12 ed.). Stuttgart: Schäffer-Poeschel.

Weber, J., & Schäffer, U. (2008b). *Introduction to controlling.* Stuttgart: Schäffer-Poeschel.

Weber, J., Schäffer, U., & Langenbach, W. (1999). Gedanken zur Rationalitätskonzeption des Controlling. *WHU Working Paper, 70.*

Weber, M. (1947). *Theory of social and economic organization (A. Henderson and T. Parsons transl.).* New York: Free Press.

Weick, K. E. (1979). *The social psychology of organizing* (2 ed.). New York, N.Y.: Mc Graw-Hill.

Weiner, B. (1985). An attributional theory of achievement motivation and emotion. *Psychological Review, 92*(4), 548-573.

Weldon, E., & Gargano, G. M. (1988). Cognitive loafing: The effects of accountability and shared responsibility on cognitive effort. *Personality and Social Psychology Bulletin, 14*, 149-171.

Welkowitz, J., Ewen, R. E., & Cohen, J. (2002). *Introductory statistics for the behavioral sciences* (5 ed.). New York: John Wiley.

Wertheimer, M. (1945). *Productive thinking.* New York: Harper & Brothers.

Westen, D., Blagov, P. S., Harenski, K., Kilts, C., & Hamann, S. (2006). Neural bases of motivated reasoning: An fMRI study of emotional constraints on partisan political judgment in the 2004 U.S. presidential election. *Journal of Cognitive Neuroscience 18*(11), 1947-1958.

Wilkinson, L., & The APA Task Force on Statistical Inference. (1999). Statistical methods in psychology journals: Guidelines and explanations. *American Psychologist 54*(8), 594-604.

Williamson, O. E. (1985). *The economic institutions of capitalism.* New York: Free Press.

Wilson, D. A. (1973). A Note on "environmental complexity and financial reports". *The Accounting Review, 48*(3), 586-588.

Wittgenstein, L. (1953). *Philosophical investigations.* Oxford: Blackwell.

Wright, W. F. (1988). Audit judgment consensus and experience. In K. R. Ferris (Ed.), *Behavioral accounting research: A critical analysis* (pp. 305-328). Columbus: Century VII Publishing.

Wright, W. F., & Anderson, U. (1989). Effects of situation familiarity and financial incentives on use of the anchoring and adjustment heuristic for probability assessment. *Organizational Behavior and Human Decision Processes, 44*(1), 68-82.

Wrona, T. (2005). *Die Fallstudienanalyse als wissenschaftliche Forschungsmethode.* ESCP-EAP Europäische Wirtschaftshochschule Berlin, Berlin.

Wrona, T. (2008). Kognitive Strategieforschung – State of the Art und aktuelle Entwicklungen In T. Wrona (Ed.), *Strategische Managementforschung : aktuelle Entwicklungen und internationale Perspektiven* (pp. 43-83). Wiesbaden: Gabler.

Wrona, T., & Fandel, G. (2010). Möglichkeiten und Grenzen einer Methodenintegration. In T. Wrona & G. Fandel (Eds.), *Zeitschrift für Betriebswirtschaft, Special Issue* (Vol. 4/2010, pp. 1-15).

Wübben, M., & Wangenheim, F. v. (2008). Instant customer base analysis: Managerial heuristics often "get it right". *Journal of Marketing, 72*, 82-93.

Yaniv, I. (2004). Receiving other people's advice: influence and benefit. *Organizational Behavior and Human Decision Processes, 93*(1), 1-13.

Yin, R. K. (2009). *Case study research : design and methods* (4 ed.). Los Angelas: Sage

Young, M. J., Bauman, C. W., Chen, N., & Bastardi, A. (forthcoming). The pursuit of missing information in negotiation. *Organizational Behavior and Human Decision Processes.*

Zimbardo, P. G., Gerrig, R. J., & Graf, R. (2004). *Psychologie* (16 ed.). Munich: Pearson.

CONTROLLING

Herausgegeben von Prof. Dr. Volker Lingnau, Kaiserslautern, Prof. Dr. Albrecht Becker, Innsbruck, und Prof. Dr. Rolf Brühl, Berlin

Band 12
Volker Lingnau (Hrsg.)
Mittelstandscontrolling 2009
Lohmar – Köln 2009 ♦ 376 S. ♦ € 65,- (D) ♦ ISBN 978-3-89936-860-4

Band 13
Anna Bassler
Die Visualisierung von Daten im Controlling
Lohmar – Köln 2010 ♦ 244 S. ♦ € 56,- (D) ♦ ISBN 978-3-89936-939-7

Band 14
Tatiana Villalobos Baum
Organisationales Lernen und Anreizsysteme nach dem Börsengang – Ein verhaltensorientierter Ansatz
Lohmar – Köln 2010 ♦ 248 S. ♦ € 56,- (D) ♦ ISBN 978-3-89936-971-7

Band 15
Jürgen Kantowski
Einsatz von Realoptionen im Investitionscontrolling am Beispiel Biotechnologie
Lohmar – Köln 2011 ♦ 248 S. ♦ € 56,- (D) ♦ ISBN 978-3-8441-0022-8

Band 16
Michael Rademacher
Prozess- und wertorientiertes Controlling von M&A-Projekten
Lohmar – Köln 2011 ♦ 368 S. ♦ € 64,- (D) ♦ ISBN 978-3-8441-0110-2

Band 17
Carmen Kühn
Psychopathen in Nadelstreifen
Lohmar – Köln 2012 ♦ 244 S. ♦ € 56,- (D) ♦ ISBN 978-3-8441-0138-6

Band 18
Jörn Sebastian Basel
Heuristic Reasoning in Management Accounting – A Mixed Methods Analysis
Lohmar – Köln 2012 ♦ 268 S. ♦ € 57,- (D) ♦ ISBN 978-3-8441-0160-7

JOSEF EUL VERLAG